# STARTING A BUSINESS IN

# FRANCE

## André de Vries

Distributed in the USA by
The Globe Pequot Press, Guilford, Connecticut

Published by Vacation Work, 9 Park End Street, Oxford
www.vacationwork.co.uk

STARTING A BUSINESS IN FRANCE
by André de Vries

First edition 2004

Copyright © Vacation Work 2004

ISBN 1-85458-306-9

Publicity by Roger Musker

Cover photograph of Rosemary Rudland, founder of
Camembert Heritage Museum, copyright © Yvan Barbieri

Illustrations by John Taylor

Cover design by mccdesign ltd

Typeset by Brendan Cole

Printed and bound in Italy by Legoprint SpA, Trento

# CONTENTS

## SETTING UP A BUSINESS IN FRANCE

## WHICH BUSINESS STRUCTURE?

## ACQUIRING A BUSINESS OR PROPERTY

## FINANCING YOUR BUSINESS

# RUNNING A BUSINESS IN FRANCE

## BUSINESS ETIQUETTE AND CORRESPONDENCE

## TAX, SOCIAL SECURITY AND OTHER MATTERS

## EMPLOYING STAFF

## MARKETING YOUR BUSINESS

## SELLING ON

## APPENDICES

## MAPS

NOTE: the author and publishers of this book have every reason to believe in the accuracy of the information given in this book and the authenticity and correct practices of all organisations, companies, agencies, etc. mentioned; however situations may change and telephone numbers etc. can alter, and readers are strongly advised to check facts and credentials for themselves. Readers are invited to write to Vacation Work, 9 Park End Street, Oxford OX1 1HJ or e-mail with any comments or corrections.

# FOREWORD

English-speakers are showing more interest in starting a business in France than ever before. Business creations by native French are also increasing, helped by changes to regulations and reductions in taxes.

English-speaking émigrés who look to be self-employed or to start a company are generally not trying to escape unemployment in the UK, but rather hope to find a better lifestyle across the Channel. Everyone is aware of the high quality of life in France, and with property still relatively cheap it is certainly not that hard to set up a viable business, be it a bed and breakfast or simply working from home.

Anyone coming from the English-speaking world to France is in for a culture shock, not least because of the very intrusive presence of the state in all aspects of daily life. It is said that you cannot do anything in France without filling in a form. Naturally enough, the subject of French bureaucracy and red tape takes up a large part of this book. No one can be expected to understand all the details of a foreign system when they start out. For that reason it is suggested that newcomers use the services of lawyers, accountants and other experts as far as possible, so that they can be free to face the challenge of setting up a viable enterprise. This book includes interviews with some 20 foreigners who have successfully set up businesses in quite varied domains, to give some idea of how things work in practice.

Running a business in France is not all that different from running one elsewhere, except that you are dealing with another language and quite a different culture. Foreigners who set out to make a better life in France tend to show a certain pioneering spirit. One cannot help but think back to the 13th century, when English crusaders roamed around southwest France hunting down Cathar heretics. Things are a little more civilised these days. Still, it is quite possible that the new invaders could convert some locals to the spirit of entrepreneurship that is so alive in the Anglo-Saxon world.

**André de Vries, Oxford**
**May 2004**

# ACKNOWLEDGEMENTS

A book such as this can only come about through the co-operation and kindness of many.

The Chambres de Commerce in Foix, Carcassonne and Lille provided a lot of basic information. I would especially like to thank Michel Olivier of the Lille CCI for the course on entrepreneurship, Patrick Delas for advice on legal matters, Béatrice Ciolczyk on taxation, and Mike Stickland on websites. I am also indebted to property adviser Sam Crabb for sharing his experience of the French scene with me.

I was fortunate to meet generous and informative interviewees, amongst whom are Penny Armstrong and family, Carole Bayliss, Malcolm and Tina Collett, Islay Currie, Freddy and Lisette De Cock, Paul Foulkes, Nick Goldsworthy, Dawn Gough, Mike Henty, Susan Hodge, George Lidbury, Terry Link, Hugo Nuyts, Jane Pensom, Tony Pidgeon, Simon Pullen, Rosemary Rudland, Steve Skews, Kate and Andrew Thorley, George Vellacott, Tim Weir, Jean Wilkins, and several interviewees who preferred to remain anonymous.

Photos used in this book were supplied by Mike Henty, Freddy & Lisette De Cock, Jane & John Edwards, Alan Walker, Susan Hodge, Steve Skews and Miranda Neame. Special thanks to Yvan Barbieri for the cover photo.

Amongst my French friends, a big thank you to Christophe Guyon, Hélène Audiot, Régis Rousseau, Mark Salik, Frédérique Dalhoum and Sandrine Trillaud for their hospitality and patience with my various requests for help.

It is a pleasure to thank Penny Ainsworth for her excellent chauffeuring in southwest France, also Peter and Heather Jeffery of Le Réseau Amical for putting me in touch with interviewees, and not least Jane and John Edwards in Verteillac, true doyens of the *chambres d'hôtes,* for their great kindness and support for my projects.

André de Vries, Oxford
May 2004

# *Part I*

# SETTING UP A BUSINESS IN FRANCE

WHY FRANCE?

POSSIBLE TYPES OF BUSINESS

PROCEDURES FOR STARTING A BUSINESS

WHICH BUSINESS STRUCTURE?

ACQUIRING A BUSINESS OR PROPERTY

FINANCING YOUR BUSINESS

# Why France?

## CHAPTER SUMMARY

- France has a well-deserved reputation as being a good place to live.
- Many French still adhere to socialist values and are strongly opposed to economic liberalism.
- France's wealth is based on self-sufficiency in primary resources rather than on trade.
- As many French are moving to the UK to find work as there are Britons emigrating to France.
- The French generally dislike taking risks when it comes to starting a business and prefer to take over existing businesses.
- There are large variations in wealth and lifestyle between the regions.
- Social security and healthcare provision are likely to deteriorate in the future.

The image of France in the eyes of the British is more and more one of a land flowing with milk and honey, and not only among the middle classes. France is the UK's most popular tourist destination along with Spain, with some 13 million visitors a year crossing the Channel. If there was any need to remind people, we can see programmes on how to buy property in France virtually every day of the week. Everyone has heard of Nippi Singh and his friend's crazy plan to start an Indian restaurant in the Ardèche.

The rest of Europe has believed for a long time – rightly or not – that life is better in France than in their own country. The German poet Schiller coined the phrase 'to live like God in France' 200 years ago. France means hedonism, uninhibited people, a great climate, superb food and wines and culture on every street corner.

There are also objective reasons for believing that life is better in France; UNESCO's quality of life index puts France in second place after Canada, another country with a strong French influence, and this is to a large extent on France's healthcare and social security system, as well as the general art de vivre. No wonder that so many foreigners would like to live there, which means, of course, making a living as well. Life cannot be an endless holiday.

In a way, going to France is like stepping back in time. There is an old-fashioned courtesy about the people which is hard to find in England these days. Life goes on at a relaxed pace, particularly in the south. There is also a rather un-British consensus that the state should look after the citizens. The French Republic is a project that everyone is meant to support. There are ideas here such as *solidarité* and *protection sociale* which are hardly known in the UK, let alone in the USA. Businesses are 'social partners' in a dialogue with the state and the trade unions. France believes that it has a duty to fight against *le libéralisme anglo-saxonne*, and the opposite of that is *la solidarité française*. The British are 'individualists' in the view of the French, which is quite strange since the British think the same about the French, but they are talking about two different kinds of individualism.

## THE FRENCH ECONOMY

The French economy has for a long time been the fourth largest in the world, and the British the fifth, although for a while in 2002 the two countries exchanged places until the euro started to appreciate in value in 2003. France is basically a rich country; it generally posts a positive balance of trade of around £10-20 billion per year, while the UK has an annual deficit of some £30 billion. Although France is not a great trading nation like the UK, and has virtually no oil or gas, because of its greater land area and self-sufficiency in many products, it imports a lot less than it exports. France has traditionally been a difficult export market. One might also add that long-standing high unemployment has depressed consumer demand for foreign imports.

France's post-war history can be divided into two starkly different eras: *les trente glorieuses* or the 30 glorious years from 1944 to 1974, and *les trente piteuses* or 30 pitiful years from 1974 to 2004. The French call the last 30 years *la crise* or the crisis, and there is not much reason to suppose that this crisis is about to come to an end in the near future.

In the 1990s France became an industrial superpower, with some world-beating industries such as Aérospatiale, the company that

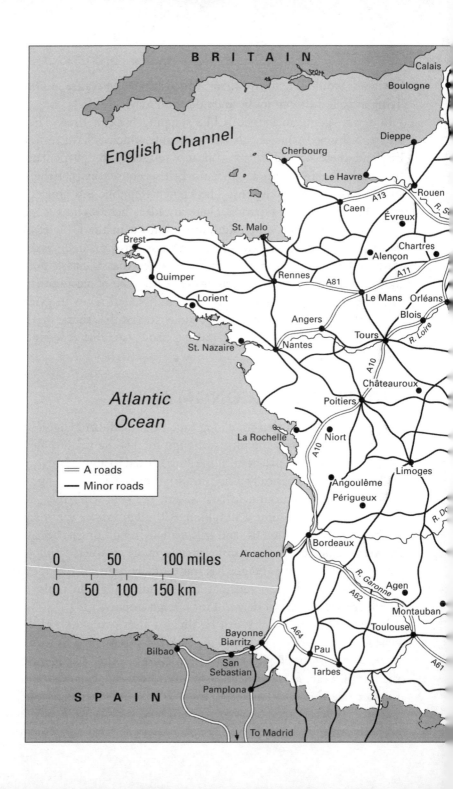

makes the Airbus together with Britain, Germany and Spain. There have also been high-profile disasters such as the bank Crédit Lyonnais and Alstom, the maker of the Eurostar trains, companies that have had to be rescued by the French state. The French like *les champions* – huge companies that bring honour and glory to France, and they are keen to support them. The TGV or high-speed train is a well-known case in point: hugely useful for those who live in and around Paris, but not that helpful if you are out in the countryside.

Periodic bursts of economic growth and the success of big companies have not helped solve the problem of high unemployment. There are simply too many disincentives for companies to take on more staff. Companies are penalised when they have 50 workers or more, so there are thousands of companies with 49 employees. The situation got to the point in the 1990s that the government brought in a 35-hour working week with the assumption that employers would automatically have to take on more workers. The idea had some initial success, but is not going to solve the unemployment problem.

### A Two-Way Street

The French approach to the economy is still to some extent based on the Marxist command economy model. The state decrees that so many jobs are going to be created, or announces a big project, and everything is expected to change. No one is very keen to consider liberalising the labour market, which would be the effective way to develop the economy, because that would mean going down the road of imitating the USA, and thus abandoning *la solidarité.*

As a consequence, France's unemployed young people are 'swimming the Channel' to try to find a job or even start a business in the UK, which is a nation of shopkeepers, as Napoleon said. At the same time the British middle classes are finding life increasingly uncomfortable in the Americanised UK, and are swimming the other way, looking for a chance to live in a more civilised society the other side of the water. Most foreigners move to France for the lifestyle rather than expecting to make a lot of money. If you have a nostalgia for a country where you pay high taxes and receive high benefits then France would be the place to go.

There are two evident obstacles to starting a business in France; one is the high level of bureaucracy – France is probably the world's most bureaucratic country – and the other is the French language. One reason young French people give for moving to the UK is the chance to improve their English. One rarely hears English-speakers expressing the same enthusiasm about mastering French, partly because those who move over to France are usually already in their thirties and have never had much experience of language-learning.

Starting a business anywhere requires similar skills. Those who have run a business elsewhere and are already successful professionals will not find it that difficult to succeed in France. The obstacles are perhaps more social than economic. Having a social life means being able to communicate with people about a greater variety of topics than the price of vegetables. Everyone who has settled down in France has the same message: the language is the key.

Many English-speaking foreigners have created a better life for themselves in France. After a few years of paying into the system they reap the benefits and enjoy a quality of life that they would never have been able achieve in their own countries.

## FRENCH ECONOMIC CULTURE

'There is no French word for *entrepreneur*', George W. Bush is reputed to have said. Everyone agrees that France does not have a particularly entrepreneurial culture, that the French are averse to taking risks, and so on. The French expect the state to look after them, in exchange for paying high taxes, or rather, high social security contributions, but the downside is that businesses also have to pay very high social charges, which in turn discourages them from setting up in the first place.

It is interesting and instructive to look at the historical reasons for the relative lack of an entrepreneurial culture in France. The modern-day situation has some echoes of the 18th century. At that time there was a popular theory that France should not export or import but rely on its own resources, and thus close its economy off from the outside world, the so-called physiocrat view of economics. France was traditionally self-sufficient in basic commodities and so pursued an isolationist policy which led to her falling behind the more go-ahead

Dutch and British. The tradition of trying to ignore what is going on in the outside world continues. France is still a rather inward-looking country, with a belief that it does not have to do things the same way as the rest of the world.

The roots of the French economic malaise can be found in the distrust of the French towards the state and large organisations and the distrust of the state towards the citizens. The Napoleonic Code, which is the basis of the modern French legal system, starts out from the assumption that people cannot be trusted. This is evident in the banking system, which is still very backward compared with the rest of the developed world. Banks are generally reluctant to lend you money, and going overdrawn is treated as a serious crime.

The necessity for the big brother state could stem from the basically anarchic nature of the French and the need to keep them under control. Or it could be that the state has made the French anarchic. That is the paradox at the centre of the French mentality. The French want to do whatever they like, but they also have an exaggerated respect for authority which seems entirely perverse to the British or Americans. Unwillingness to challenge authority and the lack of co-operation between the state and the citizens have weakened France in many ways.

The development of commerce requires both freedom from state interference, and confidence in the rule of law, factors that are still to some extent missing from the French scene. France is both a relatively corrupt country and has an over-regulated economy.

It is also worth considering the views of the German sociologist Max Weber concerning the relationship between religion and work, which he wrote about in *Protestant Ethics and the Spirit of Capitalism*. Weber believed that Catholics are more inclined than Protestants to view the world as a dangerous place ruled by the law of the jungle and this tends to discourage entrepreneurship. France's history of foreign invasions is also another factor that has reinforced a dislike of taking risks. It is a historical fact that modern capitalism arose out of Protestant cultures where work and making money became ends in themselves, once the fatalism and belief in predetermination of Calvin and Luther had undermined the drive to work for one's spiritual salvation. It is also very obvious that the French do not share the Protestant view that one can gain pleasure by self-denial.

The French Republic, of course, was founded on strongly secularist values, but this is still one of the world's most idealistic societies. This makes it difficult to bring in a more market-oriented economy, where more people have to be left to fend for themselves. There is still a large amount of paternalism about the French state and French employers. One must also be aware of the crucial importance in France of nobility of purpose, or just nobility, which has a lot of influence on attitudes to work and business. By getting rid of the aristocracy, the Revolution allowed everyone to be an aristocrat. You have to admire the French for their generosity, their refusal to do anything petty or mean-spirited, or maybe just feel irritated that you are surrounded by 55 million aristos.

Good social relations also tend to take precedence over a strict concern with profits and efficiency in France. Quality of life should not be undermined by creating a bad atmosphere in the workplace.

## FRENCH ATTITUDES TO BUSINESS CREATION

There was a seminar in Paris recently: 'Do you have to be mad to start a business in France?' A survey done for the EU by Gallup in 2001 reveals a great deal about the way French people approach business creation. They generally prefer the security of a salaried job with all the benefits that go with it: 54% stated that they preferred working for an employer to self-employment, against 49% in the UK. Note that there was not a single country in the EU where the majority preferred self-employment to employment. Opinion is more divided in UK on the benefits of employment, with 47% stating they would rather be self-employed.

France has one of the lowest rates of business creation in the European Union, with 30 creations per 10,000 population annually, compared with 65 in the UK and 71 in Germany. The French also show a stronger preference for taking over an existing business than the British. Out of all respondents, 6% had taken over a business, and 7% had started a new one, while in the UK 14% had started a new business, and only 3% had taken over an existing one. It is certainly rare for Britons to take over an existing business in France, apart from bars and restaurants.

Not surprisingly, the French see complex administrative procedures as a major obstacle to business creation, more so than the British. They are just as pessimistic about the lack of financial support. They feel a great deal of responsibility towards their staff and customers, more than the British who are more concerned about losing their assets.

## FRANCE AND THE REGIONS

France has about the same population as the UK, but twice the land area. There is a wealth of regional identities, as well as languages, some of which have reasonable survival prospects, e.g. Alsatian, Basque, Corsican and Breton. Flemish in the north-west, Catalan in Roussillon, and Occitan, which was once the language all over the south, are only spoken by enthusiasts.

The French revolutionaries deliberately tried to cut the connection between the provinces and regional identities, and created départements named after rivers which ignored traditional boundaries. While the British refer to 'the Dordogne', the French call the area 'le Périgord'. Until recently it was considered unpatriotic to insist on one's local identity, but the state has now officially recognised about 200 *pays*, or local regions, which have a useful function in promoting tourism as well as encouraging a sense of identity. As a practical measure, the huge number of local communes or municipalities are now more or less obliged to join together into larger *collectivités* in order to manage their resources more efficiently. There are some 55,000 collective entities and some 550,000 local and national politicians, many of them holding offices at several levels of government.

There are great disparities in terms of wealth and lifestyle between the regions, as one can see from the table below.

France has been in a process of decentralisation since the 1950s when the idea of the regions was first mooted. The power of the centrally appointed *préfets* (an idea that goes back to Roman times) has been reduced in favour of regional and departmental councils. Local authorities have more say in handing out grants and subsidies to new businesses, and may receive more powers in the future.

For the English-speaking foreigner, there are certain areas that hold the greatest appeal, namely those that are close to the Channel ports, and most of the eastern half of the Pyrenees and south-east France. A dry climate is a major factor, and the best areas for sunshine are the Vendée and the south-east. If your business is aimed at servicing other expatriates then you are more or less obliged to go where the other foreigners are.

| ANNUAL GNP PER HEAD OF POPULATION IN EUROS (2000) | |
| --- | --- |
| Ile de France | 35.946 |
| Rhône-Alpes | 24,113 |
| Alsace | 23,777 |
| Haute-Normandie | 22,909 |
| Champagne-Ardenne | 21,796 |
| PACA | 21,020 |
| Bourgogne | 20,974 |
| Aquitaine | 20,893 |
| Centre | 20,603 |
| Pays de la Loire | 20,437 |
| Franche-Comté | 20,261 |
| Midi-Pyrénées | 20,197 |
| Auvergne | 19,653 |
| Basse-Normandie | 19,521 |
| Bretagne | 19,345 |
| Lorraine | 19,177 |
| Picardie | 19,031 |
| Nord-Pas de Calais | 18,982 |
| Limousin | 18,859 |
| Corsica | 18,550 |
| Poitou-Charentes | 18,454 |
| Languedoc-Roussillon | 17,827 |

Property is relatively cheap all over France, outside of the Riviera. Even Paris is quite reasonable: see tables in the chapter Acquiring a Business or Property. There are considerable differences in local taxes between different areas, but not enough to make one want to avoid

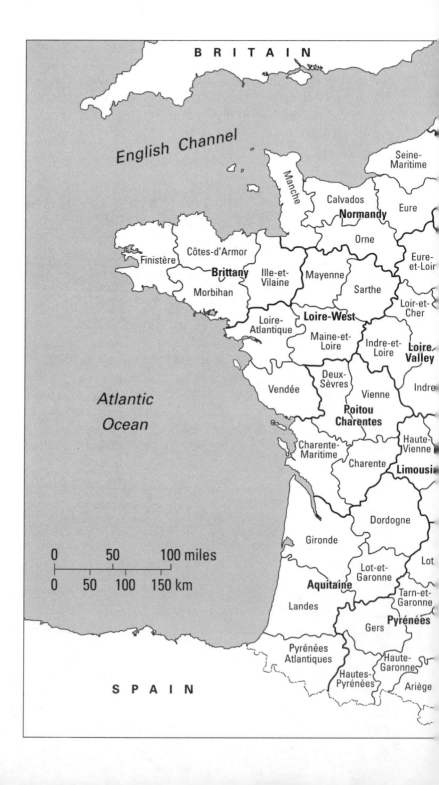

**Regions and Departments of France**

BELGIUM

GERMANY

LUXEMBOURG

Nord-Pas-de-Calais
Pas-de-Calais
Nord
Somme
Picardy
Oise
Aisne
Ardennes

Paris
Seine-et-Marne
Région parisienne
Paris et Région
Loiret

Marne
Champagne-Ardenne
Aube
Yonne

Meuse
Lorraine
Meurthe-et-Moselle
Haute-Marne
Vosges

Moselle
Alsace
Bas-Rhin
Haut-Rhin

Haute-Saône
Franche-Comté
Belfort
Côte-d'Or
Burgundy
Doubs
Cher
Nièvre
Saône-et-Loire
Jura

SWITZERLAND

Allier
Ain
Haute-Savoie

Creuse
Puy-de-Dôme
Loire
Rhône
Auvergne
Savoie & Dauphiné
Savoie

Corrèze
Cantal
Haute-Loire
Rhône
Isère

ITALY

Ardèche
Drôme
Hautes-Alpes

Lozère
Aveyron
Gard
Vaucluse
Alpes-de-Haute-Provence
Alpes-Maritimes
Côte d'Azur

Tarn
Languedoc
Hérault
Bouches-du-Rhône
Provence
Var

Aude

Pyrénées-Orientales

Mediterranean Sea

Haute-Corse

Corse-du-Sud

any particular places.

Demographic changes will have a considerable effect on the relative chances of success in different regions. Central France is generally emptying out, while the western coastal regions and Provence/Côte d'Azur will see rapidly growing populations. There is a big new market for gardening and DIY centres as more city-dwellers move out to the surrounding countryside (as they are everywhere in western Europe), with the constantly improving railway system making long-distance commuting easier. All kinds of restaurants, fast food outlets, delicatessens and high-class food shops are seeing a growth in trade, while there is also more demand for domestic employees and childcare facilities for women who want to go out to work. There are also increasing age disparities in the regions; the centre has an ageing population as the young people move away from the land, while Paris will have an increasingly youthful population. Montpellier is becoming a major attraction for young entrepreneurs, while Toulouse is already a well-established magnet to foreigners because of its aerospace and other high-tech industries.

Some areas are seeing an excessive number of British, Belgians and Dutch moving in, and rumblings of discontent from locals who feel that outsiders are pushing up property prices and changing the character of some villages and towns. The recent big growth area has been in the Midi-Pyrenees and Languedoc-Roussillon. The next areas are likely to be the previously unpopular Limousin and Auvergne. Poitou-Charente is also seeing a lot of new English-speaking foreigners who cannot afford or do not want to live in the overcrowded Dordogne or Lot.

The decline in population in the French countryside has stopped for the first time in 100 years, as it becomes easier to work from home and the internet creates new forms of business. This should all be helpful to foreigners who want to base themselves in the countryside and provide services not only to the expatriate community but also to the middle-class French who are moving out to the countryside.

# WHAT DOES THE FUTURE HOLD?

Despite its reputation as a utopia, France is not immune to the problems of the rest of the developed world. These include an ageing population and a shortfall in the provision for the social security system. One thing that is clear is that since the election of a right-wing government in 2002, and the re-election of Jacques Chirac, a programme of reform has started which will lead to a reduction of social security and healthcare benefits and a more market-oriented economy. Many new policies have been put in place to encourage small business start-ups but these do not begin to address the real problems in this area. While income tax has decreased considerably for everyone, this has never been the real issue, when compulsory social security payments are so high. France has suffered for a long time from weak governments which caved in too easily to violent protests. One can expect a period of political unrest with an authoritarian right-wing government taking on all kinds of interest groups from all shades of political opinion.

A more disturbing trend has been the growth in popularity of extreme right-wing politicians such as Jean-Marie Le Pen, who beat the socialist candidate Lionel Jospin into third place in the 2002 presidential election. The consequence has been that the current government has had to go along with more repressive policies towards immigrants, such as banning headscarves in schools. Increasing intolerance towards outsiders is a feature of the present scene, but hopefully it will not extend to the Anglo-Saxons.

# Possible Types
# of Business

## CHAPTER SUMMARY

- **Target Market.** You need to think about who your target market is going to be.
- **Façade.** It is sometimes better to have a French business name.
- **Shops.** The French see English goods as exotic and are even prepared to buy some kinds of English food.
- **Tourism.** Bed and breakfasts and *gîtes* are not guaranteed to support you, and are vulnerable to a downturn in tourism.
- **Restaurants.** This is an expanding area and it is quite possible to compete with the locals.
- **Farming.** Although still supported by EU subsidies, this could be a risky area when subsidies go down.
- **Vineyards.** These are expensive and hard work, but can provide a very satisfying way of making a living.
- **Gardening.** A growing area and one where foreigners can do well.
- **Alternative Medicine.** Expatriates need osteopaths, psychotherapists etc. Some areas of alternative medicine are more strictly regulated than in UK.
- **Running Courses.** There is a lot of scope for running courses and providing accommodation for tourists at the same time.

A good deal of initiative and determination is needed to make a go of a business in France. The safest way to go could be to set up a service for other foreigners, although you cannot afford to completely ignore the local market. The risk is that if there were a big downturn in the tourist market, or for some reason – e.g. currency movements – a lot of foreigners were to leave France, then you would no longer have a viable customer base. It is also rather more interesting to cater for the French and their tastes rather than trying to pretend that you are not in a foreign country.

Few English-speakers take over existing businesses, even though there are plenty available. Inevitably, you have to decide whether you are going to capitalise on your foreignness, or try to blend in with the scenery and keep an entirely French façade. Much of this depends on just how many foreigners there are in your *clientèle*. If half the population in your village are English-speakers (which includes Dutch, Belgians, Germans etc.) then you might have something to gain from presenting an English façade, but at the end of the day your business will succeed or fail on the basis of what you are rather than your nationality.

# SHOPS

One of the more obvious routes towards business success is to set up a shop to sell goods imported from the UK (or other English-speaking country) to homesick Britons who miss their Marmite and digestive biscuits. However, there is also a market amongst the local population for crockery, tea towels, biscuits, cakes, etc., that appear quite exotic to the French. Even if the locals turn up their noses at English cuisine they will still come to you to get their tea.

## *The English Shop*

Susan Hodge started up The English Shop in Foix, Ariège in South-west France in 2003. The website is: www.simplybritishshop.com.

*I have been living in France for 14 years. I'm running a small shop, retailing British products – food, chinaware, books, etc. The business is in my name, and I'm self-employed. I already had the property which had been previously used for business purposes by someone else. I went to the Chambre de Commerce for advice and to register the business.*

*I had to deal with various bodies such as the Répression des Fraudes, who insisted that all foods be labelled with ingredients and instructions for use in French, and that books and videos are labelled as in Langue Anglaise. The legality of this is in some doubt, so I'm seeking legal advice. I've had a visit from another department checking for price labels on everything. Then there are the health department checks as regards chilled foods, and I have a licence to sell alcohol.*

*I was not obliged to go on any training courses, compulsory or otherwise. I did have one meeting with an accountant to check on the necessary book-keeping system. I am using my local bank who hold all current/savings/mortgage accounts. Basically I told them what I wanted to do and there have been no problems. As I live in a rural area, there was little choice of banks locally. I had to ask three times for a business cheque book, and had to submit a* prévisionnel financier *(provisional budget) approved by the Chambre de Commerce before they would let me have one.*

*For tax purpose I am under the* réel simplifié régime, *not micro-entreprise. As a self-employed person I pay my social security payments to the Mutuelle de Tarn et Garonne.*

*The most difficult part of running a business in France is knowing the right questions to ask the right people at the right time. The French assume that you are 'au fait' with the way that things are done over here. Knowing what is essential and legal, as opposed to that which someone is simply trying to sell. It's like buying a property: the second time is easy, once you've found out how things should be done. It would have been helpful to know more about the legislation as regards running a business. In my case, the 'labelling of goods in French' issue, and the fact that it is illegal to sell anything at a loss.*

*Running a retail business every day brings new faces and new ways of thinking. The way that the French can be as snobby as the Brits, and how some of them see anything imported from Britain as better than the same thing found in France, Twinings tea for example. They pay more for an identical product from me than from the local supermarket because it's 'better'.*

## TOURISM

France has the image of being the world's number one tourist destination; the British make 13 million trips a year to France, although Spain actually has more tourists in absolute numbers. You may be surprised to know that the UK actually earns more from tourism than France, and employs more than twice as many people in the hotel and restaurant sector. The reasons for this lie in the make-up of the French population. As everyone has relatives in the country, they go and stay with them rather than in a hotel or bed and breakfast. Better-off French families usually have a house in the country of their own.

In recent years there has been a growing interest in 'green tourism' or *le tourisme vert*, as more and more city dwellers look for peace and quiet in the countryside. The traditional tourist market in France has been declining for some years, while the shortfall is being made up by an increase in the number of foreign visitors. The most significant trend now is 'theme tourism', which means providing activities as well as accommodation. Many foreigners find the tourist sector to be a steady earner, but it is just as well to try to hedge one's bets with some other money-making activity.

## GITES AND CHAMBRES D'HOTES

The famously popular businesses called *gîtes* and *chambres d'hôtes* are actually rather different, but they can be run from one property. The term *gîtes* originally meant a basic dwelling, but is now applied to any kind of self-catering lodgings in the countryside. In Britain they are called 'holiday cottages'. The implication is that the owner has little contact with the guests, and may not even need to live on the premises if they employ someone to deal with changeovers. If you are going to belong to the organisation known as Gîtes de France (GdF) then the building you use can be no more than two storeys high and has to be in a rustic style. There is in principle nothing to stop you from running a *chambres d'hôtes* from an apartment block in the middle of a town, but you will not receive any recognition (or grants) from GdF.

What are known as *chambres d'hôtes* are bed and breakfasts in the English sense. They often include dinner as well, which are known as *tables d'hôtes*. Literally speaking, *chambres d'hôtes* means 'guest bedrooms'. According to Gîtes de France there are some 45,000 *gîtes* in France, and 26,000 *chambres d'hôtes*. As far as registered businesses go, it seems that only about 6,000 families are able to make a full-time living in this sector, while the rest have other income. Foreigners need to realise that the market for *gîtes* and *chambres d'hôtes* is pretty well saturated and that they need to have some other source of income to survive.

The original idea of *gîtes* and *chambres d'hôtes* was to give farmers an additional source of income. As a farmer, if you run some *gîtes* on the side, you will be registered as an *agriculteur* and you will not have to register two different businesses. Before you can buy a farm to make it into *chambres d'hôtes* or *gîtes* SAFER – an organisation devoted to promoting farming – has the right to match the highest offer on the property. It is up to your notaire to contact anyone who has pre-emptive rights to make sure that they do not intend to exercise them.

The majority of bed and breakfasts are not run by farmers these days. Some *gîtes* or holiday homes are run by Britons and other foreigners who remain resident in their own countries and run them from a distance. There is nothing illegal about this, as long as they pay their taxes to one country or the other. In principle, it is easy to enough to buy properties, advertise them in the UK, and employ a local person to change the sheets and deal with the key handover.

Running *gîtes* is a great deal easier than running *chambres d'hôtes* as you are not required to have contact with your guests. In the case of *chambres d'hôtes* things are very different. Many guests expect to have contact with owners. In a sense the world is coming to your door, and you need to be friendly with whoever turns up, regardless of how you may feel about some of your guests. Even how you answer the telephone is of crucial importance. The advice is to smile when you talk on the telephone; your attitude does come across. Your guests need to feel at home, while having their own space. It is essential to keep rooms clean, and to change bed linen once a week, towels twice a week. The rooms should be decorated in a neutral style, in light colours. Avoid imposing your personal tastes on the guests; i.e. no garish paintings or odd colour schemes.

There are of course regulations to be observed. If the *chambres d'hôtes* or *gîtes* are your main business then you will need to be registered with the Chambre de Commerce. Before you even consider buying property to let out furnished, you must be aware that in principle you are not permitted to rent out furnished property in communes with 10,000 inhabitants if you are classed as a professional landlord, i.e. the majority of your income comes from rentals, or where rental income exceeds €23,000 a year. This restriction may be waived where a property is regularly let in a tourist area. If you rent out 6 furnished bedrooms or more then you are officially a hotel, and subject to more stringent safety regulations, and a lot more red tape, including VAT.

Before buying a property with a view to renting it to holidaymakers, you need to make a hardheaded analysis about the attractions of the place:

- Is the place easy to get to?
- Are there any cultural attractions nearby?
- How far is it from the sea/mountains/lakes?
- How will it look in a photograph?
- How much income do I need to make it viable?
- How many weeks of the year do I want to use it myself?
- Can I get a grant to renovate the place?
- How much will it cost to furnish?
- Can I install a swimming pool?
- Are there any shops nearby?
- What other services can I offer to make the business viable?

If you are looking for grants then you will need to register with Gîtes de France, an organisation originally intended to help farmers which is run by the Conseils Généraux. There are advantages and disadvantages to belonging to Gîtes de France. They will tell you how to equip your *chambres d'hôtes,* and what you can charge people to stay (see box below). You will also be given a minimum number of months that you have to remain open each year. You can cancel your contract with GdF every year before 30 June, otherwise it continues by default.

## CHARTER FOR CHAMBRES D'HOTES

**Gîtes de France requires you to fulfil numerous conditions to run a *chambres d'hôtes:***
- garden and living room must be included
- separate entrances for you and your guests
- breakfasts are served by the owner, and must be 'generous'
- no more than 5 bedrooms and 15 guests in total
- bedrooms are graded separately
- 2-*épi* rooms must have a private bathroom, but can have

> shared toilet (up to 6 persons)
> - 3-4 *épi* rooms are fully en suite
> - curtains and bed linen must match
> - minimum furnishing of a wardrobe with coat-hangers, shelving, bed-side table and lamp
> - adequate sound insulation
> - walls, floors and ceilings in perfect condition
> - rooms and beds need to be of a certain size
> - safety and hygiene regulations must be observed
> - the Gîtes de France symbol can be displayed as long as you pay your subscription.

Once you have been inspected by Gîtes de France (GdF), then you will be given an *épi* (wheatear) rating, and you can display the Gîtes de France plaque on your wall. Individual rooms are graded separately on a scale of one to three *épis*, so you can quite easily have two rooms with three *épis* and one room with two *épis*. You will of course be listed in the GdF guide. Tourist offices will direct potential customers to you, rather than to people who have not registered with GdF; they may not even be aware of the existence of any other bed and breakfasts. The downside is that you will need to pay 12-15% of your takings to GdF. Many foreign owners find GdF's interference in their business intolerable and do not get involved with them. You should be careful about taking grants via GdF because this could lead to problems if you decide to pull out of their organisation (see below).

## Upgrading facilities

Any *chambres d'hôtes* or *gîtes* business needs publicity, and whatever happens you will need to put money into becoming known, at least initially. There are umpteen websites and organisations that can publicise your business. Further ideas are given in chapter 10, *Marketing Your Business*. If your guests are satisfied, then your reputation will soon spread; word of mouth is the best publicity. The best way to maximise takings is to install a swimming pool. Beyond that, you need to provide further services that will bring people to your door. These could include running courses with guest teachers, such as painting, creative writing, cookery, etc. Or you could offer guided hiking, using local people, or visits to local craftsmen. Many guests come to visit cultural attractions, so it is as well to bone up on the local history, or at least provide a range of guidebooks to the area. It is worth considering that the average *chambres d'hôtes* guest is a sophisticated professional in their forties with a high disposable income, so you need to try to cater for their tastes.

An extension of *chambres d'hôtes* are *tables d'hôtes* (the guest table), i.e. you cook your guests meals. Usually these are only supplied in the evening. They are a plus point in country areas where your guests may have to go a long way to find a restaurant. Supplying meals can increase your profits but it can also be a strain, and it is a good idea to have cooking facilities for your guests as well. If you are officially registered as offering *tables d'hôtes* then there are rules about the kind of food you can serve. The food has to be fresh and ideally grown by yourself, or otherwise bought from local farmers. If cooking is not your forte, you might be best advised to have your *chambres d'hôtes* near some restaurants.

### Twitching in the Ariège

Nick Goldsworthy is an ornithologist who runs a *chambres d'hôtes* at Lescure near St Girons in the Ariège with views of the Pyrenees. He has been living there since 1992 with his wife and two children.

*Initially we spent a year researching the area. We sold our house in the UK, but then sterling dropped by 30% so we were undercapitalised when we moved to France. The original idea was to offer nature and bird-watching tours; our customers would stay elsewhere in the area. We didn't want just to offer bed and breakfast as there were so many other people doing the same thing. One of the greatest problems was the cost of advertising: over time the RSPB and other organisations raised their rates to commercial levels and so it became impossible to advertise with them. We offered tours for botanists and ornithologists; they often asked if they could stay with us and lost interest when we said that they would have to stay elsewhere, so eventually after 5 years we decided to do bed and breakfast as well. Sometimes groups of* botanists or bird-watchers stay for a week or 10 days. Otherwise it's open to anyone. We also rented the place out to the BBC at one time.

We still do botanical and ornithological tours; many customers are early retirees picking up old hobbies. If somebody wants to see orchids we can guarantee them fields and fields full of orchids. If they want to see a particular bird they may have to walk for several hours before they see one, but we don't offer guarantees. Others are specialists finishing their studies.

We went to Gîtes de France, who were very pleasant at first. They gave us a lot of good information about tax and social security. They brought WWF France along and suggested that we go for Gîte Panda status, since we were outside a national park. We paid to be in their magazine and didn't get a single client. In the end they became too unreasonable. They wanted me to knock two rooms together because one of them was 20 cubic centimetres too small, so we quit them.

One aspect to watch out for is the cooking. It took me 18 months to figure out an answer to the question 'Why don't you British say bon appetit?' If you have French people staying with you then you can't offer them 'Stewed Rabbit'. If you call it 'Civet de Lapin' then they are quite happy to eat it. If it hasn't got exactly the right ingredients then you can't say that a dish is French, but it's OK if you say it's Scottish.

Starting out with this business was difficult because I needed a Chambre de Commerce number before I could get a Carte de Séjour, but then I needed a Carte de Séjour to get the Chambre de Commerce number. Then you have to register with Sécurité Sociale so you can make contributions. When we filed our first declaration we were too poor to pay any contributions so they sent our money back. I would advise dealing with these offices at any time other than in March when they are preparing their annual accounts.

## Gîtes

There are considerable advantages to renting out gîtes rather than doing bed and breakfast. The guests look after themselves; your job is to make sure the place is clean and that sheets are changed. You will need someone to deal with keyholding, and changeovers between guests, if you cannot do this yourself. Gîtes are generally rented by the week and will accommodate more than two people at a time. You can also have special offers for weekends. If you are a member, Gîtes de France requires you to rent out the *gîte* by the week and for a minimum number of months of the year, usually six months. Out of season you can rent out *gîtes* to house-hunters or others for months at a time but this does require attention to having a suitable letting contract (see below).

---

## GITES

Gîtes de France distinguishes between several kinds of *gîtes* of which the most common type is the *gîte de séjour*. The conditions for such a *gîte* as laid down by GdF are:

- The *gîte* must be accessible by car.
- It must be in a commune with fewer than 5,000 inhabitants.
- There must be a communal space.
- A kitchen or cooking facilities must be available to guests.
- For a 3 *épis gîte* there has to be a washing machine.
- Beds and mattresses must be of a minimum quality.
- There has to be some open space around the property, preferably with garden furniture and barbecue equipment.
- The owner is not required to live on the premises but must be within 15 km.

In the case of another GdF-recognised *gîte*, the *gîte d'étape*, this has to be located on a recognised signposted hiking trail, and the owner has to be nearby to give information to hikers. A greater degree of comfort is also required, e.g. heating. There is also a *gîte de pêche* which has to be equipped for fishing.

---

If you are simply looking to rent out holiday homes, including cottages, apartments, villas, chalets, etc. then you can register with the organisation Clévacances ('Key holidays'), who will list you on their website and in their catalogue for an annual fee. It is compulsory to draw up a contract for the letting. You can rent out by the week or by the weekend. See www.clevacances.com.

Running *gîtes* is a very seasonal business: the core months are July and August. Often the rooms will be unsuitable for use in cold weather. It is a good idea to consider supplying some added services, such as sport facilities, rented bicycles or internet access. Giving your *gîtes* some kind of ecological theme can attract more customers. Furniture and equipment for your property need to be adequate but not elaborate, as there will inevitably be breakages. It is best to buy plain, light-coloured local furniture that fits in with the surroundings. Older French houses tend to have dark wallpaper and are badly lit by British standards; holidaymakers prefer bright, light colours. Crockery and cutlery should be as cheap as you can get away with.

It is essential to have electric kettles, cooking equipment, and adequate rubbish facilities. It is sometimes suggested that you leave some food for arriving guests if you are not cooking for them, but it is best to avoid perishables such as flour, rice or porridge, as they will attract insects.

**Grants from Gîtes de France.** Before you do any work on a property, or even buy it, look into the possibility of applying for grants for the building work. Grants for *gîtes* are distributed by the local Conseil Général – the departmental government – through Gîtes de France, which is organised on a regional basis. The amounts available vary considerably. If you are lucky, GdF may match the amount you spend. In other areas, the *département* may have little money to hand out. If you do not follow GdF's instructions to the letter then grants will be withheld. One Dutch couple in the Ariège lost their grant after the work had been done because they failed to send in a particular form.

There are conditions attached: you have to agree to allow GdF to handle the letting and publicity for 10 years during the summer in return for a cut of your takings of some 15%. It has the final say in what kind of facilities your *gîtes* will have, and grades your premises in its catalogue with one to three *épis* or wheatears. They will tell you the minimum number of weeks of the year you can rent your *gîtes* out; six months is quite normal. If you sell the property within 10 years then the grant will be repayable.

There are plenty of other organisations that can hand out grants, starting with the European Union (see the chapter Financing Your Business). The most important person to talk to is the local mayor, who not only knows about possible grants, but also has the power to approve building permits. Mayors can be very helpful, or in some cases irrationally obstructive and difficult. Just pray that you have a good mayor in your commune. You should also contact the local *Office du Tourisme* or the *Syndicat d'Initiative*, whose function is to promote all kinds of small businesses and investments as well as tourism. If you are buying a listed building or one with special historical associations, there will be more generous grants available, but any renovations will be subject to more stringent requirements. Whatever kind of renovation you plan to do, all the plans and estimates must be approved first before any work is started, otherwise you will not receive the grant. You should have the estimates or *devis*, as well as valid planning permission before you even think of buying your property.

## Financial viability

It is essential to understand that very few people make a full-time living out of *gîtes* unless they have a large complex, or several of them in different places. It is quite feasible to leave the letting to an agent, who will collect up to 15% of your rental takings. If you live far away, then it is best to install a telephone that only takes in-coming calls, and phone up from time to time to see if people are staying at the place, otherwise agents may pocket the money for themselves.

If you would like to do a training course in how to run *gîtes* then there are monthly courses held in Warwickshire and the Charente/Dordogne borders. Look at www.gitescomplexes.co.uk, or contact Tim Williams on 05 45 98 08 56 in France.

## How Much Can I Charge?

The core letting season for *gîtes* is very short; at most 12 weeks a year, and even as short as 8 weeks: July and August. The average number of weeks in the year that *gîtes* are rented out is 17 according to GdF. This can be stretched if you are in the south, or can offer some additional activities. The other months are 'shoulder months'. In the colder months you can only charge half the rent you would in the summer. It must be said that many areas in the south of France are saturated with *gîtes* and *chambres d'hôtes*; there are other people who have had the same idea as you. A swimming pool greatly increases the market-ability of your B&B. It is easy enough to check up on prices by looking at websites belonging to *gîtes* owners, or in catalogue. A good-size 4-bedroom house with swimming pool can fetch as much as €1,000 a week in the high season.

Most *gîtes* can only fetch a low rent out of season, but *chambres d'hôtes* can keep going all the year round. There are prospective property buyers travelling around most of the year looking for a welcoming place to stay in the countryside. If you offer other attractions, such as battlefield tours or winter sports, then you can do as well in the winter as the summer, but by and large many *gîtes/chambres d'hôtes* owners go on holiday in the quiet season if they have no family commitments.

**Taxation Issues.** Most *gîtes/chambres d'hôtes* opt for the status of *micro-entreprise* which simplifies the whole bookkeeping process. If the net income from rentals exceeds €23,000, or constitutes more than 50% of your household income, then you are considered a professional landlord, and you will be required to register as a business and pay higher social security taxes on the income. Farmers can include their income from tourism under *bénéfices agricoles* as long as they opt for the *régime réel,* if their tourist income does not exceed €30,000 or 30% of their income per year. There are also issues relating to local property taxes, and the *taxe professionnelle.* For further information see 'Taxation' in chapter 8, *Tax, Social Security & other Matters.*

**Legal Issues.** Short-term lets of holiday homes come under the *Location Libre* regime, the basic rental law dating from 1948, which protects the owner as long as they observe certain conditions. If the right conditions are not observed, and the tenants refuse to leave the property, there will be major legal costs involved in evicting them (unless it is your principal residence). Amongst other things:

○ The property should be fully furnished.
○ The rental must be for no more than three months.
○ The tenants need to have a principal residence elsewhere.
○ The property is only to be used for holidays.

It is advisable to draw up a written contract – *contrat de location* – which includes an inventory of the contents of the property, the *état des lieux,* drawn up in the presence of both parties. This is to protect you in case tenants do damage to your place. There should also be clauses concerning nuisance to neighbours. For more information on longer-term letting, consult *Letting French Property Successfully,* by Stephen Smith and Charles Parkinson, published by PKF Guernsey.

# RESTAURANTS

Incredible as it may seem, there are a number of Britons and other foreigners who are prepared to take on the French in their holy of holies, the *resto.* Most will employ French chefs and stick with a more or less French menu. There is probably little mileage to be made from offering bangers and mash, although it has been done. One British dish that has really caught on recently is apple crumble, and it is even served on the TGVs as *crumble de pommes.* Most other British food is generally looked down on.

Running a restaurant involves one in a whole range of inspections and health and safety regulations.

### *A Vertical Bistro*

Mike Henty is an accountant who moved to the Dordogne in 1992 to run a bed and breakfast. In 2002 he started the Bistrot Verticalle in Verteillac.

> *The building we took over was once a butcher's, and then used for tea dances. For 35 years it was used as a stockroom for the general store across the road. We have now split the ownership of the building between ourselves and the owner of Galérie Verticalle, an art gallery. We own the ground floor and the cellars.*
>
> *There are a lot of formalities to opening a restaurant, which you have to do in a certain order. There's a rule for everything, and a way of getting round things. You can't argue with them. The best thing is to ask them to help you out. For example, I made a toilet with wheelchair access that was vetoed by the health and safety, because it*

*had two doors close together which would be difficult to get through, so I had to remove the inner door. If you put in a new toilet then it has to have disabled access. There has to be a ramp from outside. The kitchen had to be tiled and separate basins and chopping surfaces put in for meat and vegetables, and we had to put in a new floor and ceiling. My wife is the chef; the waitresses and the* plongeur *(washer-up) are French. We are only open between mid-May and mid-October, and the staff have short-term contracts.*

*The local French have not supported us much. The chemist next door complained about the fumes from the extractor fan affecting her daughter, but this was completely impossible as the smoke would have to have gone around a couple of corners. Then there was the terrace out the front. I got the approval of the* maire *and the planning office to put up an 8 by 1.5 metre terrace on the pavement. One day I came back and found a white line painted on the pavement. The chemist had complained that my terrace stuck out too far so the* maire *had painted a line.*

*The business is an* Entreprise Individuelle. *I do my own accounts because I'm a qualified accountant, but most Britons would have an accountant. We have chosen not to be a* Micro-Entreprise, *because we want to claim depreciation, having invested a lot in the building and equipment. If you go for* Micro *status, then you are taxed on 28% of your turnover whereas our profit margin is less than that. We use the* BIC réel simplifié *on our tax return. We are not VAT-registered as we're below the limit. We do have to pay our employees' contributions, however, which adds 50% to the wages bill. We need to serve 20 full meals a day to reach our break-even point.*

## HOTELS

A fair number of hotels in France are run by foreigners. Some experience in the tourist trade is useful if not absolutely compulsory. Just as with a shop, a hotel can be bought and sold as a *fonds de commerce* i.e. the business is sold separately from the building, which is then rented. An example of a hotel run from a rented apartment can be found in the chapter *Acquiring a Business*. It is much more usual to buy the building, since hotels in country areas are not that expensive, but you are then responsible for maintaining it. Running a hotel means observing a lot of regulations. When you are given a star rating you are also told the minimum price you can charge per room, a measure intended to prevent unfair competition.

## A Family Hotel

The Armstrong family took over the Hôtel du Perigord hotel and restaurant in Verteillac, Dordogne in 2002 and have worked hard to restore it to its original condition. Penny Armstrong previously managed a large hotel complex with 60 apartments near Cannes.

*We took over a working hotel in November and hoped to renovate it in stages. This didn't quite go to plan, as the dust from the building work made it impossible to run a restaurant at the same time. We thought it would just mean redecorating it but there was a lot more involved. By March 2003 we were able to open for business, while still leaving some rooms to be refurbished later on.*

*Someone from the Chambre de Commerce came along when we arrived and told us what we had to do. This meant installing fire doors and alarms, stripping all the polystyrene tiles off the ceilings, and bringing the kitchen up to the required standards. The doors have to resist a fire for a certain number of hours. As there was no one available to do the work for 6 months, we had to do it ourselves.*

*There are five bodies who come and inspect you. The health inspector comes anyway every year. We have a Category 4 licence that allows us to sell any kind of alcohol without food. The business registration number or SIRET, arrived automatically. We are an entreprise individuelle. The TVA is not sorted out automatically. The notaire deals with it, and the fact is advertised in the local paper. For your first year you have quite a lot of leeway. You can let it mount up till the end of the year and then pay it. After that it becomes monthly or quarterly. When people come and eat here they pay 19.6% TVA. The stuff you buy is taxed at 19.6% or 5.5%. You can claim TVA back on your capital expenditure.*

*As regards finance, as I had worked in the hotel business before, I knew what to expect. We knew what the turnover was from the previous owner; we calculated that we would be at break-even for the first year.*

*We have gone out of our way to keep the existing customers. We don't serve shepherd's pie and Yorkshire pudding. In this location we serve country cooking. If you are on the Côte d'Azur you have to serve haute cuisine. We use the vegetables that are in season; the English* brocanteur *(junk-shop owner) next door supplies us with pumpkins, courgettes etc. We grow our own tomatoes. If someone gives us a load of rhubarb then we have rhubarb crumble, which the French greatly enjoy. There are also the mushrooms; you need to take them to the local pharmacy to make sure they're not poisonous. It's part of their job to tell you.*

*We were already aware of the nature of running a hotel/restaurant, i.e. split shifts. It is physically demanding work and the hours are long. On the other hand you meet a lot of people, and it is very satisfying to see everyone laughing and joking and having a good time. During the summer it gets very hot in the kitchen; even with the air-con going full blast it can be like Dante's inferno in there. It got up to 46 degrees in 2003 and that was outside.*

*Getting the right staff is crucial. When I worked near Cannes there was a Human Resources section. Here I would say that you need either the longest trial period possible, or use a limited term contract. This is allowed in the hotel business for a 4-month season. If you get good staff you don't want to lose them. On the other hand, if the contract is unlimited, they can go off sick for months and you don't see them. As an outsider in France, you must be careful what you do. Getting good advice is not easy.*

When you employ staff, as you will need to, their contracts and wages are subject to the *Convention Collective Nationale des Hôteliers Cafetiers Restaurateurs.* The nearest DDTEFP will inform you.

## BARS

In order to start a bar you are certainly going to have to take one over from someone else. Because of the French policy of not creating new licences for spirits there is virtually no possibility of starting from scratch. The bar/café is another French icon, but one which can be adjusted to your liking. The present trend is towards theme cafés; getting hold of some photos and authentic trinkets to stick on the walls is the thing to do now. You will need to consider your target market; if you are looking for a young crowd then consider putting in free internet access. If you want the more traditional type of customer, then a pool table and 'baby-foot' (table football) are the thing. For a sophisticated crowd, try a literary theme, and supply some books.

**Licensing Laws.** To run a bar, you require a Category 4 drinks licence, which enables you to sell spirits and all kinds of alcohol without serving food as well. As part of a campaign against alcoholism it is official French government policy that the number of Category 2, 3 and 4 licences is limited depending on the population of the commune. If the quota of licenses has not been used up, or the population increases, then new licences can be created, but this rarely happens. Generally, licences have to be bought and registered with the *mairie*. Once a business selling alcohol ceases to exist, then the licence disappears after three years unless someone takes it over. Category 4 licences are particularly valuable and can be worth €25,000 or more when a bar is put on the market. Restaurants can obtain a drinks licence that allows the sale of alcohol with food only. A declaration has to be made to the *Bureau de Déclarations* of the *Direction des Douanes et des Droits Indirects* (French customs and excise).

Beverages are classified under five types, depending on alcoholic content, and basic ingredients. This is an abbreviated list:

Group 1     0-1.2 degrees
Group 2     1-3 degrees
Group 3     up to 18 degrees
Group 4     apéritifs and spirits
Group 5     all alcoholic drinks

To allay any uncertainty, the list of possible drinks licences is given below:

*petite licence restaurant*   Group 1-2 drinks, accompanied by food *grande licence restaurant* All groups, accompanied by food

| | |
|---|---|
| *Licence 1* | Non-alcoholic drinks, or with traces of alcohol under 1.2 degrees |
| *Licence 2* | Group 1-2 drinks |
| *Licence 3* | Group 1-3 drinks |
| *Licence 4* | All Groups. |

If you want to sell tobacco, then a licence is also required from the *Direction Régionale de Douanes* (customs and excise). All spaces used by the public are subject to regulations concerning smoking areas. Each smoker must have a certain number of cubic metres of air around them. A sign has to be put up to show where people may smoke. Other areas must be properly ventilated. If you are uncertain about the rules, contact the local *commissariat de police.*

## CAMPING AND CARAVAN PARKS

Running a campsite has considerable attractions. Space, fresh air and no one sleeping in your house. On the other hand, you need to be fairly tough to deal with unruly campers, and the investment required is considerable. Being able to speak several languages is a great advantage. As far as foreigners go, the campsite business has for a long time been dominated by the Dutch, who have always been keen campers and are tough enough to deal with troublemakers. While the use of tents remains popular, sales of caravans have been falling steadily as more and more holidaymakers choose to travel in camping cars. The Dutch particularly like camping cars, as they can bring all the food they need with them from Holland, and thus avoid spending too much money locally.

As with everything else in France, there are regulations aplenty. In the first place there has to be a *bloc sanitaire* with WCs, washbasins and showers. Septic tanks (*fosses septiques*) are the norm in campsites; old-style cess pits (*fosses à lisier*) are on the way out and are not allowed for new sites. Secondly, you need an electricity supply for lighting and for the caravans and camping cars.

If you are planning up to six 'pitches' or room for up to 20 people, then you will only be required to make a declaration to the *mairie* about the facilities you are installing, hence they are known as *terrains déclarés*. You are not allowed to put up cabins or shacks, and you will need permission to station a caravan on the site permanently.

Above six pitches or 20 guests, the formalities become far more complicated. You will first need to apply for outline planning permission – the *certificat d'urbanisme* – and obtain an *autorisation d'aménager*, permission to construct the campsite. The facilities will also have to be more luxurious, including hot showers, drinking water taps, proper rubbish disposal facilities, somewhere for the guests to shelter in bad weather, and at least 150 sq.m. per pitch. Trees are a requirement to screen the campsite from your neighbours, as well as to supply shade. The campsite needs to be near your house or farm, with access to the building for campers. The prefecture will check that the land is sufficiently flat and grassy, and that there is adequate access. They will classify your camping as either an *aire naturelle de camping* or the more luxurious *camps de tourisme*. The *camps de tourisme* are further subdivided into *camps de tourisme aire naturelle*, which can remain open six months of the year, and *camps de tourisme saisonnier*, which can only stay open two months a year, but can have far more pitches per hectare. There is another type of *camp de tourisme*, the *camps de loisirs*, where pitches are rented out for at least a month, and where mobile homes may be stationed for long periods. Mobile homes are not allowed on some camping sites, and there are plans to build more separate sites for them. The prefecture awards stars depending on the degree of comfort you can offer to campers.

### Camping Alternative

Freddy and Lisette De Cock currently run the alternative holiday centre Joia in the Ariège. Their first project was in the Hérault.

*In 1982 I was working in my family's furniture business. For a long time we had dreamt of a place in the countryside where people could relax and develop spiritually and physically. We came to hear of a derelict sheep farm owned by a Belgian in the Parc Régional de la Haute Languedoc which was available to rent. In the first place we had to go through a lot of administrative red tape, which included trips to Paris, all of which lasted 18 months before we could actually get started.* We were registered with the Chambre de Commerce in Béziers as a SARL *(private limited company) under* tourisme, location chambres, camping et restauration. *We paid social security contributions to URSSAF.*

*We decided to go for an aire naturelle – a type of campsite that allows space for up to 25 pitches or 75 people. We couldn't run a camping à la ferme as we were not running a farm, and we didn't want to have a starred campsite; the main emphasis was on a lot of space. We had to have the basic three showers, three toilets and three washbasins for the camping. There were also rooms available for those who wanted to be indoors. Apart from offering yoga, meditation, tai-chi and similar activities, we also asked the campers to lend a hand with the work. In the spring we had volunteers staying to work.*

*After 10 years we bought a nearby hotel whose owner had gone bankrupt, at an official auction. Five years later, however, we decided that we wanted to buy our own place. The regulations were constantly getting stricter, and we wanted to invest in something that was our own. It wasn't possible to buy the campsite so we terminated the rental contract and went looking in the Ariège. We now run the alternative holiday centre, La Joia (see below).*

Running a campsite is a very seasonal business. To be viable each pitch needs to be occupied 30 nights per year at least. You may also consider offering other services such as home-made produce or meals. A swimming pool will pull in more customers, but there are strict regulations about where they can be built and they have to be fenced off to stop children from falling in. Proximity to a sports centre or recognised hiking route will help your business, as will renting out mountain bikes. Local cultural sites are also an advantage. Camping car owners generally have a high disposable income and are likely to be interested in cultural monuments, so bear them in mind.

The usual profile of a campsite owner is someone who likes camping themselves and has done a lot of it. During the summer you will not have a moment to yourself, the rest of the year there won't be much to do. Neither the investment required, nor the returns, are that immense. Subsidies are available up to about €2,500 from the Conseil Général on condition that you are a member of Gîtes de France; contact the local Relais. To get an *épi* (wheatear) rating you need to be a member. Some départements have much higher subsidies; the Pas-de-Calais has been offering up to €100,000 for the construction of three-star camping sites.

If your campsite is on a farm, you can get an official label *Camping en Ferme d'Accueil* from the local Chambre de l'Agriculture as part of the *Bienvenue à la Ferme* initiative (see www.bienvenue-a-la-ferme.com). You will be expected to show guests around your farm and help them to find out about the traditions of the area.

The best source of information about campsites is the *Fédération Française de Camping et Caravaning* (www.ffcc.fr) who publish magazines and other essential publications (see below). By joining them you can benefit from various services, including insurance against cancellation by customers.

**Formalities.** The campsite business was originally viewed as a branch of agriculture, so you will pay your social contributions to the Mutualité Sociale Agricole. From the taxation point of view you only have to inform the tax authorities that you are running a non-commercial business (BNC). While membership of the Chambre de Commerce is not required, it would be wise to talk to them, and above all to the local *maire* before you even think about trying to open a campsite. You will also need to talk to the local Département de l'Equipement (DDE) concerning planning permission for construction of a campsite, if you plan to have more than six pitches.

### Some Useful Addresses

*Agence Française de l'Ingénierie Touristique,* 2 rue Linois, 75740 Paris Cedex 15; ☎01 44 37 36 00; fax 01 44 37 36 69; www.afit-tourisme.fr. Agency set up to improve tourist facilities in France.

*Fédération Nationale des Gîtes de France,* FFCC, 78 rue de Rivoli, 75004 Paris; ☎01 42 72 84 08; fax 01 42 72 70 21; email info@ffcc.fr; www.ffcc.fr.

*Fédération Nationale de l'Hôtellerie de Plein Air,* 105 rue Lafayette, 75010 Paris; ☎01 48 78 13 77; fax 01 42 85 41 39; email: fnhpa@club-internet.fr; www.fnhpa.fr. National campsite owners union.

### Useful Publications

*Le Guide Officiel des Etapes Touristiques Camping-car 2003,* from FFCC. Annual listing of camping-car only sites.
*Le Guide Officiel du Camping-Caravaning 2003,* from FFCC. Annual listing.
*Les Textes Officiels,* from FFCC. Official documents related to campsites.
*L'Hôtelier de Plein Air.* Journal of the *Fédération Nationale de l'Hôtellerie de Plein Air.*
*Liaison.* Official magazine of the FFCC. See www.ffcc.fr.
*L'Officiel des Terrains de Camping,* from FFCC. Magazine advertising campsites for sale.

# FARMING

Most people would not immediately think of going to France to run a farm, and yet there are many Britons, Irish and other nationalities taking over abandoned or working farms in France, with the active encouragement of the French authorities. The image of farming in France is quite different from what it is in Britain. The countryside and farms are somehow a fundamental aspect of French identity. Eight per cent of the population still works in agriculture, and almost everyone in the city has relatives who still farm. French farming has, though, been hard hit by the drift from the land to the cities, leaving a lot of abandoned farmhouses and land.

The French government considers the preservation of the traditional French farm a priority and offers help to foreigners who want to take farms over. The main grants are for young farmers, defined as under 35, although the limit is usually stretched to 40. Land is very cheap, especially in central France, where the population is ageing very rapidly, and most young people want to move out. Taking France as a whole, about 2-2.5% of farms are owned by foreigners, but the figure goes up to 5% in Normandy, with the main concentration close to the Channel ports. Most foreigners seem to settle in well in France. Although they are not going to get rich – one family of English farmers estimate that they make £15,000 a year on a turnover of £80,000 – at least they have the chance to buy their own farm at a reasonable price. There are plenty of heartwarming stories about newcomers being helped out by their neighbours, having tractors dragged out of the mud, etc. There is also a darker side: English-speaking farmers leaving because of the hostility of the locals: the problem seems to me most acute in the Limousin and Auvergne, where the inhabitants are notoriously suspicious of outsiders. One unhappy English farmer in the Dordogne, who prefers to remain anonymous, said that 'You would have to be mentally deranged to take over a farm in France.' Fortunately, this is not most people's experience.

Land is relatively cheap by British standards, starting from €1,000 a hectare up to €100,000 or more for vine-growing land. An average for good arable land is €4,000. The cheaper land is to be found in the central swathe of France going from the Vendée across to the Alps. The price is dependent partly on whether there are EU quotas. To make the farm viable, you need sufficient land, livestock and guaranteed subsidies.

One organisation that has become well-known for helping British and Irish farmers to move to France is Eurofarms, run by George Lidbury, who is himself half French and comes from an agricultural/property background. The website is very informative: www.eurofarms.com. There are also Terres d'Europe-SCAFR and Europe Ruris, organisations that have mainly settled farmers from the Netherlands and Belgium into France (see below for websites).

### Regulations

Farming is a highly regulated profession, and you need permission before you can start up. The system is weighted towards encouraging young farmers with experience of farming to take over farms as older people retire. This has proved a successful policy; the average age of farmers in Brittany has, for example, gone down from 50 to 40 in the last 10 years.

Buying a farm might seem a straightforward operation, but there is no certainty that you will actually be permitted to buy, because of the existence of the organisation called SAFER, which has the right to match the highest bid on a piece of farmland. Farmers can also sell their land direct to SAFER, who will then sell it on at the same price, with a small charge for administration. No farmland can be sold in France unless SAFER has been informed first, which is usually done by the notary handling the sale. Once SAFER has assured the seller that they do not wish to buy the land, then the sale can go ahead. See their website: www.safer.fr.

There is then a further obstacle, namely that you need permission to run a farm. The département decides who can farm and where. You fill in an application form – the Demande d'Autorisation d'Exploiter (currently CERFA 11534*01) – which is submitted to the Direction Départementale de l'Agriculture et de la Forêt or DDAF. There are variations in the application forms between départements, depending on local policies. A complete form, including the letter you need to send to the DDAF can be found on www.cerfa.gouv.fr.

If your application is accepted you will send a declaration to the Centre de Formalités des Entreprises, which in this case is your local Chambre d'Agriculture (see under chapter 3, *Procedures*). Your social security organisation is the MSA (Mutuelle Sociale Agricole) and you will pay taxes under *bénéfices agricoles* (see chapter 7, Running a Business). You are subject to land tax – *taxe foncière* – which you would not pay in the UK. For more information on taxes see chapter 8, *Tax Social Security and other Matters.*

### Grants and Loans

In order to qualify for grants you are required to enter into a contract with the state, known as the *contrat territorial d'exploitation* (CTE). This specifies what kind of farming you are allowed to carry on, respect for environmental norms, and so forth. The organisation handling the forms is ADASEA. More details on the nature of their requirements can be found at www.adasea.net. The application form is also available on the internet: search on Formulaire à Remplir par les Nouveaux Demandeurs d'Aides.

Grants are mainly for young farmers, and are divided between outright grants (*dotation d'installation aux jeunes agriculteurs* or DJA) and soft loans (*prêts bonifiés pour la reprise d'exploitation* or MTSJA). You will need a properly costed plan for the first three years of operation, worked out with an expert. You will also need to show that you are paying to the agricultural social security organisation, MSA, and send an *Extrait Kbis* (proof you are registered as a business) if you are operating as a company. The application is passed on by ADASEA to the DDAF. The amounts that you can expect to receive as grants depend on where you are and how large your family is, and whether you work together with your wife or not. The highest grants go to those in mountain areas, and those who work in partnership with their spouse. Amounts vary from €8,000 to €17,300 for flat arable land, to between €10,300 and €22,400 in the mountains. One of the absurdities of the system is that grants are treated as income and taxed. The maximum soft loan or MTSJA is €110,000. There are a great number of smaller grants, rebates and free management support, all of which your local Chambre d'Agriculture will be able to tell you about.

**European Union Policies.** The present outlook for French farmers is less positive that it has been. With the expansion of the EU, a great number of impoverished Eastern European farmers will be looking for subsidies. French farmers have until now been heavily subsidised, and paid to produce, or even not to produce. The writing is now on the wall for them, and they will need to diversify in the same way as UK farmers have been forced to do.

### Sources of Information

The Chambres d'Agriculture Départementales, and to a lesser degree the Chambres d'Agriculture Régionales, offer advice and support to farmers. They are in turn supported by the APCA, the Assemblée Permanente des Chambres d'Agriculture, and SUAF, Service d'Utilité Agricole de Formation, which deals with training.

The most detailed information available is on the French Ministry of Agriculture website: www.agriculture.gouv.fr. The ministry's official name is Ministère de l'Agriculture, de l'Alimentation, de la Pêche, et des Affaires Rurales (MAAPAR).

The organisation Terres d'Europe-SCAFR (*Société de Conseil pour l'Aménagement Foncier Rural*) deals with informing prospective foreign farmers: see www.terresdeurope.net. An English version is in the pipeline.

For prices of land see www.europeruris.com/prixterres.html, or the journal Espace Rural 2003. APCE publish five brochures on setting up a business in the countryside: *Entrepreneur du Paysage, Les Marchés de l'Environnement, Exploitant Agricole, Exploitation Forestière* and *Entreprendre à la Campagne*, which are relatively cheap. These are easiest to obtain by going to the APCE's bookshop at 14 rue Delambre, Paris, or by paying with a French cheque or Carte Bleue (debit card).

The most crucial source of information is your local Chambre d'Agriculture. These can usually be found by typing www.[name of département].chambagri.fr. Regional, and some departmental chambers can be found by searching on Chambre d'Agriculture + de + name of region/département. Examples are www.pdc.chambagri.fr (Pas-de-Calais), www.allier.chambagri.fr and www.cra-normandie.fr.

# VINEYARDS

These come under Agriculture but belong to another world from the average farm. For one thing the price for a good *terroir* or the unique soil and conditions for making the perfect wine is out of this world and can reach €1,000,000 per hectare (2.47 acres) in Champagne and Bordeaux. In the Languedoc you might pay as little as €15,000 per hectare, while the Entre Deux-Mers near Bordeaux has land for as little as €30,000. Everything depends on the *terroir.* In theory, most of France is suitable for growing grapes, except the north-west. Normandy is rather too wet and specialises in apples and pears, while the tradition of vine-growing died out in Brittany in the 16th century.

Taking over a vineyard requires very big initial investments and a long waiting period before you see any returns. If new vines have to be planted, then you will be waiting 6-7 years before you see any wine. This is something that you should watch out for when you consider buying a vineyard. The seller may forget to tell you that the vines need to be replaced. This business is also very vulnerable to the vagaries of the climate, as well as being very hard work. On the other hand, the satisfaction of selling your wine to the French and the lifestyle can hardly be beaten.

George Vellacott has owned a farm and vineyard in the Dordogne since 1989, where he produces an Appellation Bergerac red called Casse Bessou.

*We were living on a property that was surrounded by a farm, so when it came up for sale we thought it was an opportunity that was too good to miss. We have 37 hectares, of which 30 are a white limestone type of land, only good for subsistence farming, and 7 hectares of what is called* argile au calcaire, *or clay over limestone, which is suitable for growing grapes. The previous owner had let the vineyard run down, which we were aware of when we bought it, but we could not at that time have known how much energy and money we would have to put into re-establishing the vines, and for a number of years we wondered whether it was really worth it. It was an extremely steep learning curve. Now we have really turned the corner and gain a lot of satisfaction from what we do.*

*The previous owner had a contract with a local* cave coopérative *which takes the grapes and turns them into wine. We chose not to renew the contract with the co-op and instead we bottle our wines ourselves. About 60% of the grapes are Merlot, 40% are Cabernet Sauvignons, and there is a little Malbec, locally called Cot. We are on the Monbazillac plateau which is famous for its sweet white wines; these are produced on north-facing slopes that favour late ripening whereas our vineyards face south. Geologically the land is the same as Monbazillac.*

*It's a moot point whether you can make a decent living from a vineyard of 7 hectares. It would be possible if you did everything yourself. We have an agreement with a neighbouring vineyard known as a* métayage – *which could be called a shared farming agreement in English – whereby they process our grapes into wines, while we just deal with the* immobilier, i.e. *the vines and the post and wires. There are local people with 20 hectares who send their grapes to the co-op and they manage to get by. In my case, my main line of business is an agricultural equipment company based in the UK which exports to*

*France. The vineyard is a subsidiary occupation.*

*The main point that I would make about coming to start a business in France is that you absolutely must learn the language. I've seen all too many people with great schemes who have got into all sorts of difficulties because they couldn't speak the language. It really can't be overemphasised that the language is the key to everything here.*

For information on property agents who sell farms and vineyards, see chapter 5, *Acquiring a Business.*

# GARDENING AND MAINTENANCE SERVICES

There is a growing demand for landscape gardening services, not only for expats but also among the French, and this is very much connected with demographics, as more and more city dwellers head to the outskirts of the cities and find that they have big gardens to look after.

Other types of maintenance service are also sought after. The usual situation is for a couple to offer several services at the same time, including house-sitting. Some of this work is done by people who are not registered with the authorities. There are issues here regarding taxation and social security, which affect the employer just as much as the person who is doing the work. In the big brother French state, the minute someone comes to your property and does any work you are responsible for their social security payments, i.e. you have to inform URSSAF. There are measures in place to make it easier to employ people in your home. The consequences of not informing the authorities can be unpleasant financially for the employer, and worse for the employee. There has been recently been a case in the Dordogne where someone with 6 gardening jobs 'in the black' was sent to prison. The crime the person committed was *le travail dissimulé* and the authorities have snoopers out looking for perpetrators, the logic being that if you work in the black then you are being deprived of your social security rights. Further information can be found under chapter 9, *Employing Staff.*

### Garden Design

Jake and Jean Wilkins have a successful garden design business, Kerbreizh Services, based at Combourg in Ille-et-Vilaine. Brittany.

*Six years ago we came to Brittany for a week's holiday and fell in love with the area, so we decided to go and live there. We didn't know how we were going to make a living, but I had an English teaching diploma which would allow me to find work teaching French people English.*

*To begin with we didn't buy a property. We contacted the people we had stayed with and rented a gîte for six months. It was in the winter, the place wasn't insulated, and the only heating was a wood fire. We were so naïve that we ordered a load of green wood, which of course wouldn't burn. Still, I got a job teaching English, and my husband got work helping a builder. After a while, we did the usual British thing and bought a ruin, for £12,000. We moved into a caravan on the site and set to work.*

*Then one day my husband said: 'I'll buy a lawnmower, and cut grass.' I told him he must be joking, but that was the beginning of our gardening business. The business is now doing very well. Our customers are British and French individuals. Mainly they live in satellite towns around St Malo and Rennes; we work within a 50 km radius of Combourg about halfway between the two cities. Because of the large-scale house-building programmes around many French towns there are a lot of new gardens to be designed or landscaped. While we started with other expatriates, we also do a lot of work for the French; in the past year most of our work has been for the locals, due to the temporary slowdown in the foreign property market. Since we live in France it is natural that our customers should be French. For this reason we have adopted a French, or rather Breton, business name: Kerbreizh. It is best if we appear to be French, at least from the outside.*

*To begin with we started out as a* Micro-Entreprise; *now our turnover has gone over the* Micro-Entreprise *limit we are TVA-registered, but we are still self-employed. There is no advantage right now in becoming a limited company. We have our SIRET number and employ a couple of French workers. We have to pay their social security contributions – we come under the Agricultural regime, not URSSAF – and this is one of the major headaches of running a business here. You have to be very prudent because on a certain day you are asked to pay your employees' contributions, so you have to put money aside.*

*The requirements of British and French customers are totally different; it has been a great education working with two Frenchmen, and they have learnt a lot from us as well. The French want entirely different things as regards fencing, paving, driveways, you name it. We use the best materials available, and offer the highest standards of workmanship, so the customers will have something that will last. Our competitors who work in the black may offer cheaper services but their customers are not happy at the end of the day.*

*In running this business we've learnt how the French tick. One thing that I would say is that you must have all the work you are expected to do written down on the* devis *or binding estimate. It happens that customers say: 'While you're here do you think you could do this, or that', and then they refuse to pay because it didn't appear on the estimate.*

# ARTISANS

## BUILDING AND OTHER SERVICES

Working as a builder in France is a classic way to make a living, and one that attracts a lot of fly-by-night characters as well. There are also many well-established foreign builders who do everything by the book and give satisfaction to their customers. Property magazines will not accept advertisements from tradesmen who are not properly registered. Many builders have undertaken work for other foreigners once they have finished working on their own properties. An important part of the business is knowing how to establish estimates or *devis* for work to be done. Speaking English is an advantage with foreign customers as there is less likely to be misunderstanding about what is included in the estimate. Builders (and other tradesmen) also need professional insurance to guarantee their work for 10 years (the *garantie décennale*) or other statutory period.

## The Builder

Islay Currie at one time ran a building company, Construction Currie, in the Dordogne. He is now a Cambridge-based estate agent handling property in France.

*In the 1980s I had made some profit from selling a share in a house in Cambridge, so not having any other projects, I decided to buy a pile of stones in France. After working on the house in the northeast Dordogne, I had made contacts with tradesmen, builders merchants, etc. so I started to do some work for a friend. I then registered with the Chambre de Commerce who sent me on the compulsory training course you have to do. This was very practical, but of course a lot of Anglos don't understand what is going on. So I was set up with a trading name – Construction Currie – and a VAT number and off I went.*

*There was a tricky moment when the Chambre des Métiers asked me what experience I had of building, so I told them I had a degree in civil engineering and 11 years as a partner in a building firm, and they were quite happy with that. I had actually worked for some years in Cambridge in a building co-operative. There is no official qualification for being a builder – although there is for electricians and plumbers – so it's rather a grey area.*

*Once you are properly registered you receive a business number – SIRET – which legally entitles you to trade. This must be printed on your letterhead and on estimates or* devis. *As in the UK, there are estimates and binding quotations. The* devis *is a contract; you can only charge more than is stated if you do work that is not on the* devis. *Where you cannot actually know how much the work is going to cost – e.g. the foundations of a house, you can give a* devis provisoire *or non-binding estimate.*

*Basically I worked for other foreigners; I leafletted foreign cars – putting a leaflet under the windshield wiper. I was offering a general building service, a one-stop solution for whatever people needed. Although the company was called an Entreprise Générale de Bâtiment this has no legal or tax significance. For tax purposes I was a self-employed person. I almost exclusively employed French sub-contractors, and paid them a lump sum. They were not officially my employees.*

*As a builder you are required to have insurance in case you go out of business, and to cover the 10-year guarantee on your work – the* garantie décennale. *The biggest problem is the overheads. Accident insurance, retirement insurance, sickness insurance are all very expensive and are taken out with private companies. As a self-employed person you have to earn an awful lot to get by. On your tax return you just put your profits. Your contributions are worked out on the basis of the previous year. If your figures for the following year are significantly lower than for the previous year, you are financially crippled for a year. Then again, the system is great if you are benefiting from it.*

*The situation is even worse if you are employing people because of the huge overheads. If you hire your employees out to other people, you have to charge the customer a very high rate, so they are paying an indirect tax.*

*Many foreigners see trouble coming and decide to close down, but continue working in the black for a while. To stay within the law, you have to cancel your registration. I closed down my own business after about four years in the correct manner. I now run Currie French Property Services, an estate agency registered in the UK.*

## Other Services

There are many other services that one could offer to homeowners, such as **plumber, electrician, roofer, fencer,** etc. These all come under the *artisan* regime, and are registered with the Chambre des Métiers. You can start up as long as you can show that you have experience; there are no qualifications as such for some of these jobs, or they may not be comparable to those in France. All prospective *artisans* are required to go on a four-day training course with the Chambre des Métiers to give you some basic idea about how to run a business.

Along with the builders, there are also a number of UK architects and surveyors who have set up in France. The French do not recognise the profession of 'chartered surveyor', the nearest thing being an 'expert immobilier' which could also be a property valuer. Most surveyors are builders or architects who do some surveying on the side. Architects are also a regulated profession, and you would need to be registered unless you were based in the UK and just going over to France from time to time.

## Taxation Issues

You will enter your earnings under *Acquiring* (BIC) on your tax return. There are various choices to be made about how you want to be taxed. You can function as a *micro-entreprise* without reclaiming TVA. Normally, builders will charge 5.5% TVA for services, plus TVA at 19.6% or 5.5% on building materials, and reclaim TVA on materials they buy. For further information see chapter 8, *Tax, Social Security & Other Matters*.

## Other Artisans

If you make anything with your hands then you are an *artisan,* and this includes brewing beer. Steve and Jane Skews run a **brewery** and farm in the Orne, Normandy. Steve Skews (see below), started out making dolls' houses and miniature models, before he got into brewing in a big way. Their website can be viewed at www.le-brewery.com.

> *We originally produced cider, but as all the apple trees were blown down in the great storm at the end of 1999, we decided to turn to brewing. Cider-making is considered an agricultural activity by the authorities, while brewing is artisanal. This proved to be quite a problem as the local Chambre des Métiers had no forms that fitted our category of business, so it took a long time to actually register the business. There are in fact only six breweries in Normandy. On the other hand, the French customs and excise, the Direction de Douanes, were extremely charming and helpful. I had brewing qualifications from the UK, but I still had to go on another brewing course to satisfy the authorities here. Then there was the whole labelling scene; you have to satisfy the DDCCRF (Répression des Fraudes) that your label doesn't mislead in any way. And of course we had to have a budget provisoire to satisfy the Chambre des Métiers that our business would be viable. All in all it was 8 months before we produced our first bottle of beer.*
>
> *Getting a licence to brew is difficult in itself. Because you are making*

*a product to be consumed by the public which contains alcohol, a number of regular checks have to be carried out. DASS – the food hygiene inspectorate – were going to send someone round who only had experience of inspecting Camembert factories, on the principle that brewing and cheese-making both involve microbiological testing. In the end we had to bring over our own British brewery inspector at our own expense. Even the hop plants had to have a passport, because hops are not a native French plant.*

*Because brewing generates a lot of effluent it is absolutely essential to install satisfactory filtering systems to prevent pollution. We had to design a whole system consisting of a* lagunage, *a* dégraisseur, *and sand filters. The use of large amounts of water means that you have to be inspected by the Police d'Eau – the water police – to see that you are not polluting the environment. They also check up on farming effluent.*

*We have replanted with traditional types of apple trees, but it will be 10 years before we can produce cider again on a large scale. The idea is to keep the tradition going. Our business is complex as we are also running a working farm at the same time, so we are both* agriculteurs *and* artisans. *We pay social security contributions to the MSA for farmers. We are an EURL, a limited company with one partner/director.*

*I would say that far too many Britons underestimate the difficulties of starting a business here, and there are plenty who have failed and gone home. We have had a lot of people coming round who are thinking of imitating us but without the necessary training or commitment. Some are even prepared to sell products that could be downright dangerous for your health!*

## OTHER SERVICES

It is by no means essential to run a business that only caters for other foreigners. If you have some French, or can learn quickly, there are plenty of opportunities for those who are imaginative enough to take them. One English journalist, Rosemary Rudland (who appears on the back cover of this book), was daring enough to start a **Camembert heritage museum** right in the centre of Camembert. Her story is given below.

Another approach is to transfer your UK-based business to France, and if you can do everything over the internet then this is quite a simple operation. There is an increasing market for website design and other internet services for expats based in France. A number of Britons have started up hand-holding services for newcomers, or run community websites. There are also people who make tailor-made directories of local services for foreigners, along with general hand-holding for incomers.

## Relais Camembert

Journalist Rosemary Rudland bought an old cottage on the village square in Camembert, Normandy, and made it into a heritage museum, the Relais de Camembert. She also put up another building to sell farm produce from.

*I built the shop itself from scratch in the* colombage *style; we made it just under 20 sq.m. thus obviating the need for a permis de construire. The mayor of the village raised an objection to my déclaration de* travaux, *which then went to the planning office – DDE – who then passed it onto the* préfet, *who in the end overruled the mayor. Before I could start up I had to go on a week-long course run by the Chambre de Commerce, where they introduce you to a notaire and an accountant. They do ask you a lot of questions about why you want to start a business. I also took the precaution of meeting the local heads of departments, such as the fire department, health department, the Département de l'Équipement in Alençon, so I knew exactly what I was doing when I filled in the forms. I wanted to sell local produce to visitors; as I didn't know which farmers to approach I talked to the oldest person in the village who took me around to everyone he knew. They were very supportive and provided me with personal bits and bobs for the museum. I looked out for local arts and crafts to sell.*

*If you sell drink then you need a variety of licences ranging from the most basic one allowing you to sell soft drinks to the one that lets you sell strong spirits. In my case, the customers could drink alcohol as long as they ate something with it at the same time. To avoid the complications of a restaurant licence, I only sold pre-packed food, which the customers unwrapped and ate outside. Otherwise you would need separate washbasins for knives and washing your hands; it all gets very expensive and complicated. If you don't observe the regulations then your business can be instantly shut down. I didn't prepare sandwiches or cut anything up by hand on the premises.*

*It's important to be well-informed when you start out. There are new subsidies coming out all the time. I was able to get a subsidy because I was setting up the first business of this type in a commune with fewer than 2,000 inhabitants. Only the first business can have this subsidy.*

*I'm an* Entreprise Individuelle, *but not a* Micro-Entreprise. *While you can go from* Micro-Entreprise *to SARL you can't go back down again if things become difficult, so I chose to declare my earnings under the* régime réel – *that is, I'm taxed on my real earnings, or* bénéfices commerciaux. *I wouldn't have run the business without an* expert comptable *or accountant. Filling in the tax return would be simply too difficult.*

*When I started the business I said it would be for five years, and I've done it for seven now. Right now, I have closed the shop for a while in order to write a book about – what else – Camembert. If you want to stop your business you need to do it at the end of March, June, September or December, otherwise you will pay more taxes for the following three months. But having been registered, I can start up again whenever I like. I still run gîtes and grow apples which we take to the local pressoir to turn into cider. The cider is* appellation controlée *and has won three gold medals.*

## ESTATE AGENTS AND MORTGAGE BROKERS

Estate agency is a regulated liberal profession. Unlike in the UK, not just anyone can start up as an *agent immobilier.* You need professional qualifications and a licence from the Chambre de Commerce. According to the Loi Huguet of 1970, estate agents must have:

- a diploma in law, e.g. DEUG
- or a baccalaureate or other degree, and one year's work experience in an estate agency
- or 10 years' experience in an estate agency.

Anyone who acts as an *immobilier* without a *carte professionnelle* is liable to a heavy fine and a jail sentence, and this has happened to some foreigners who, while knowing the law, worked with *notaires* selling properties in France. The *carte professionnelle* has to be renewed every year. For an inside view of the estate agency business it is worth reading Alan Biggins' *Selling French Dreams* and *A Normandy Tapestry* (www.normandy-tapestry.com). Biggins worked in a grey area of the law for a while, before he had to concede that the regulations made it too difficult for him to be an estate agent in France.

Estate agents' commissions vary from region to region, and are on a graduated scale depending on the value of the property. The minimum is around €2,200. With very cheap properties the commission can be up to 20%; above about €250,000 the commission will not exceed 2.5%. Up-market properties in Paris or in tourist areas also attract high commissions; the total commission is unlikely to be less than 3%; the normal range is 5% to 10%.

Estate agents must have a minimum guarantee fund or bond of €125,000 and be members of an organisation of estate agents, such as FNAIM. Without a bond you cannot receive payments from buyers directly; they would have to go into a notaire's blocked account. Professional indemnity insurance is a necessity.

The *immobilier* has a time-limited mandat or mandate from the seller to negotiate on their behalf. This can be a basic mandate or *mandat simple* that is granted to several agents, or a *mandat exclusif* which limits the freedom of the seller to using only one agent.

Apart from estate agents, there are also property consultants or search agents who look for properties for potential buyers and offer all sorts of hand-holding services, which can include arranging flights and stays in France, and advice on dealing with the buying process. Some of these businesses offer genuinely useful services. Unfortunately, there are also a number of charlatans who have jumped on the bandwagon, who give bad advice to property buyers in various ways, as well as persuading them to buy properties at inflated prices. Property consultants or search agents are not usually registered as businesses in France, but operate from the UK.

## Other Financial Services

Along with estate agencies, there are quite a few British **mortgage and insurance** brokers who have set up in France. The most high-profile of these is Abbey National France, who are based in Lille. Such companies have to observe French regulations, of course, and function like any French business. Their main selling point is being able to communicate in English. There are similar businesses run by Dutch and German speakers.

## The Mortgage Broker

Carol Bayliss and her husband have been in France since 2000.

*We live in Alpes Maritimes, Côte d'Azur, although our business is conducted across the world for English-speaking people who want to purchase property anywhere in France. Our clients come from as far away as the USA, UK, Australia and New Zealand, Estonia, Poland – all over the place. In the UK my husband was an Independent Financial Advisor and I primarily worked as a company accountant, and also had my own Will Writing business. We decided that, as we love France, and especially the Alpes Maritimes, we would try and move there. We thought we had every chance of making a living here.*

*We started MortgageFrance from scratch. All this was brought about because my husband had developed an allergy to daylight and had to try to keep out of the light as much as possible. We needed to develop a business that we knew and that could be run as simply as possible by internet, telephone and fax communication.*

*For financial services, my husband joined an international network of financial advisers. We tried advertising in some of the local English publications. Some ads were successful and some weren't, and they cost a lot of money. Contacts with French lenders happened automatically as we started arranging mortgages for existing clients or for new referrals. For MortgageFrance we enlisted the help of the team who run a very successful information website for local expats. I wrote the scripts and they built our website. We were, and still are, very pleased with what we have made.*

*We have taken advice on many occasions from a* taxe avocat *regarding the setting up of MortgageFrance, whether to run it as a sole trader, partnership or a SARL, and it is going to be a SARL or limited company. Consideration had to be given to the continuation of the business should one of us die – my husband has children from a previous marriage and the succession laws in France are very complicated. Also it was necessary to understand some of the tax structures relating to each type of business. We have a separate accountant who has helped with yearly tax returns, explaining the various invoices we receive from government departments, helping us get into the French system, etc.*

*Our bank, Société Générale, and in particular our bank manager, have been very helpful. He explained as simply as he could about the banking system and is usually available to talk to direct by phone. Generally, I would say the banking services here are strange but efficient, but we very rarely go into a bank. All our transactions are done with Carte Bleue (debit card).*

*Running a successful business is no more difficult than anywhere else. Obviously there is the element of translation difficulties and misunderstandings because of that, but in the main it is very much the same as it was in the UK, only with sunshine and palm trees. We live in a very transient part of France. People come and go all the time including those who come here trying to make a go of it. A lot of long-term residents wait and watch to see if you're going stay – why should they deal with someone who may disappear in a few months time? My greatest joy is picking up the telephone and someone saying 'Oh, you speak English!'*

*We meet loads of interesting people. There are the highs of getting a mortgage completed, and the frustrations as well. In France you must expect the unexpected but you'll still be caught unawares, for example, the local* mairie *deciding that it wants some of the land of a property being purchased. A house being bought by one of our clients burning down. A vendor dying during the mortgage process and an illegitimate son being found. Snow causing chaos to the postal service and nearly preventing the delivery of a mortgage cheque. Some lenders don't use bank transfer but send the money through the post. Most notaires will accept a photocopy as proof that the money is coming. There are disputes over land. Family disputes. And the latest – a fire in a sorting office in the UK has destroyed a compromis de vente on its way to a client.*

*We do not charge our clients for our services. We receive our remuneration from the French lenders we introduce business to. The financial services side is regulated. There are rules and laws (mainly relating to tax) that have to be adhered to – considerations of nationality, residency, earnings and taxation. The mortgage side is regulated by the French lenders. Their lending criteria are very strict and cannot be deviated from. We had to go on some more or less compulsory training courses first. There is so much to learn living and working in a foreign country.*

## PARAMEDICAL PROFESSIONS

There are a number of British **therapists** and other **alternative practitioners** working in France, and the number is certainly growing, as the English-speaking population continues to grow. Anyone offering paramedical services is working under the *professions libérales* regime. Some professions are regulated while others are not. If you come under a regulated profession you will be required to join a professional organisation and adhere to their *déontologie* or professional ethics. There is a wide range of unregulated alternative professions who have a considerable market with the French themselves, but you have to be very careful not to infringe on the privileges of the conventional medical profession. Only qualified medical doctors are allowed to practice acupuncture, which means that the profession of acupuncturist has not developed as much as in the UK. Homeopathic medicines can only be prescribed by an authorised medical doctor. There is scope for **herbalists** (*phytothérapeutes*) and **naturopaths** as long as they belong to a recognised professional organisation. **Chiropractors and osteopaths** are less regulated but should belong to a professional organisation.

Simon Pullen has worked in France as a chiropractor since 1999. He lives in Eymet, Dordogne.

*We used to live in a small village near Bournemouth, where I practised as a chiropractor. We became tired of the stress and pace of life in the UK, and we also had concerns about educating our children. Our children then were 6 and 10, and so we knew that if we were to change and go to France, we would have to do so then, so they would be able to learn the language. The healthcare system in France is also far superior to that of the UK. I started out relying on my 'O' Level French from school, but I was used to speaking French as my parents lived in France.*

*Another interesting point: it is usually quite easy to open a business without all the red tape you would have in the UK with planning permission/change of use. Generally, you pop along to the* mairie, *tell them what you want to do, and they will tell you there and then if there is a problem with that. Usually you just get on and do what you want (unless you are changing the appearance of the property you are working from). Here in the Bastide of Eymet, they are very strict about what happens to the façades.*

*I work as a chiropractor, offering chiropractic treatment to the local French and English community, and anyone else who passes through from time to time. Given the French passion for all things medical, it's a good business to be in. I am registered as a* profession libérale, *as I work alone. It is roughly the equivalent of being self-employed in the UK. Starting out was not as complicated as people often make out. The first step was to get registered so that I could then apply for a Carte de Séjour. This was very straightforward. I simply went to the local URSSAF office, and they helped me complete a relatively easy form for registration. The rest then automatically happens. They notify the tax authorities etc., and in due course you are 'welcomed' into the system. I received my SIRET and SIREN numbers which show that you and your place of work are registered. These are very important as they are often required before you can access certain aspects of business life, such as professional bank accounts etc. Other than that, when you have your premises, it is very straightforward to run the business.*

*Up until March 2002, chiropractic was actually illegal in France, although there were some 300 plus practitioners in the country. So, up until then, there were no regulations. You had to register yourself, as stated above, to work, and pay taxes as a chiropractor, even though the profession was illegal. It was quite bizarre really. Now, following legalisation, regulations are being drawn up for the profession to follow. This is a long process as you might imagine. So at the moment, we all continue as before in a state of blissful 'non-interference'. I belong to the French Chiropractic Association. They are very active and are very good for our profession. They do all the negotiating with the government regarding the establishment of new regulations for the profession etc. They also arrange group professional insurance for their members, run seminars etc. I had to go on a short course initially with the association when I first arrived in France. Other than that, at the moment nothing is compulsory, though this will change as new regulations come into force.*

*I did not seek any advice when we moved here. I do however use an accountant with regard to preparation of my annual accounts and completion of tax forms etc. I think this is very important, when you are in a country where the taxation system is foreign to you. It does also give the tax authorities greater peace of mind if you use a registered accountant. I am classed as a* Micro-Entreprise; *I'm taxed on my overall earnings, with a fixed percentage of deductions. I don't charge and cannot claim back any VAT until I reach a certain threshold where VAT becomes applicable. Chiropractic fees will in due course be exempt from VAT following legal recognition of the profession.*

*I haven't had the need for any particular help from a bank. They are usually keen to offer small working overdraft facilities, unsecured, and they are always offering financial aid for capital expenditure. Generally, I find the banking services quite good. I have recently changed banks, and I find that the bank I am with now is more efficient than the bank I was with. So there is variation in performance.*

*If you have made sure that you know how the various systems work here in France, then you should not have many problems. The slowness with which certain organisations respond to enquiries can be frustrating, but you soon come to accept that as part of life over here. Generally, if you have any difficulty in any aspect of your business, it is always wise to ask someone for some direction. There is a wealth of* fonctionnaires *who are usually only too willing to help and give advice and information. The country is run by these people.*

*The thing I find most amusing here are the bizarre looks and comments I get when I hand my French lady patients a gown to wear, at the same time as advising them to keep their underclothes on. In France, they are used to just stripping off to nothing, and being examined by anyone who might enter the room. In the UK, all female patients must be gowned and that is something that I always adhere to here in France. I had one patient who, on putting on her gown, launched herself from the changing booth like an ageing ballerina, did a twirl, to show off her 'new' gown, and then proceeded to try to do a dance with me. I am generally amazed that the number of French patients who come to me is far greater than the English. Establishing myself in Eymet (often referred to as 'Little England'), I expected to see far more English people than French, but they come to me, by word of mouth, the way most things work over here, knowing full well that I am English. I'm very pleased with this attitude.*

### Psychotherapists

At the end of 2003, the French National Assembly threw out a proposal to make psychotherapy a regulated profession, mainly because of the hostility of the medical profession, who are fighting hard to prevent psychotherapists from receiving official recognition. Psychotherapy is to some people more or less equivalent to mind-control or a cult. There is certainly a demand for English-speaking therapists amongst the expatriate community, and for the moment anyone can set up as a therapist as long as they inform the local tax office that they are becoming self-employed. Psychoanalysts can only practice if they belong to the national society of psychoanalysts, which means first being thoroughly analysed yourself.

## ENGLISH TEACHING AND TRANSLATING

Teaching English has been a useful standby for many newcomers to France. Some kind of qualification is useful, namely the CELTA, or Certificate in English Language Teaching to Adults. Many English teachers are salaried employees working for language schools (who underpay them), or for local further education colleges known as Groupement Etablissement Formation Continue. According to French law, if you work on someone's premises on a regular basis, then you cannot be considered an *indépendant;* while if you are a *formateur* or trainer, who has short-term contracts with a company or other organisation, then you can apply for the status of *indépendant.* Naturally, if you work from home, or set up your own language school then you are part of the *professions libérales.*

Teaching English to the French is a pleasant occupation. They are respectful of teachers (even the less competent ones). They expect teachers to lecture them, which may be a bonus if you are not too sure about what you are doing. English teaching is very much a matter of your personality and is very much dominated by women, who tend to have more empathy for students' needs than males.

The subject of English teaching leads on to translating; many translators have been English teachers at some time or other. This is one type of work that can be done anywhere. The translation business has developed from the old days of the typewriter and fax machine into a virtual market place that never sleeps, but there is still a basic amount of linguistic competence needed. Unless you can understand everything you read in French – making allowances for the odd obscure term or phrase – it is not worth kidding yourself that you can make a living as a translator.

The French into English translation market is extremely competitive and difficult to get into. You will require a degree in French and a masters degree in translation, unless you have some other expertise to offer. It is absolutely necessary to specialise in one area, such as:

- law
- financial
- engineering
- technical
- medical
- pharmaceutical
- patents

If you have qualifications in one of these areas in addition to good French, then your chances will be greatly improved. Many successful translators have started out as engineers working in France who were asked to translate in-house texts. Obtaining an in-house job as a translator is an ideal way to start, but this may be easier to find in the UK. There is a general view among translation agencies that if you translate into English then you should live in an English-speaking country, on the assumption that after a few years in France your English will deteriorate and you will lose touch with what is happening at home. This can, of course, be balanced against the fact that you will understand the French system better if you live there. There are some companies who prefer to deal with a translator who has a SIRET or French business registration.

It is important to remember that your final product is in English, so you must be able to produce a text that is free of grammatical or spelling mistakes, with correct punctuation and layout. A reliable computer with suitable software, and a professional-sounding e-mail address are further prerequisites.

If you are not put off by the foregoing, then the next step is to find a mentor, i.e. a more experienced translator. You can register yourself with some websites where jobs are put out for bidding, e.g. www.proz.com, www.translatorscafe.com. If this doesn't work you can try bombarding agencies and potential customers with your CV. It is a chicken-and-egg situation; you need experience to get work, but no one will give you work unless you have experience. There are also people who will try to take advantage of translators by paying them too little or not paying them at all. It is advisable to verify client credentials through the websites mentioned above.

If you are involved in interpreting then you will have a degree in the subject, and will most likely work for an international organisation such as the European Parliament or the Council of Europe. There are also sworn translators in France, known as *traducteurs assermentés*, who are registered as such with the courts and are called on to translate legal documents such as birth and marriage certificates. Generally, only the bigger cities keep lists of traducteurs assermentés.

Finally, it is necessary to point out that there is very little literary translation work available. Most of the work there is goes to highly qualified translators, as it requires a more advanced knowledge of French and a greater degree of writing talent than the other specialities.

## Employment Status

Translators and interpreters are reckoned to belong to the unregulated liberal professions, and are mostly self-employed *indépendants*. As this is a job that can be done from home there are few overheads involved. If you use a part of your rented dwelling as an office then you are allowed to deduct one-third of the rent from your profits, as a matter of course. However, you are then deemed to be renting the room to yourself, so the amount is then added on to your property tax. There may be some advantage even so.

## The Translator

Jane Pensom has lived in France for 30 years, and has 5 children, all of whom have grown up in France. Having achieved complete fluency in French, and on the basis of her long experience of living in France, Jane launched a new company At Your Service in Carcassonne in 2003, which provides hand-holding services for foreigners settling in France, as well as translation and language tuition. Jane also runs a small English library in Carcassonne.

*Having taught English for many years I decided that it was time to launch my own business. I found the easiest way to go about this was to use the services of a consulting company: Conseil Entreprise Marketing Formation or Cémafor for short based in Narbonne and Carcassonne. Unless you are a genius with French forms then it is the best way to do it. At the time I was unemployed, so I was able to get a* chèque conseil, *a sum of money provided by the state that you can use to get consulting services.*

*When I visited my adviser with my project, he told me to find an office and to look for sources of finance. My consultant put together a dossier and we went to the bank together; it was not easy and it took a long time to get the money. As an unemployed person I had the right to a €4,000 loan which I only have to start paying back after 12 months.*

*For the moment I'm an* indépendant *in a* profession libérale *which means that I can't employ anyone. I fill in a normal tax return. As of the start of October 2003 it will be possible to begin an SARL for €1, which will reduce my tax bill and also allow me to employ someone. I am also hoping to obtain the status of 'sworn translator' or* traducteur assermenté. *This means you are registered with the local* tribunal de grande instance *and are officially an expert. I've sent out my CV and references; the* gendarmes *came to visit me at my shop and at home.*

*The basis of my business is to provide advice and help to foreigners coming to buy property in France or live here. With my local knowledge I can warn them about the hidden traps involved in searching for property, such as estate agents not telling buyers about serious environmental problems in the neighbourhood. I often translate for people when they go to notaries or get married. I offer a 10-hour package to be used as and when people want after they have already bought their house.*

*The bureaucracy here is trying. The best thing is to stand back and not tear your hair out. The system does work, even though it shouldn't. I was put in a Catch-22 situation when I wanted to get my stationery printed; they said I had to have my SIRET (commercial register) number first which I couldn't get till March 1st even though the commercial register already had it. I needed it to correspond with EDF and other services. In the end the Chambre de Commerce told me the number before the official date. At the end of the day, if you can't cope with French bureaucracy you shouldn't come and live here.*

## WORKING WITH ANIMALS

This might not be the most obvious thing to do, but there is a big market with foreign residents who want their pets looked after while they are away, or who are keeping their animals in France before they take them to the UK. A market has arisen for US residents who are able to bring their pets into the UK more easily after they have been in France for 3 months. It is obvious that such potential customers would rather go to someone with an English name than a French one. Some French kennels and catteries have tumbled to the ruse and use names like **'Cat Sitting'** or **'Dog's Hotel'** to attract foreigners. The numbers of such establishments can be easily gauged by logging on to www.viva-vous.net/services/pension-chien-chat.php a website that claims to list all the canine and feline hostelries in France.

In order to run kennels or catteries (*pension de chiens et pension de chats*) you do not require any prior qualifications. There are no qualifications as such in France for this profession. You need to contact your Chambre de Commerce since you are effectively running a hotel for animals. If you are offering services, such as an animal beauty parlour, then you are in the area of *professions libérales* which also means registering with the Chambre de Commerce. One English couple in Livarot, Calvados has made a successful business out of toilettage de chiens.

If you have experience, then breeding dogs or cats is another potential area to consider. In this case there are regulations, and specific training courses in France, which you will have to take if you cannot show qualifications from elsewhere. Once you breed more than one litter or *portée* a year, then you are considered a professional breeder and you have to go through the whole process of registering with the Chambre d'Agriculture as such. Note that whether you breed dogs or fish or mushrooms, these are all considered agricultural professions and comes under *Bénéfices Agricoles* on your tax return.

## ALTERNATIVE CENTRES

France is in some ways an ideal place to run courses to refresh tired northern Europeans with **spiritual and alternative fare**. The availability of cheap land, the help that is on offer from the authorities, and the attractions of France to holiday-makers have to be weighed against the red-tape and over-regulation that tend to strangle French businesses trying to get off the ground. Idealism is certainly not enough, as Freddy and Lisette De Cock have found with their alternative centre Joia in the Ariège:

*After running a campsite in the Haute Languedoc for 15 years, we decided to move to the Ariège, closer to the Pyrenees. We found a piece of land near a lake, with views of the Pyrenees, and in the middle of a forest, but without running water or electricity. In the first place we started a limited company SARL Joia. The idea was to have a* village *de vacances which would allow us to offer more or less any activities we liked without having to apply for everything separately. This time the administrative paperchase took us three years, but of course we were working on the project at the same time. For the first year in 1998 we rented part of the local municipal campsite to run our courses.*

*We have received a lot of help from the mayor and the region. After 15 years in the Haute Languedoc we had excellent references from the previous mayor which were a great help, and we could show 15 years of accounts.*

*The locals were quite suspicious of us at first, but when they saw that we were hard workers they accepted us, and we now have excellent relations with everyone around us. The Ariège is known as* La Terre Courage; *they respect people who see things through. The Chambre de Commerce, prefecture and collectivity of communes helped us to obtain 27% regional and EU subsidies on the basis that our project would stimulate tourism in the area. There is less money available now. In order to get the subsidies you have to respect all the possible norms and prepare very detailed dossiers.*

*In the form of company we've chosen, I am the* gérant minoritaire *– executive director and minority shareholder – which allows me to be a salaried worker, and thus have all the associated benefits. While I pay income tax (IR) on my income, the profit made by the SARL is subject to corporation tax (IS) and is distributed to the shareholders who also pay their own taxes.*

*I work with an accountant and a* juriste, *someone who deals with the legal side of running a business, but doesn't plead in court. The company accounts are published in the* Journal Officiel *and can be viewed by anyone on Minitel as well.*

## COMMERCE AMBULANT

Markets are still very much a part of French life and are not likely to lose their popularity. They are under threat from supermarkets and conventional shops, and also a law promoted in 1996 by the current Prime Minister, Jean-Pierre Raffarin, which limits the number of days that shopping centres can rent out stands to market traders to two days a week. Actually working on one requires a lot of stamina and determination. You can expect to get up very early in the morning. Some markets in the South go on into the night during hot weather. The simplest approach is not to sell takeaway food, which involves a lot of additional expense and regulations. There are some 60,000 market enterprises in France, and about 7,000 new ones are created every year, according to APCE. The average investment is €85,000.

If you go outside your own commune to trade from market stalls or by the roadside, and you have no shop premises, then you are considered a *commerçant non-sédentaire*, but this does not mean that you have no fixed abode. For non-EU citizens it is necessary to have a *carte de commerçant*, to start a registered company, and to have lived regularly in France for the previous 5 years, and have a fixed domicile in France for the previous 6 months. Market traders require a carte *professionnelle non-sédentaire*, available from the *préfecture* and renewable every for two years. Various documents are required, including proof that you have professional and civil liability insurance. Traders without any fixed abode are *commerçants forains*. This status is only available to EU citizens; other foreigners cannot become *forains*.

Being a market trader is a business like any other: you have to be registered with the Chambre de Commerce, or Chambre des Métiers (if your principal activity is making things), and produce your *Extrait Kbis* from the Registre de Commerce et Sociétés. In order to sell on the public highway, or outside a market, you need the permission of the *mairie*. Otherwise you should approach the market *placier* – the one who gives out the places. It is usual to pay the *placier* a sum of money (which may or may not be declared to the taxman). Market stands cannot be bought or sold by the traders. The markets themselves are run either directly by the *mairie*, or by a specialised company as a concession.

The Direction Départementale de la Concurrence, de la Consom-mation et de la Répression des Fraudes is responsible for seeing that all your goods are correctly labelled etc. For food, drink, hygiene, and safety, you need to contact the Direction Départementale des Affaires, Sanitaires et Sociales. You will pay rental for your stand, a tax on the stand, and the *taxe professionnelle*, on top of the usual income taxes and social security payments.

For the small-scale market trader, life would seem to be difficult.

The profits to be made are not that great, and the routine of going round the French markets with your van can become wearing. Only for the very determined.

For more information it is worth getting hold of the APCE brochure *Commerce Ambulant* (order from www.apce.com) or contacting the *Fédération Nationale des Syndicats des Commerçants Non Sédentaires*: www.fnscns.com, the market traders trade union.

## OTHER SERVICES

### Ski-ing Resorts

Working on the ski slopes and **providing services for skiers** is an area of business that is rather separated from other French businesses in most people's minds. It does, quite naturally, favour those who are keen on winter sports, and who know the ski slopes well. This is evidently a seasonal business, and it may even be possible to register your company in the UK and only operate in the ski season (see chapter 4, *Business Structures*). On the other hand, it will be difficult to make a living out of one ski chalet operating for only part of the year. If you choose to remain in France all the year round then you can still continue to make a living by catering for hikers and climbers. Chalets and hotels in good locations cost millions; the investment required is beyond most people's means. On the other hand, if you can think of an original service you can offer, then you may do very well.

### Battlefield Tourism

There is a thriving market in **battlefield tours**, which is naturally dominated by retired army personnel, or military historians. The tours are generally offered in conjunction with accommodation. There are only two areas of France where this kind of business can function, namely Calvados near the Normandy landing beaches, and north-west France, i.e. the Somme, where there are still a lot of signs of the World War I.

## Running Courses

The scope for running courses is as unlimited as your own imagination. If you already have *gîtes* or *chambres d'hôtes* then you are in a good position to organise something, such **arts and crafts, painting, yoga, wood-carving, language courses,** etc. The accommodation has to be suitable, and the course should include some sightseeing and visits to local craftspeople if relevant. As a trainer, or *formateur*, you are in a *profession libérale*, for which you need to register with the Chambre de Commerce, the same body that looks after *gîtes*. Another possibility is not to register a business at all in France, and do this in the summer only.

## Personal Services

An example of a business initiative that one might prefer not to copy is the case of Margaret McDonald, who was sentenced in 2003 to 4 years in prison for running an international prostitution ring from Paris using multiple mobile phones. The most ironic part of her story is that she was able to advertise her services in the *International Herald Tribune* under the guise of an escort agency. The services were not cheap at €500 a time.

# Procedures for Starting a New Business

## CHAPTER SUMMARY

- ○ EU nationals still require a residence permit to stay for more than three months, even though France is in the EU.
- ○ No one has the right to remain indefinitely in France unless they can show that they have sufficient funds to support themselves.
- ○ Applications for a residence permit have to be accompanied by at least eight personal documents, but it is no longer necessary to make official translations in advance.
- ○ You need to know the names, dates and places of birth of your parents for many official documents in France.
- ○ Residence permits have to be renewed periodically.
- ○ US citizens have to apply in advance for a long-stay visa, and complete eight copies of the same form.
- ○ EU citizens do not require a work permit.
- ○ If you want to start a business in France, you will have to register with the chamber of commerce or trades, and usually follow a compulsory training course.
- ○ There are strict rules about registering a business.

# RESIDENCE AND ENTRY

France does not encourage immigration, but it does look favourably on foreign investment, and is generally welcoming to those who can contribute something to the local economy and, preferably, create jobs. While France is part of the European Union, there are still formalities to be gone through if a citizen of another EU country wants to settle down here. British citizens are entitled to live and work in France on the same terms as French citizens, as long as they have a *carte de séjour*, or residence permit. Citizens from newer EU member states, i.e. Cyprus, Czech Republic, Estonia, Hungary, Latvia, Lithuania, Malta, Poland, Slovakia and Slovenia do not have the right to go to work in France until at least 2006, and possible later, depending on what the French government decides. The situation for non-EU citizens who want to start a business is much less certain.

# OBTAINING A RESIDENCE PERMIT

## *EU Nationals*

Nationals of other EU countries (Austria, Belgium, Denmark, Eire, Finland, Germany, Greece, Italy, Luxembourg, the Netherlands, Portugal, Spain, Sweden, the United Kingdom and other countries due to join) have the right to settle permanently in France, under certain conditions. Swiss citizens have similar rights. In the case of the UK, your passport must state that you are a British Citizen, meaning you have the right of abode in the UK. If you have another type of British passport, contact a French consulate in your home country to find out whether you can move to France.

Travelling to France is easy enough for British citizens. The French immigration authorities may not even look at your passport. Once in France, you have the right to remain for three months to look for a job, without registering with the police or any other authorities. There will be no stamp in your passport, so it is not that easy for anyone to know how long you have been in France. If you plan to look for a job or start a business, you should apply for a *carte de séjour* (residence permit), before the three months are up. In the first instance, go along to the nearest *préfecture de police* (police station), or *mairie* (town hall or municipal office) to apply. It can take several months to obtain. In the meantime you will be given a receipt (récépissé) which will enable you to legally take up a profession. Britons who own property in France, and want to stay there for longer than three months at a time are officially also required to have a *carte de séjour*: if you come and go several times a year, you can manage without it.

The law passed on 26 November 2003 (no.2003-1119) states that EU citizens no longer need to apply for a residence permit (i.e. *carte de séjour*) if they wish to remain in France without working. They can apply at their *mairie* for a *carte de séjour* if they wish, which will be granted to them if they do not represent a threat to public order. EU citizens who wish to work in France must still apply for a *carte de séjour*. The precise implications of this law are still not entirely clear but it is clear that until you make yourself known to the authorities you can remain as a tourist for as long as you like. There still remains the fact that you will not be able to obtain certain public services without some kind of *carte de séjour.* You also need to be tax-resident somewhere.

**Documents.** A number of documents are required to apply for a *carte de séjour:* a valid passport, four passport photographs, a birth certificate, and a marriage certificate, if you have one. If you are a single parent with dependent children, you will need proof that your children can leave the UK. The authorities may require you to have your birth and marriage certificate officially translated and legalised, although this seems to be happening less and less. Certainly if you get married in France you will need a legalised translation of your birth certificate. Even original British documents are not necessarily considered legally valid; translations have to be legalised. If you use a translator in France, they must be sworn in, or *assermenté,* all of which adds to the cost, of course. Any old translator from the yellow pages will not do. Finding a translator who is *assermenté* is difficult in the UK so you are best advised to find a translator through a British consulate in France. If you are in southwestern France (e.g. Dordogne or Lot) your nearest consulate is in Bordeaux. Documents can be legalised by a French vice-consul, i.e. stamped and signed, in the UK. In France, documents are legalised by a notaire. It is advisable to have several copies made of documents and have them all legalised, as you will need them in the future. At some point you are also likely to be asked for copies of your parents' and grandparents' birth certificates: these can be easily obtained from the Family Records Centre in London (☎0870-243 7788; e-mail certificate.services@ons.gov.uk; www.familyrecords.gov.uk).

**Financial Resources.** As well as all the above, you need to have proof of financial resources. If you already have work, or have been offered a job, you can use your contract of employment; you can also ask your employer to make out a *certificat d'emploi* on headed paper, confirming your passport number, the date you started work, and your salary. If you plan to be self-employed, you will need some proof that you are a member of a professional body and that you have registered with the local *chambre des métiers* or *chambre de commerce.* If you are planning to stay in France without working, you will need bank statements, again witnessed by a notary. If your income is less than the French minimum wage or SMIC – about £8,700 a year – you may be refused a *carte de séjour*. The authorities seem to accept that two people can live together on this amount. Whether you own your property or not is irrelevant. On the other hand if you show that you have a certain amount of capital (how much is not precisely clear) then this rule is often overlooked.

**Proof of Residence.** If you have bought a property, your notary can supply a *certificat* giving proof of residence. If you rent, then rent receipts will be adequate proof. If you are staying with friends, and not paying rent, then your friend will need to supply an *attestation d'hébergement* and proof of their identity. Naturally, if you are paying someone rent and they are not declaring it, then no *attestation d'hébergement* is likely to be forthcoming. Further proof of residence includes phone or electricity bills (from EDF/GDF) with your name and address.

Local officials can react in very different ways to applications for a *carte de séjour*. As is the way here, much depends on the whim of the official. You need to be well prepared, and patient if obstacles seem to be put in your way. Getting irate with the local petty officials will make future contacts a lot more difficult.

---

## DOCUMENTS REQUIRED FOR THE *CARTE DE SÉJOUR*

- ○ Passport, with copies of the main pages, stamped as *copie certifiée conforme* by the *préfecture* or *town hall*.
- ○ Four passport photographs of each member of your family.
- ○ Birth certificate, with an official translation if requested, notarised by a French Consulate or French lawyer.
- ○ Marriage certificate/divorce papers/custody papers (officially translated and notarised only if requested).
- ○ Certificate from the town hall stating that you are living in *concubinage notoire* if you live with a common-law partner.
- ○ Proof of residence: *certificat* from the notary who handled your house purchase, or rent receipts, or *attestation d'hébergement*

> from the person you are staying with.
> O  Proof of entry. Your travel ticket may be sufficient; or ask the immigration police when you enter the country.
> O  Proof of employment.
> O  Proof of financial resources.
> O  You may be asked for proof that you have no criminal record.
> O  Medical certificate (for non-EU citizens).

**Renewing your residence permit.** The first *carte de séjour* is for one year. You need to apply for a renewal before it runs out. EU citizens will usually receive a 10-year residence permit as long as they are in regular employment in France. You will have to prove that you have paid all your taxes. The permit is then renewed again for five or ten years at a time. The same documents as above are required, except that you will not need to produce your children's or parents' birth certificates. Certain categories of resident do not automatically receive a 10-year residence permit:

O  Students or anyone who has been unemployed for more than 12 months: a one-year permit. If you are still unemployed after the permit has expired it may not be renewed.

O  If you become unfit to work, other rules will apply.

O  Economically inactive persons (mainly pensioners): a five-year permit.

If you change address within France, you are required to inform the police in your new place of residence, so the address on your *carte de séjour* can be changed.

## Remaining in France

If you have worked in France and want to stay on you should fall into one of the following categories:

O  You are of pensionable age in France, and you have worked for at least the last 12 months and lived in France on a continuous basis for more than three years.

O   You have lived in France on a continuous basis for more than two years, and have stopped working as a result of permanent disablement resulting from an occupational accident or illness that entitles you to a pension paid by the relevant French body, and you fulfil other residency requirements.

O   After living and working in France for three continuous years you become a frontier worker (*frontalier*) and remain resident in France.

O   You come to live in France after retiring in another EU state, or you come as an economically inactive person: you need proof of income and adequate social security cover (see above).

### *Residence Permits for Non-EU Nationals*

Non-EU citizens require a Schengen visa to enter France: normally this allows you to stay for 90 days (*visa de court séjour*). Citizens from some countries – in particular, the USA, Canada, Australia and New Zealand are automatically allowed to stay for 90 days in the Schengen area (which includes France). If you come from these countries you will need to apply for a *visa de long séjour* well before you leave if you want to stay more than 90 days. In the USA you should count on 2 months to receive your visa. The application form for the *visa de long séjour* can be found at: www.service-public.fr/formulaires/index.htm. The requirements are similar to those for the *carte de séjour*, but you will need a certificate of good conduct from the state police, health insurance and proof of financial resources. Family connections with France, or a statement from a French citizen promising to support you financially, will also help.

## WORK PERMITS

EU citizens do not require work permits; they only need to follow the same regulations as French citizens as regards self-employment and business formation. They have exactly the same rights as French workers.

## Carte de Commerçant

Non-EU citizens who wish to start a business of any description will require a *carte de commerçant étranger*. This applies to whatever business it is you want to start, although in practice it is mainly given to traders, and it is officially translated as 'trading card'. The official French text states that it is required for any foreigner who wishes to carry on an industrial, commercial or artisanal activity, unless a special dispensation is granted. Citizens of Iceland, Norway, Liechtenstein, Andorra, Monaco and Algeria are exempted from this ruling. If you already possess a residence permit in France, then there is no need to apply for a *carte de commerçant*, but you will still have to go through the process of applying to start a business.

France does have a bilateral convention with the USA (and several African countries) which simplifies the procedure for obtaining the *carte de commerçant*. Paradoxically, there is no such agreement with Canada. Where certain conditions are fulfilled, US citizens can come to France to run a business, namely:

O you can fulfil the requirements for regulated professions
O your planned activity does not constitute a threat to public order
O you have not been found guilty of any crime that would disqualify you from running a business in France.

The *carte de commerçant* is also given to foreign directors, partners and chairmen of French companies or branches of foreign companies. There are two different processes for prospective sole traders and for directors of companies, but at the end of the day, the decision rests with the *préfecture* in the département where you want to run your business. In theory, you should receive a *carte de commerçant provisoire* within three weeks of applying at the *préfecture* (assuming you have the right of residence), and if there is no rejection, then the provisional card becomes valid for one year. A renewal request has to be entered at least two months before the card expires.

French embassies do not particularly wish to publicise the fact that US citizens have a right to start a business in France. The experience of Terry Link, an American journalist, given below should alert you to the kinds of obstacles that could be put in your way. In the normal course of events you apply for your *visa de long séjour* (which usually corresponds to the *carte de séjour*) at the same time as the *carte de commerçant*. The application is to be made at the nearest French consulate or embassy to you. If you want the *carte de commerçant* but not the *carte de séjour* then the application is made directly in France. The *carte de commerçant* is actually a type of identity card that mentions the word *'commerçant'*.

If you come from a country which does not have a bilateral convention with France, then you will be required to present a budget for the first years of your business activity, backed up with a guarantee or actual funds deposited in a bank to cover the first years of activity. The type of application you need to fill in depends on what business structure you choose, i.e. as a sole trader or a limited company, or whether you are taking over an existing business or starting a new one. Details of the documents you will have to provide are obtainable from French consulates or from the *préfecture* where you plan to start your business. They can also be found on the internet at: www.diplomatie.gouv.fr under 'Entering France'.

## Useful Addresses

*French Embassy in London*: 58 Knightsbridge, London SW1X 7JT; ☎ 020-7201 1000; www.ambafrance-uk.org.
*French Embassy:* Cultural Department, 23 Cromwell Rd, London SW7 2EL; ☎ 020-7838 2055.

Visa enquiries should be sent to the French Consulate:
*French Consulate:* Service des Visas (Long Stay Visas), 6A Cromwell Place, PO Box 57, London SW7 2EW; ☎020-7838 2048. Open 9-10am for long-stay visa applications only. Closed on UK bank holidays and French public holidays.
*French Consulate General:* General Inquiries, 21 Cromwell Rd, London SW7 2EN; ☎020-7838 2000; fax 020-7838 2118; www.ambafrance-uk.org. Open 9am to midday Monday to Friday; also 1.30-3.30pm Tuesday to Thursday.
*French Consulate at Edinburgh & Glasgow:* 11 Randolph Crescent,

Edinburgh, EH3 7TT; ☎0131-225 7954. Open daily 9.30-11.30am for visas.

*French Embassy & Consulate General:* 4101 Reservoir Rd NW, Washington DC 20007; ☎202-944-6195; www.ambafrance-us.org; www.consulfrance-washington.org.

There are French consulates in: Atlanta, Boston, Chicago, Houston, Los Angeles, Miami, New York, New Orleans and San Francisco.

**British Embassy and Consulates in France.** Documents are issued from Paris. The Consulates-General can issue forms, which you then send to the British Embassy in Paris. The Consulates-General can issue emergency passports valid for one journey. Addresses of Consulates-General are given above.

*British Embassy:* 35 rue du Faubourg St Honoré, 75008 Paris Cedex 08; ☎01 44 51 31 00; fax 01 44 51 32 34; www.amb-grandebretagne.fr.

*British Consular Services Paris,* 18bis rue d'Anjou, 75008 Paris; ☎01 44 51 31 00; fax 01 44 51 31 27.

*British Consulate:* 18bis rue d'Anjou, 75008 Paris; ☎01 44 51 31 00; fax 01 44 51 31 27; e-mail consulare-mailparis2@fco.gov.uk.

*British Consulate:* 353 bvd du Président Wilson, 33073 Bordeaux; ☎05 57 22 21 10; fax 05 56 08 33 12; e-mail postmaster.bordeaux @fco.gov.uk.

*British Consulate:* 11 Square Dutilleul, 59800 Lille; ☎03 20 12 82 72; fax 03 20 54 88 16; e-mail consular.lille@fco.gov.uk.

*British Consulate:* 24 rue Childebert, 69002 Lyon; ☎04 72 77 81 70; fax 04 72 77 81 79; e-mail britishconsulate.mail@ordilyon.fr.

*British Consulate:* 24 ave du Prado, 13006 Marseille; ☎04 91 15 72 10; fax 04 91 37 47 06; e-mail MarseilleConsular.marseille@fco.gov.uk.

**US Embassy and Consulates**

*United States Embassy:* 2 ave Gabriel, 75008 Paris; ☎01 43 12 22 22; fax 01 42 66 97 83; www.amb-usa.fr.

*United States Consulate:* rue St Florentin, 75001 Paris; ☎as above.

## The American Connection

Terry Link was a journalist in San Francisco who decided to move to France to open a *chambres d'hôtes*. He has published a book – *Adapter Kit France* – aimed at US citizens who want to move to France. His bed & breakfast is in the beautiful town of Caunes-Minervois, near Carcassonne in the Aude.

*I started out by going to the local French Consulate in San Francisco and put in all the necessary application papers. When I told them I wanted to open a* chambres d'hôtes, *they told me I had to have the location before actually making an application, in other words, they could not process an application for me to operate a bed and breakfast that did not physically exist. So after several trips to France, my wife and I found a building that we thought would be suitable and made a down-payment, planning to return in several months, in which time the sale would be completed.*

*After I had purchased the property, I filed all the necessary documents and after being told that everything appeared to be in order, I said rather off-handedly that I was leaving for France in a few days. At that point, the official told me that I was not permitted to leave, or at least to go to France, until everything had been approved and I was notified. This is a requirement that is now stated on the consulate's website, but had never before been mentioned to me. I had already bought the non-refundable plane tickets. So I said something about how I had every right to go and see my property and left.*

*In the meantime, in France, I first went to the Chambre d'Agriculture who told me that Gîtes de France was only for French people and were quite hostile. After this rebuff from the Aude Chambre d'Agriculture, we simply continued with our plans for a* chambres d'hôtes. *On the other hand, the* mairie *was helpful in the sense that we were accepted for what we were.*

*Back in San Francisco our three adult children, who continued to occupy our home after we left, forwarded any important mail to us. In fact, there was nothing at all from the consulate – no* carte de séjour, *no rejection of our application, nothing. In the end I called from France and asked them what was going on, and they told me that they had already written to me rejecting my application. At that point, they said, the time to contest the rejection had passed so there was nothing I could do. Because my children forwarded me every other piece of mail that was important but nothing from the consulate, I believe that the consulate never sent a rejection of my application, thus allowing the deadline to contest it to pass. There was a rejection which they showed me in their files, stating that the village did not need a* chambres d'hôtes *and that I was not qualified to open such a business as I had been a journalist all my adult life. I don't think they discarded my application, but that they simply withheld notification that the application had been rejected.*

*It was now necessary to regularise the situation in France, so we went to the* préfecture *in Carcassonne with all my papers. Finally, I got the* carte de commerçant *and the* carte de séjour. *The* carte de séjour *was renewed annually for the first three years, as was the* carte de commerçant étranger. *After that I received a* carte de résident *and no longer needed the* carte de commerçant.

*What happens when you apply to a French consulate – part of the Ministry of Foreign Affairs – for a* carte de séjour *is that the application is processed for proof of birthplace and nationality, financial sufficiency, not wanted by the police – all the sort of things that are best handled outside of France. When your application is approved, what you actually get is a sort of a temporary permit that you take to your local* préfecture *(i.e. the local office of the Ministry of the Interior) with proof of address in France etc., where the actual* carte de séjour *is issued. In other words, it is a two-step process with each ministry playing a separate role, although commonly perceived as simply 'getting a* carte de séjour'.

*My advice to non-EU citizens is to always try to work with the system and follow the rules; at least if you try then you cannot be blamed for not doing the right things. However, if you are planning on starting a business the first thing is to talk to the local Chambre de Commerce and other local people in France before you go to the French Consulate in your own country.*

# SOURCES OF INFORMATION

Getting advice is one of the main factors in ensuring the survival of your business in the first difficult years. Other factors are whether you have formal qualifications or previous experience of your job.

Attitudes towards taking advice and who you take it from are very different in France from those in England. While 20% of the British would ask their bank for advice, only 10% of the French would. This is not surprising given that banking services are unsophisticated compared with the UK and USA, and the laws against usury prevent banks from lending money that easily. On the other hand, the French see their Chamber of Commerce or Chamber of Trades as their best source of advice, which would probably not have occurred to most British people until they came to France. According to the EU survey, 40% of French entrepreneurs will go to a Chamber of Commerce or Trades, while only 20% of British would think of doing so. The French also see other people who have successfully started a business as good sources of advice, as well as tax lawyers and business start-up consultants.

There are now numerous business consultants who will guide you through your business creation. If you are starting out from the position of being unemployed in France, you are entitled under the ACCRE scheme to a *Chèquier Conseil* (Advice Chequebook), with six cheques worth €45.75 to be spent on business advice from a state-approved private agency. An hour of advice costs €61, and you make up the remaining money yourself. Chambres de Commerce organise free half-day seminars on starting a business in different towns in each département two or three times a month. There are 5-day courses which will set you back between €90 and €130. If you are planning to start up a business classified as *artisanal*, in which case you are dependent on the Chambre des Métiers, then a 4-day training course is compulsory, on the assumption that artisans are less educated and need to learn management skills. If you are starting a shop or other business defined as commercial you may come under pressure to take a training course, depending on which area you are in and what you are going to sell. The general aim is to introduce you to an accountant and a lawyer who will try to put you off going through with your project. Many a foreigner has sat through several days of such a course without understanding a great deal of what was going on. Nonetheless, you will at least be introduced to some useful contacts.

It is worth contacting the nearest Boutique de Gestion (Management Shop). These are state-sponsored offices that provide help and information to potential entrepreneurs, and they can guide you for the first three years of setting up a business. If you have been unemployed in France then you can participate in seminars free of charge and have at least one individual session as well. The Boutique's services are available to everyone, but they are generally not free. There are some 260 Boutiques de Gestion in France, to be found in the phone book, or via the website: www.boutiques-de-gestion.com. They will generally not be able to provide advice in English.

## Books and Leaflets

The French love writing about business and taxation and so on. The problem again is whether you can understand French business jargon. The more technical books are expensive and may just confuse you. The Agence Pour la Création d'Entreprises publishes very clear, jargon-free books in a series for budding entrepreneurs. APCE also sell dossiers and *fiches professionnelles* on various professions and businesses, listed on their website at www.apce.fr. If possible, visit APCE's bookshop at 14 rue Delambre in Paris (a stone's throw from the Gare de Montparnasse) to see their stock. The real bible for business creation is APCE's *Créer ou Reprendre une Entreprise,* published every year at the start of February with the latest information. It can be consulted at a *Centre de Documentation* in the Chambre de Commerce. APCE's books can be ordered from www.amazon.fr, while their brochures are most easily obtained in person, or by sending a French cheque. At the other end of the spectrum, there are the books published by the legal publishers Delmas on various aspects of enterprise creation which are only suitable if you can understand legal French. In between there are the publishers Eyrolles (www.eyrolles.com) and Puits Fleuri (www.puitsfleuri.com). Publications from Dunod (www.dunod.com) and Vuibert (www.vuibert.com) can also be recommended. The Lyon Chamber of Commerce has also launched a range of publications: see www.ceral.org.

To sound a note of caution: because of the big changes to business regulations and taxation starting from August 2003, many books are now out of date. It is advisable to check information with the offices concerned before you take anything as gospel truth. You will need to make an appointment if you wish to speak with an adviser at the Chambre de Commerce etc., or the Centre des Impôts (local tax office). They can usually see you the following day.

The best source of free dossiers on various professions is the Paris Chamber of Commerce and Industrie website: www.ccip.fr. Other CCI websites have far less information. The CCI de Bayonne in the Basque country has translated part of its website into English (see www.bayonne.cci.fr), perhaps acknowledging the fact that Bayonne was the last British outpost in southwest France at the end of the 100 Years' War. Local offices of the Chambres de Commerce/Métiers/ Agriculture can give you dossiers and leaflets, but these are only a fraction of the information that you actually need. Every CCI has a Centre de Documentation or Centre de Doc as they call it, with a lot of statistics about the typical turnover per employee of the kind of business you may wish to start. These statistics are published as books by the Centres de Gestion Agréés, non-profit accountancies attached to CCIs. They will tell you how much money a similar business is actually making in your area. For more information see the chapter *Acquiring a Business.*

### Internet

There is now a great deal of information about starting a business in France on the internet, almost entirely in French but generally free. The downside is that you have to know French well enough to be able to find the information that is relevant to you. You can try to start from the French Embassy website in your country, which will direct you towards official French sites. You can register on the APCE website for free daily and monthly e-mail newsletters on current legislation and developments in small business regulations. Past dossiers are also available on the same site.

## Useful Websites

www.acfci.org. Assemblée des Chambres de Commerce et de l'Industrie.

www.apce.fr. French business creation agency. Most extensive site.

www.ccfgb.co.uk. French chamber of commerce in UK.

www.ccip.fr. Paris Chamber of Commerce site, with free dossiers.

www.cgpme.org. Confédération Générale des Petites et Moyennes Entreprises. Small business federation.

www.contrats.biz. Ready-made contracts and forms, against payment.

www.credoc.fr. Centre for research into consumer and social habits.

www.entreprendre-en-france. Information for all kinds of businesses.

www.greffe-tc-paris.fr. Paris Commercial Court site with details on how to register new businesses. Partly in English.

www.microentreprise.net. Very small businesses.

www.patrimoine.com. Useful information on taxation, finance, etc.

www.service-public.gov.fr. Official government site with many forms and explanations.

www.tpe-pme.com. Site for small businesses, with a lot of useful dossiers.

# CHAMBERS OF COMMERCE AND INDUSTRY

French Chambres de Commerce et d'Industrie (CCIs) have a far higher profile than their equivalent in the UK, and are regarded as the place to go for information and help by entrepreneurs; part of your business tax goes towards financing them. There are, of course, also the Chambres de Métiers for *artisans* and the Chambres d'Agriculture for *agriculteurs*. The Chambres des *Professions Libérales* are a fairly recent phenomenon, and only represent liberal professions (see below); they have no statutory role.

After the mayor of your commune your Chambre is probably the most important point of contact for aspiring business people. It is not always obvious which Chambre you should go to for help. For example, if you breed dogs then you are an *agriculteur*, if you train them then you are a *libéral*, but if you keep kennels then you are a *commerçant*. The distinctions will be made clear below, as well as under the sections on different types of business. Lists of all Chambers of Commerce and similar organisations can be found on the website www.apce.fr by clicking on 'E-mail' via which you can search on each département.

French CCIs are also present abroad; there are no less than 19 of them in the USA, but only one in the UK. They are orientated towards helping people to invest in France, or to export to France. They can function as a useful initial point of contact before you go over to France, and they will be able to supply some general information about French business culture and practices, and market studies (at a price). All chambers of commerce outside France are listed under www.uccife.org. A few addresses are given below:

*Franco-British Chamber of Commerce:* 31 rue Boissy d'Anglas, 75008 Paris; ☎ 01 53 30 81 30; fax 01 53 30 81 35; www.francobritishchambers.com.
*Chambre de Commerce Française en Grande-Bretagne:* 21 Dartmouth St, London SW1H 9BP; ☎ 020 7304 4040; fax 020 7304 7034; e-mail mail@ccfgb.co.uk; www.ccife.org/gb.
*French-American Chamber of Commerce (New York Chapter):* 1350 Avenue of the Americas, 6th floor, New York, NY 10019; ☎ 212-765 44 60; fax 212-765 46 50; e-mail info@faccnyc.org; www.faccnyc.org.
*Union des Chambres de Commerce et d'Industrie Françaises à l'Etranger:* 2 Rue de Viarmes, 75001 Paris; ☎ 01 55 65 39 21; fax 01 55 65 39 38; e-mail info@uccife.org; www.uccife.org.

## CATEGORIES OF PROFESSION

In accord with the French – or maybe one should say EU – mania for systems every profession and business has its own category and number. The first main distinction is drawn between 'commercial' and 'civil' professions, because of the different types of law involved. Buying and selling, or transforming raw materials to sell, and the more tangible services are commercial professions. The more intangible liberal professions, agriculture, renting out property and management services are civil professions. Businesses come under one of three main categories: *libéral, commercial, artisanal* (or *industriel*) and *agricole*. For taxation purposes you have to choose one of these as your main activity, even though you may carry on two or three at a time. The type of legal entity you choose to operate under is a separate matter. There are limits on what type of business structure you can use. More significant is the impact on how you are going to pay your taxes and what kind of accounts you keep

## PROFESSIONS LIBERALES

The term 'liberal profession' covers a vast array of jobs. In the French system, anyone who carries on a money-making activity comes under *profession commerciale* or *profession civile*. Anyone who buys or sells (*commerçants*) or makes things (*artisans*) comes under the category of commerce; the rest are presumed to be exercising a liberal profession. If what you are offering is intangible, e.g. anything intellectual, or a service, then you come into this category.

With the rapid expansion of the service economy about 66% of French workers are considered to be in liberal professions. Many of them work for employers, while others choose to be independent. There is no requirement for them to be self-employed, or to set up a company or partnership, but many of them do. The great increase in outsourcing and short-term contracts means that many workers have no choice but to go independent.

The *professions libérales* are divided into regulated (*réglementées*) and unregulated (*non réglementées*). In the former category you find doctors, legal professions, surveyors, dentists, opticians, nurses and other paramedical workers. The only categories likely to affect foreigners are those of architect, insurance broker and surveyor. These are professions where membership of a professional body is obligatory, and with their own ethical requirements or *déontologie*. Your professional body can suspend or terminate your right to carry on your profession if you break their rules. Because of their nature, you need to bring proof of your qualifications with you if you are going to register for a *profession réglementée*. There are mechanisms for recognising the qualifications and experience you have gained elsewhere, as detailed at the end of this chapter.

The heading *professions libérales non réglementées* covers so many weird and wonderful jobs that it would be impossible to list them all. There is no definitive list, as people invent new professions every day. If you are undertaking an unregulated profession then there is no need to show qualifications when you register. Some of the relevant professions include:

| | |
|---|---|
| *analyste programmer* | computer analyst |
| *architecte d'intérieur* | interior designer |
| *céramiste* | potter |
| *concepteur de sites internet* | web designer |
| *consultant* | consultant |
| *chiropracteur* | chiropractor |
| *diététicien* | dietician |
| *formateur* | trainer |
| *géologue* | geologist |
| *ingénieur* | engineer |
| *maître d'œuvre* | master builder |
| *ostéopathe* | osteopath |
| *photographe* | photographer |
| *professeur* | teacher of music, sports, etc. |
| *psychothérapeute* | psychotherapist |
| *rédacteur* | editor |
| *sculpteur* | sculptor |
| *traducteur* | translator |
| *travaux à domicile* | home worker |

The more unlikely professions include astrologers, tarot card readers, clairvoyants and radiesthesists – termed 'paranormal professions' – and others such as dog-handlers, medievalists and speleologists. Anyone offering computer services, web design, etc. comes under unregulated liberal professions. It follows that there is no actual necessity to have any training in what you are doing, although you might not get a lot of customers without any letters after your name.

**Business Ethics.** Those who work in the regulated liberal professions will belong to a professional association and are subject to strict professional ethics. The non-regulated professions are not entirely free of ethical restrictions, however. Everyone who works in the liberal professions is bound to maintain professional secrecy, i.e. not divulge names of clients to others, except to the taxman. You can be fined up to €15,000 and imprisoned for up to a year for breach of professional secrecy.

With the so-called intangible professions, customers cannot demand tangible results. If you are dealing with computers and suchlike, then they can sue you if you commit a serious professional error. You can take out professional liability insurance if you want.

**Administrative Jungle**

Freddy De Cock, who has been running alternative holiday camps in France for more than 20 years, has the following advice:

*A lot of foreigners see France as a kind of paradise where they can leave all their problems behind, but I've seen a lot of people who have come here full of enthusiasm and been defeated by the French system.*

*Basically, I see three different kinds of people coming here: the first are those with a small income who come here looking for some kind of salvation. The second are those who have sold a home or business in their own country and who come to start a business here; some succeed and some don't. The third are the well-off newcomers who are generally over 50, have taken early retirement, and have no kids to worry about, who can just come to enjoy themselves. The third category is becoming increasingly common.*

*In our case, we started from nothing, and did everything by the book. We have always done our best not to get involved in court cases, and to get on with the local people. At the end of the day, you have to work just as hard in France as you do at home, and on top of that you are confronted with a wall of bureaucracy. Moving to France to run a business can put a lot of strain on relationships; business failure is often accompanied by divorce or relationships breaking down.*

# PROFESSIONS COMMERCIALES

As one might assume, commerce covers buying and selling goods. It also covers renting out furnished rooms, which includes hotels. Your first point of contact is the nearest Chambre de Commerce et Industrie

(CCI). If you run a shop then you will be subject to a great number of regulations and inspections. In the first place, you will most probably take over an existing shop but sell quite different goods. Most shops are leased; what you will buy are movable fixtures and goodwill built up by the previous owner, known as the *fonds de commerce*. A *fonds de commerce* never includes the building the shop is in. You can also buy both the building and the *fonds* at the same time. Buying a shop is not at all the same thing as buying an ordinary property. There have to be extensive checks on the history of the business to ensure that you are not taking on someone else's debts. Generally, the notaire has to present a declaration that the business's debts have been 'purged'. The concept is further explained in the chapter *Acquiring a Business*.

If you rent out furnished rooms, and this is your main occupation, or the income exceeds €23,000, then you are required to register with the Chambre de Commerce. More information about this type of business is given in the previous chapter. You will pay tax on your *bénéfices industriels et commerciaux* (BIC).

## PROFESSIONS ARTISANALES

The word *artisan* conjures up old-fashioned craftsmanship and sometimes inflated prices for handmade goods. Again it is all a matter of keeping rural traditions alive. If you employ up to 10 workers, then you remain an *entreprise artisanale*; above this you become an *industrie*. The basic difference between *artisans* and *commerces* is that the former transform basic materials into something, while the latter sell things.

---

**The Electrician**

Paul Foulkes has been working as an electrician in France since 1999. He is based near Brive-la-Gaillarde in Dordogne, but works in several départements, including Dordogne, Corrèze, Haute Vienne and the Lot.

*I first approached the Chambre des Métiers, who asked me to have my qualifications translated by an official translator, who was not very good, by the way. As I had done an apprenticeship in engineering and was a qualified electronics engineer (my last job was with British Aerospace in avionics), they accepted that I could be trusted as a household electrician.*

> *Anyone who comes from the UK will have the same problem: doing the wiring may be easy enough – the wires are colour-coded – but then you have to learn the regulations.*
>
> *For someone who is going to be an electrician, then the best advice I can give is to find good suppliers who supply good materials. It's a mistake to go for cheaper materials, and to chop and change suppliers. I attend training courses run by suppliers as a way of extending my expertise. The rewiring will be checked by* Consuel *(the state electricity watchdog) to see that it is safe, but they do not check the electrician's work unless something is wrong. Different départements have very different standards regarding what they will allow.*

The types of job covered by the title *artisan* include:

| | |
|---|---|
| *brasseur* | brewer |
| *couvreur* | roofer |
| *ébéniste* | cabinetmaker |
| *électricien* | electrician |
| *entrepreneur de bâtiments* | builder |
| *installateur de clôtures* | fencer |
| *mécanicien* | mechanic |
| *menuisier* | carpenter |
| *plombier* | plumber |

Artisans tend to be sole traders who work with other artisans on a self-employed basis, or in local co-operatives.

## PROFESSIONS AGRICOLES

Anyone who wants to get involved with farming or related activities should first approach the local Chambre d'Agriculture who will be very happy to tell you everything you need to know. There are a number of incentives in place to encourage foreigners to set up as farmers in France. A good point of contact is the website www.eurofarms.com, run by George Lidbury, a consultant who assists English-speaking farmers to set up in France. The situation for French farmers is likely to become more difficult soon, as subsidies are to be reduced and new countries join the EU. Farming also covers forestry which could be an attractive profession as there is no income tax on the sale of wood, but only a tax on the land where the trees grow. It also covers breeding fish and other animals, plant-breeding, making cider and growing fruit and vegetables.

If you are a salaried or non-salaried farmer or farm manager you will pay your pension contributions to MSA (Mutualité Sociale Agricole). Income is taxed under bénéfices agricoles (BA) on your tax return. For more information see section on 'Farming' in the previous chapter.

# REGISTERING YOUR BUSINESS

### *Preliminaries*

Before you consider going to the *Centre de Formalités des Entreprises* (CFE), you must be entirely clear that you are permitted to exercise your chosen profession. If you practise a regulated profession then you have to be registered and approved by the professional body you belong to. Your Chamber of Commerce will tell you about restrictions on practising a profession. If you are planning to run a shop you should contact the *Direction Départementale de la Concurrence de la Consommation et de la Répression des Fraudes (DDCCRF)*.

No one can register a business without an official address (*domiciliation d'entreprise*). Sole traders – *entreprises individuelles* – are no longer required to have a registered office, or *siège social*. There are restrictions on using rented property to run a company from: see chapter 5, *Acquiring a Business*. You can get around this by using an official *pépinière d'entreprise* (business nursery) or *société de domiciliation* (mailbox address).

It is equally important to go to your local Centre des Impôts to find out what kind of tax regime you are going to come under depending on what form of business structure you choose. Once you have chosen a business structure it is difficult to downsize. You can always go from being a sole trader to a limited company, but it is much harder to go the other way without a lot of administrative problems. It is advisable to look carefully at the types of business structures on offer (see chapter 4, *Business Structures*) well before you think about going to the CFE. In order to make an informed decision, go on some courses or talk to some experts at your Chambre de Commerce. You must also plan ahead for TVA (French Value Added Tax) and the possible consequences if you make the wrong choices.

You also need to think about the time of year that you are going to start up, because of the various payments which have to be made in tax and social security contributions during the year. It is a matter of consulting your advisor. The time of year that you close down your business is more crucial in order to avoid unnecessary payments.

Chambres de Commerce (and other Chambres) require you to present some kind of projections, generally called a *plan financier prévisionnel* as to how your business is going to survive the crucial first three years, before you can be registered. This is particularly necessary if you are opening a shop. You will not get the necessary licences unless the authorities are convinced that your business plan is going to work, nor will the banks lend you money. Because of the taxation system, everything operates on three-year cycles. If you can survive three years, then supposedly, all will be well.

The main requirement is that you take professional advice, and are able to present your estimates for profits in the first three years. The details of financial and business plans are dealt with in the chapter *Financing Your Business*. It is worth considering the following checklist first, to see if you have been working on the right lines:

O   Decision on nature of business.
O   Contact the Chambre de Commerce/Métiers/Agricole.
O   Make a market study.
O   Drawing up a financial plan.
O   Consider how you want to pay taxes.
O   Look for grants.
O   Choose your business structure.
O   Find suitable business premises.

### A Name for Your Business

Choosing your business name – *la raison sociale* – may seem the easiest thing in the world, but it does deserves some thought. The French tend to favour far-fetched puns or wordplay, which may be fine as long as your name does not break the rules of French grammar, which could offend some people. It may be as well to avoid the very obvious, because shop names, and names of branded products are copyright. To find out if your name is going to land you in hot water, you can contact the Institut National de la Propriété Industrielle (www.inpi.fr) and ask them to conduct a search to see if the name you want to use is already taken. Some business consultants advise you to register your name with INPI straight away; you will have to pay to register it anyway so it is safer to find out immediately whether you can use the name you have thought of. You can also see directly if the name has been used in a website domain by looking at www.whois.net. If you plan to sell a product with a label on it, then you have to clear the name with INPI. The basic charge is around €230 to register three trademarks or ideas. You will receive a certification known as an *Enveloppe Soleau* that allows you to prove that you thought of a trademark first.

## *Registration*

Whatever kind of business you are registering, be it an *entreprise individuelle* or a limited company, you will have to submit a *déclaration*. By French standards, this is a relatively simple procedure. Depending on the type of business you will submit your form to the relevant Centre de Formalités des Entreprises. For self-employed people this is Form P0 (*personne physique*); for companies it is Form M0 (*personne morale*). The CFE is located in one of a number of places:

| | |
|---|---|
| *agent de commerce* | Greffe du Tribunal de Commerce |
| agricultural profession | Chambre de l'Agriculture |
| artisan | Chambre des Métiers |
| artist | Centre des Impôts |
| *association loi 1901* | *Préfecture* |
| *commerçant* | Chambre de Commerce |
| *profession libérale* (EI) | URSSAF |

The form has several identical sheets which are distributed to various organisations, who then pass on the details to other organisations if need be:

- ○ Registre de Commerce et des Sociétés/Registre des Métiers
- ○ DGI (tax office)
- ○ URSSAF (for social security)
- ○ INSEE (national register)
- ○ Inspection du Travail (Health and Safety Inspectorate)

The M0 form is intended for new business creations. Form P0 is a declaration that you are commencing or restarting a non-salaried activity. Note that the CFE as such is merely a letter-box for all the other organisations you have to deal with. CFEs were set up to simplify the initial approach to registering a business. They will only carry out a basic check to see if you have given sufficient information, but they are obliged by law to pass on the various copies of the form to the right organisations on the same day they receive your form. You can also present yourself directly to the Greffe du Tribunal de Commerce (Clerk of the Commercial Court) if for some reason you think that there is an emergency (i.e. you are trading illegally) and they will then pass on your details to the CFE. If you employ salaried workers (stated on the application form) then your details will be passed on to the Inspection du Travail, and the social security bodies responsible for your employees. You will in all cases need to submit a declaration that you have not been found guilty of any crime that would prevent you from carrying on your profession: the *attestation* (or *déclaration*) *de non-condamnation*. For EU and French citizens this is an *attestation sur l'honneur* (on your honour), i.e. you do not have to obtain a document from the police to prove that you have no criminal convictions. Non-EU citizens will need to provide proof of their lack of a criminal record in order to obtain a *carte de commerçant*. Further documents to be provided are listed below.

---

**Documents to be Submitted by Foreign Self-Employed Persons**

- ○ P0 and TNS
- ○ Copy of your *carte de commerçant* or *carte de séjour* or *carte de résident*
- ○ *Attestation de non-condamnation*

> ○ Copy of your marriage/divorce certificate
> ○ Copies of your diplomas or official permission to carry on your profession
> ○ Your commercial tenancy agreement or proof of address of your registered office
> ○ Property deeds; deeds related to purchase of business

You do not have a free choice of compulsory pension and sickness funds. You will be informed by the CFE which *mutuelles conventionnées* are available to you. Contributions come under either the *régime de base* or the *régime complémentaire obligatoire* meaning both are compulsory. There is no need to make approaches to a fund directly, unless you want additional protection beyond that required by law.

How you fill in the *déclaration* is crucial. You will specify the nature of your business, the type of tax regime you want to choose, and how you are going to deal with TVA. You will also give details of your marriage regime in French law (see p. 162) and whether your company is going to employ anyone. If you make a mistake on your *déclaration* then you will be given 15 days to correct it, otherwise you start again.

You will also fill in Form TNS for non-salaried workers, i.e. *travailleurs non salariés* (unless you are opting for the status of *gérant minoritaire* or salaried director). You will be given the name of the pension and sickness funds relevant to your profession by the CFE, and this is entered on the TNS form. The form is passed on to the social security organisation URSSAF, or to MSA if you come under the agricultural regime.

The CFE also passes your details to the Greffe du Tribunal de Commerce who enter you on the Registre de Commerce et de Sociétés, or Répertoire des Métiers if you are an artisan. Only sales agents (*agents commerciaux*) go directly to the Greffe du Tribunal de Commerce to be registered. You cannot legally trade until you receive your *Extrait K* or *Kbis* (the extract from the RCS) from the Greffe du Tribunal de Commerce. Since 2004 when you go to register your business the CFE will give you a *Récépissé de Création d'Entreprise* (receipt) which will allow you to obtain headed notepaper but not start trading without waiting for your *Extrait Kbis* to arrive. The RCE includes your SIREN number and your Code NAF, and remains valid for one month.

## What Happens Next

Finally you will receive your official business number or SIRET. This is given to you by the national statistical organisation, INSEE, when they place you on the national business register (RNE). Your number comes in two forms: the basic one – the SIREN – has 9 figures and is used by the authorities in their dealings with you. Following the 9 figures there is the code for your Régistre de Commerce et de Sociétés or the Régistre des Métiers. Thus your SIREN will look like this: 123 456 789 RCS 011. If you are a *profession libérale* then there are only the 9 figures.

The number that you quote on your letterhead is the SIRET which has an additional 5 numbers (the NIC number) and allows for the possibility that you might run several different businesses in one name. The first four numbers identify your establishment, the last number is a control number. The 14-figure number has to appear on your headed paper, invoices, estimates etc. In addition there is the name of the town where you are registered.

You will also receive a Code NAF (Nomenclature des Activités Françaises) consisting of three numbers and a letter which gives the nature of your principal business. It is vital that you have the right code as it determines which social security organisations you will make your contributions to. The complete list can be found on the Paris Greffe website: www.greffe-tc-paris.fr. The Code NAF was known as the Code APE until 1 January 2003. It is quite possible to have more than one Code NAF, and to be running two different businesses (or more) at the same time, but you will still need to have one main activity, and this will determine who you pay social security contributions to, something that can have a big effect on your finances.

If you are registered for TVA, and deal with other EU countries, then you will also need a *numéro de TVA intracommunautaire*. This consists of the letters FR followed by two numbers, and then your 9-number SIREN. This has to appear on invoices for cross-border transactions in the EU.

If you are a *commerce* or *société* you are registered with the RCS and you will receive a confirmation from the Greffe du Tribunal de Commerce that you have been properly registered in the form of an *Extrait K* (for EIs) or *Kbis* (for other companies). This is an *extrait d'immatriculation*, a copy of your registration; the original remains with the Greffe. Note that anyone can order an *Extrait* from the RCS on demand for any company for a small payment, via www.infogreffe.fr. Basic information is free.

Once your registration has been passed, an extract will be published in a local newspaper (*journal d'annonces légales*). Within 15 days of the publication, the announcement will also have to be placed in the national *Bulletin Officiel des Annonces Civiles et Commerciales* (BODACC), which is done for you by the Greffe du Tribunal de Commerce. Any changes to your company's status, or its closure, will be announced in BODACC for the benefit of third parties. Finally, your company also has to be registered with the Institut National de la Propriété Industrielle (INPI), which protects trademarks and patents (see above).

## CHANGES TO YOUR COMPANY'S STATUS

Any event that changes the information that should be kept by the Greffe must be reported via the CFE or to the Greffe directly within a month. This could include: change of name, transfer of the registered office, change in the directors/associates, removal of your married partner (*conjoint*) from the register, change in the capital, etc. This is a requirement so that third parties can be aware of what is happening to your business. The relevant forms and details can be found on your Greffe's website.

---

### PERMITS

There are a number of organisations whose job is to check up on health and safety and other regulations. Some give out permits. It is a good idea to approach these organisations first to see what their requirements are. These organisations include:

**DDASS.** *Direction Départementale des Affaires Sanitaires et Sociales.* Checks up on sanitation and hygiene in public places, and also on disabled access.

**DDJS.** *Direction Départementale de la Jeunesse et des Sports.* Supervises businesses dealing with children and young people, and also sports activities.

**SDIS.** *Service Départemental d'Incendie et de Secours.* Checks on fire and safety provisions. Sometimes referred to as *la commission de sécurité.*

**DDE.** *Direction Départementale de l'Equipement.* Gives out building permits, and also permits to place advertisements by the roadside.

**DSV.** *Direction Départementale des Services Vétérinaires.* Deals with food hygiene as well as animals.

**DDCCRF.** *Direction Départementale de la Concurrence de la Consommation et de la Répression des Fraudes.* Enforces laws on the numbers of people allowed in public places, labelling of goods, hygiene in markets and also regulations applying to bed and breakfasts.

**Inspection du Travail.** This is the Labour Inspectorate, and forms part of the Direction Départementale du Travail, de l'Emploi et de la Formation Professionnelle (DDTEFP). Their job is to enforce employment regulations, and inform workers of their rights.

**Police d'Eau.** Body that polices use of waterways and water supplies by businesses.

# MUTUAL RECOGNITION OF QUALIFICATIONS

The European Union Treaty enshrines the freedom of EU citizens to undertake a self-employed profession in another member country. This is of particular significance if you intend to set up in a *profession libérale réglementée* (e.g. lawyer, architect, optician), or with certain types of *profession artisanale* such as builder and electrician. In the liberal professions recognition should be automatic. Where there is too much of a difference between British and French qualifications you could be required to undertake further training or be subject to an assessed period of supervised practice.

There are two main directives concerning mutual recognition of education and training (89/48/EEC and 92/51/EEC). The first concerns higher education, the second qualifications gained through any post-secondary course of more than one year or work experience. This means that National and Scottish Vocational Qualifications (NVQs/SVQs) and their equivalents are recognised by the EU. The organisation responsible for providing information on the comparability of all academic qualifications is the National Academic Recognition Information Centre (NARIC) in each EU country. For France this is the NARIC based in Paris (www.education.gouv.fr/sup/default.htm). You should go through your UK or French Employment Agency (ANPE in France) rather than contact NARIC directly, otherwise you will be charged for the service. You can look at www.naric.org.uk if you want more explanation in English, but you should not contact NARIC in the UK if you are going to work in France.

If you have experience but no skills, you can apply for a European Certificates of Experience. These are handled by the Certificates of Experience Team in the UK, which is part of the Department for Education and Skills. Their role is to implement Directive 99/42/EEC (the so-called Third Directive) concerning the mutual recognition of experience gained in a profession in EU member countries. A certificate costs £105 and takes 15 days to process. Contact: DFEs, Certificates of Experience Team, Qualifications for Work Division, Room E3B, Moorfoot, Sheffield S1 4PQ; ☎0114 259 4237; www.dfes.gov.uk/europeopen. A considerable amount of information on professional bodies and EC Directives can be found on the EU website http://citizens.eu.int.

Should you have registered a business in the UK, you can obtain a Letter of Introduction from your local UK Chamber of Commerce. The Chamber will validate your registration document and provide a covering letter which will be recognised anywhere in Europe. The cost is £20-40.

## LEGAL ASSISTANCE WITH
## STARTING A BUSINESS

You can obtain legal assistance from UK-based lawyers who are qualified in French commercial law. There are also lawyers who specialise in taxation: *taxe-avocats*. If you are thinking of turning a residential property into a bed and breakfast, it is advisable to obtain advice in English before you actually buy a property. Some names of UK-based legal practices are given below:

*Blake Lapthorn Solicitors:* Holbrook House, 14 Great Queen St, London WC2B 5DG; ☎020-7430 1709; fax 020-7831 4441; www.bllaw.co.uk. Has an in-house team of three French lawyers.
*John Howell & Co*: The Old Glassworks, 22 Endell Street, Covent Garden, London WC2H 9AD; ☎020 7420 0400; fax 020 7836

3626; e-mail info@europelaw.com; www.europelaw.com; ☎020 7420 0400; fax 020 7836 3626; e-mail info@europelaw.com; www.europelaw.com. A team of English, French and Dual Qualified lawyers working in a Law Firm specialising purely in 'foreign' work.

*Howard Kennedy Solicitors:* ☎020-7636 1616; www.howard-kennedy.com. Large London firm dealing with the top end of the market. Ask for Anthony Slingsby.

*The International Property Law Centre:* The International Property Law Centre, Unit 2, Waterside Park, Livingstone Rd, Hessle HU13 0EG; ☎01482 350850; fax 01482 642799; e-mail internationalpr operty@maxgold.com; www.maxgold.com. Contact senior partner and solicitor Stefano Lucatello, an expert in the purchase and sale of French, Italian, Portuguese and Spanish property and businesses, and the formation of offshore tax vehicles and trusts.

*Russell-Cooke:* 2 Putney Hill, Putney, London SW15 6AB; ☎020-8789 9111; fax 020-8780 1679; e-mail Delasp@russell-cooke.co.uk; www.russell-cooke.co.uk. Large firm with French law and property department, headed by Dawn Alderson, qualified in both English and French law and member of the Bordeaux bar. Bordeaux office: 42 place Gambetta, 33000 Bordeaux; ☎05 56 90 83 10; fax 05 56 90 83 11.

*Stephen Smith (France) Ltd:* 161 Cemetery Rd, Ipswich, Suffolk IP4 2HL; ☎01473-437186; fax 01473-436573; e-mail stephen@step hensmithfranceltd.com; www.stephensmithfranceltd.com. Stephen Smith is the author of *Letting Your French Property Successfully,* published by PKF Guernsey.

# Which Business Structure?

## CHAPTER SUMMARY

O There is a far greater variety of company structures than in the UK or USA.

O Most foreigners choose to operate as sole traders – *Entreprises Individuelles* – and some as private limited companies – SARLs.

O The degree of liability depends on the business structure you use.

O Once you choose a legal structure you cannot go down the scale, only up.

O You can now protect your principal residence from creditors if you are a sole trader.

O Limited companies are expensive to register but useful for raising capital.

O A limited company can now be started with 1 euro capital.

O Certain types of companies make it possible to avoid heavy social security contributions.

O It is legal to register a company in the UK and operate in France.

# A FLURRY OF ACRONYMS

There is a superfluity of business structures in France, most of them rather obscure. These have all kinds of acronyms like SARL, SAS, and so on, something the French are very keen on. Apart from your business structure, you can be classed as a TPE (*Très Petite Entreprise*) or as a PME (*Petite et Moyenne Entreprise*) for the purposes of certain business organisations and government bodies (e.g. the Secrétariat d'Etat aux PMEs); these terms only refer to the size of your company. The type of structure you choose has implications for how your earnings will be taxed. One also has to consider the situation regarding TVA or Value Added Tax. You have some freedom of choice in this respect if you are a small company.

Most foreigners operate as sole traders without going to the trouble of setting up an entity such as a limited company. Some 68% of businesses are sole traders. Smaller companies have fewer restrictions, although not as regards raising capital. It certainly cannot be stressed enough that it is wiser to start out as a sole trader and then go for a limited company status than to begin with a more complex structure and then find it is impossible to downsize without closing down the whole business.

# COMMONLY USED BUSINESS STRUCTURES

## ENTREPRISE INDIVIDUELLE

The simplest way to start up as a self-employed person or *indépendant* is to go along to the Centre de Formalités des Entreprises (see previous chapter under 'Registering your business') and inform them of your *état civil*, marriage regime, address, nature of your business etc. There is no requirement to raise capital or publish statutes, nor are there any charges to pay. Your only obligations are to keep records of your receipts and expenses, and to pay your taxes and social security contributions on time. This certainly appears to be an attractive option, but there are also drawbacks. **You have limitless and indefinite liability for all business debts, but your house can be made safe from creditors (see box).** This form of business structure is popular with those who work from home or who run a small shop. Most foreign sole traders start out as *entreprises individuelles*, and then consider whether they want to go for limited company status. It is easy to go from EI to a EURL or SARL, but not the other way.

> **Liability of *entreprises individuelles***
>
> In principle no distinction is made between a sole trader's professional and private assets. But in accordance with Article 8 of the Loi Dutreil, which came into force on 1 January 2004, you can now make a declaration of non-seizability (*déclaration d'insaisissabilité*) in front of a notary, which will render

> your principal residence safe from creditors. The declaration is registered with the *Bureau des Hypothèques* (land registry) and has to be published in the local official newspaper. If you do not make this declaration then your home can still be seized by creditors.
>
> Professional and private assets are separate in limited companies, but you can choose to use your home as collateral. The French authorities discourage the use of your principal residence as collateral, but at the end of the day you can still use your home to raise a loan if you want.

## *Taxation and Social Security Implications*

Sole traders are taxed on their income under the taxation regime of their choice, i.e. *micro-entreprise, regime simplifié* or *régime réel.* They will pay *impôt sur le revenu* (income tax) according to the rates in force. They cannot be considered unsalaried workers if they have any kind of regular employment contract with their own company or a third party. The question is whether there is a relationship of subordination to an employer.

For the first two years of their activity they will pay social security contributions at a fixed amount of €2,580 (rate for 2004) for the first year and €1,874 for the first half of the second year (amounts can vary if you earn too little or too much). From 2004 it is possible for non-salaried workers to spread the first year's payment out over 5 years. From the third year the contributions will be based on their real income, with the exception of incapacity and death insurance which continues to be a fixed amount. *Micro-entreprises* can now start paying on their real income from the first year of trading. See under 'Social Security' in the chapter *Tax, Social Security and Other Matters* for further details.

## BASIC REQUIREMENTS OF A FRENCH COMPANY

- ○ There are at least two partners (except EI/EURL).
- ○ The partners intend to work together.
- ○ Share capital is paid up within a certain time.
- ○ Shareholders share in the profits and losses.

> ○ The articles are published in a *journal d'annonces légales.*
> ○ The articles are deposited with the Clerk of the Commercial Court.
> ○ The company is registered with the RCS, via the CFE.
> ○ A summary of the articles is published in BODACC.
> ○ The company has a registered office.
> ○ Directors must be qualified if the company exercises a regulated activity.
> ○ Directors must meet certain requirements regarding nationality, good conduct and conflicts of interest.
> ○ Partners in a company can be another company.

# EURL

The *Entreprise Unipersonnelle à Responsabilité Limitée* is in essence the equivalent of a *Société à Responsabilité Limitée* or private limited company. Your letterhead will state that you are a *SARL à capital de ...,* i.e. no one will know that you are the single partner, unless they enquire at the Registre de Commerce. Creating an EURL assumes that you intend to remain a sole trader and is permitted for non-regulated liberal professions, *commerçants* and artisans. Legally speaking, the EURL comes under commercial law and not civil law, whatever the nature of your activity. When you create a company you are also creating a new legal personality or entity with legal rights and obligations – a *personne morale* in French. The Articles of Association have to be published in a local newspaper that prints official announcements (*journal d'annonces légales*) in the same district as your registered office, as well as in the national BODACC (which is done for you by the clerk of the commercial court). The costs add up to some €260 for artisans, less for other businesses. Since the passing of the Loi Dutreil in August 2003 you only need to put up one euro in capital. Before this time it was necessary to come up with €7,500 as share capital. The implementation of this measure has been delayed, but it should now be working smoothly. In theory it may also be possible to register a business on-line in the near future; the measure has been held up over a dispute about electronic signatures.

The advantages of the EURL are considerable. There is only one partner (*associé*), so there is no one who can vote against you at a meeting. Your liability is limited to the amount you have chosen to put up as capital, and can be as little as one euro, but you will have more credibility with business partners and customers if you can put up more; the amount will be on your letterhead. There are constraints on your freedom from liability which are examined below. It is simple to transform your EURL into a SARL if you so wish. You can also choose between income tax (IR) and corporation tax (IS) as regards your taxation regime.

Certain types of business cannot be run as EURL, including:

o   insurance companies
o   investment companies
o   savings companies
o   credit companies
o   tobacconists
o   companies involved in sport

There is a special form of EURL for farmers known as an EARL. There is a limitation on EURLs in that the single partner can be another company, but not another EURL.

## Articles of Association

The articles or *statuts* need to include a minimum amount of information. The first is the amount of capital, which now only needs to be one euro. If you decide to pay up more capital you have a choice of paying in cash (*apports en numéraire*) or using assets as capital (*apports en nature*). Intangible assets such as 'goodwill' cannot be used as capital, even if they have a certain value. There is an inspector who will decide the value of your physical capital contribution – the *commissaire aux apports*. If you use a property on which there is an outstanding loan then a notary has to register the fact with the *Bureau des Hypothèques* (land registry). In other cases you can draw up the articles of association yourself, or use a lawyer or notaire. Further details of the articles to be included are given below under SARLs.

Your business has to have a registered office (*siège social*), which can be a rented business location or a letterbox company address. You can also now register your company at your principal residence for a period of two years without having to ask the landlord's permission as long as you do not store goods or receive customers at home.

## *Liability*

The freedom from liability for the partner of an EURL is not quite as total as one might at first think. Apart from your liability for the sum of the capital subscribed, situations which render you personally liable include:

- Pledging your property or other assets as surety.
- Not separating private and company assets.
- Misstating the amount of capital paid up.
- Acting as a *de facto* director when you have employed a director.

Directors of EURLs and other companies have wider liability than partners, but it is rare for an EURL to have a director other than the single partner. The unique partner always has the right to override decisions by the director, and to view documents relating to the company's activities going back at least three financial years. The regulations governing the conduct of directors are similar for every type of company. The details are given below under SARLs.

The authorities can 'requalify' an EURL if they consider that it is not functioning properly as a limited company and turn you back into an *entreprise individuelle*.

**Social Security Implications.** A partner who is not a director of the company is considered an unsalaried worker (*travailleur non-salarié*) and not obliged to belong to a social security fund. If they gain remuneration as a director then payments have to be made into a social security fund in the same way as a sole trader does under the *commerçant* regime. Where you employ a third party as the director of your EURL (*gérant salarié*), they are considered a salaried worker (except with respect to unemployment protection via ASSEDIC), and they will pay social security contributions on their salary, while you as the employer will also pay their part of the contributions (*part patronale*). For further information on social security, see the chapter *Tax, Social Security and Other Matters*.

**Taxation and Company Accounts.** An EURL cannot opt for the status of *micro-entreprise* but has to keep full accounts and pay taxes according to the *régime réel* (either *simplifié* or *normal*). You have a choice between income tax (IR) and corporation tax (IS). The subject is treated further in the chapter *Tax, Social Security and Other Matters*.

# SARL

The other type of limited company often used by foreigners is the SARL, the *Société à Responsabilité Limitée*. **This is essentially no different to an EURL, except that there are at least two up to a possible total of 50 partners. The advantages of limited liability are the same**, as are the obligations of directors and partners. It is a popular form for those who expect to expand their activities and want greater credibility with customers and other businesses. An EURL can be turned into a SARL by selling one or more shares to a new partner.

It is generally said that one should avoid a situation where there are two partners each with 50% of the shares as it then becomes difficult to take decisions if they disagree. Within a family context, where two or more partners are also directors and they hold more than half of the shares together then both are considered to be *gérants majoritaires* (majority executive partners) with the potential for great difficulties in taking decisions. You can always agree on a mediator in cases of deadlock. There are risks involved in getting someone to agree to be a partner in your company when they have no real involvement – the so-called *associé de complaisance*. If they disappear or fall out with you then it could become impossible to take basic decisions on the status of the company.

**Items to be mentioned in the Articles of Association of a SARL**

Name of the company

Type of company (SARL)

Names and *état civil* of partners

Purpose of the company

Capital

Form of contribution to capital

Number of shares

Registered office

Name of auditor (*commissaire aux comptes*) where applicable

Intended lifespan of the company, up to a maximum of 99 years

Details of the commercial court in whose district the company is to be registered

Authority given to directors or to other parties

Conditions for calling General Meetings

Means by which partners are kept informed of developments

Conditions for the liquidation of the company

The basic details of the company have to be registered with the Registre des Commerces et des Sociétés via the Centre de Formalités des Entreprises (see previous chapter).

## Liability

Partners are liable up to the amount of the share capital they have subscribed to. If you put in one euro, then your liability is one euro. As in the case of the EURL, however, partners can be held personally liable for a greater amount if they pledge their assets as security for loans, etc. Their liability is much greater if they are also directors of the company. The company can be held liable for the actions of its representatives even when these are not related to the purpose of the company in its constitution, unless the company can prove that the third party knew that the company's representative was acting beyond their authority.

## Directors

A SARL (or any other company) must have at least one director or *gérant* who represents your company to the outside world. The director is a salaried worker, and their salary is tax-deductible under business costs, but the company will have to pay full social security contributions as for salaried workers. Non-executive directors can also have an employment contract with the company and they are then treated as salaried workers. Directors of EURLs and SARLs have wider liability than partners. In particular they can be held liable for any mistakes that they commit in their running of a company. Any actions that break French company law render the director liable. Fraud, negligence, misuse of company funds (*abus de biens sociaux*), distributing fictitious dividends, false accounting, and non-compliance with social security regulations, all render directors open to civil claims for recovery of debt. A director of a company can make the company itself liable for their mistakes, or they can be held liable as individuals, depending on whether their actions were carried out in the name of the company or not. Actions that fall outside the purposes of the company's articles of association or violate one of the articles also render directors liable.

The nomination of directors must be communicated to the Registre des Commerces et des Sociétés (RCS), and published in the local *journal d'annonces légales*. The Clerk of the Commercial Court (Greffe du Tribunal) will arrange for the publication in the national BODACC journal. This is normally done after the articles of association have been registered. Any change in director also has to be publicised in the same way. Only adults above the age of 18 can become company directors.

Under certain circumstances you can be disqualified from being the director of a company, or from starting one. If you have been declared bankrupt (*faillite, banqueroute*) then you are disqualified for at least 5 years. If you are convicted of a financial crime, e.g. tax evasion or fraud, then you are banned for at least 3 years. Crimes involving violence or harassment imply a lifelong ban, but it is possible to appeal to have the ban lifted. Where the company operates in a regulated environment, directors will need to be qualified to work as managers. Non-EU citizens need to have a *carte de commerçant* to become directors.

The articles of association will include clauses placing limits on what a director can do, e.g. the debt he can make the company liable for. The director and partner are obliged to meet for the Annual General Meeting (*assemblée générale annuelle*) during which the company's accounts are approved and changes to the articles (statuts) decided. The director is legally required to send the annual accounts and a report on their management during the year along with other relevant documents to the partner 15 days before the AGM. After the AGM the accounts and management report are submitted to and published by the RCS, where anyone can read them. An auditor is required if two of three conditions are met:

o Balance sheet exceeds €1,550,000.
o Turnover (CA) before tax exceeds €3,100,000.
o Number of salaried employees exceeds 50.

**Tax and Social Security Implications.** The SARL's income is taxed according to the *régime réel simplifié* or *normal* which requires accounts to be kept. Where the partners in the SARL are family members they can opt to pay income tax, or *impôt sur le revenu,* known as a 'transparent' regime, where each partner pays taxes on the profits in their own name. In this situation the company is known as a *SARL de Famille.* Otherwise the SARL will pay corporation tax or *impôt sur les sociétés* on its returns. The *gérant minoritaire* partner with up to 50% of the shares who is also a director can be a salaried worker, which gives the potential to go back into the social security system without too much difficulty, although they are not allowed to pay into ASSEDIC, the salaried workers' unemployment fund (the same applies to all salaried company directors). They can of course pay into a private fund to cover the risk of unemployment.

### Gérant majoritaire or minoritaire?

It is now common for a company to be run by a *gérant minoritaire* or minority director (one who holds 50% or less of shares) who is paid a salary, while the rest of the shares are held by the *gérant majoritaire* or majority director who may have no active role in running the company. The majority director holds more power; if he or she has 75% or more of the shares (including shares held by their spouse and children), then they can take virtually any decisions they want in relation to the company. A minority director with less than 25% of shares cannot block decisions made by the majority.

A comparative table of the amount of social security contributions and tax paid by *gérant minoritaires* and *majoritaires* is given in chapter 8, *Tax, Social Security and Other Matters*, under 'Social Security'. The *gérant majoritaire* is better off in money terms, but receives less social security protection and a lower pension.

## SA

The *société anonyme* is the equivalent of the Public Limited Company or PLC in the UK. Listed stock market companies are all SAs. Generally only multinationals or very large companies would try to set up a SA in France, simply because of the complex requirements for the organisation of such a company. A SA has to have at least 7 shareholders to start up (there is no upper limit on the number of shareholders), and a share capital of €37,000. The capital can be paid up in the form of physical assets (*apports en nature*) or in cash (*apports en numéraire*). In the first case the assets have to be valued by a professional auditor, the *commissaire aux apports* and fully paid up at the time of incorporation. The cash element has to be paid up to at least 50% of its value at the time of being subscribed, with the remaining 50% to be paid up within 5 years of the registration of the business. Where properties, business goodwill, business leases and the like are used as capital contributions then transfer taxes of 4.89% are payable if the property is transferred from a company paying income tax (IR) to one paying corporation tax (IS). This is a general regulation for all companies.

The principal inconvenience of the SA is the requirement for a Management Board with between 3 and 18 administrators, who have to be shareholders, whether persons or companies. Where the capital is under €150,000 one can make do with a Board of Directors of between 2 and 5 members. A SA always has to have a Chairman of the Board, and a Director General, who may be the same person. Accounts are always audited and presented to the AGM for approval.

The SA can raise money on the stock market once its capital passes 1.5 million French Francs, or approximately €223,000 (the amount is due to be rounded down to take into account the euro).

Shareholders are only liable for the share of the capital they subscribe to, as long as they do not act as directors, whether officially or unofficially. Shares can be freely traded or transferred between family members in ascending and descending line, spouses and between shareholders. The constitution of the SA can include clauses putting constraints on the sale of shares to outsiders.

The Chairman of the Board is a salaried employee of the company and subject to the normal regime for salaried workers, whether they are a shareholder or not.

## SAS/SASU

In keeping with the acronymomania of the French, these are two more forms of limited liability companies that are becoming quite popular these days. The SAS or *Société par Actions Simplifié* (simplified PLC) is a sort of mini-SA with less of the limitations and complex administration. It was first set up in 1994 in order to create a flexible type of SA which was in the first place used by big SAs to create small subsidiaries, in order to give French companies a format more like those available in the English-speaking world. The SAS was reformed in 1999 and many of the original restrictions removed, so as to make it easy for anyone to create a SAS. There are general similarities with the SA in that the share capital is at least €37,000. A SAS cannot be listed on the stock market, but can issue bonds and securities. There is a chairman, but almost total freedom concerning the appointment of directors or other officers and the type of management structure. The chairman/managing director can fulfil all the management roles if they wish; usually the roles are split between two people.

### Advantages of the SAS

- No requirement for a board of management.
- Chairman can also take on role of managing director.
- Chairman and spouse are treated as salaried workers and pay IR on

their salary.
o   Tax on sale of shares is only 1%.
o   Great flexibility regarding organisation of the company.

Shares can in principle be freely bought and sold, but usually there are restrictions which prevent the sale of the shares for a certain period of time or only allow the sale under certain predetermined conditions. The founders of a SAS generally look to keep the same shareholders for a long period of time to stay in control of the company. The tax on the sale of shares is limited to 1% of their value, making it a cheaper operation than selling a conventional business. The SAS does not cease to exist with the death of the chairman.

The main attraction of the SAS is for entrepreneurs who are looking for investors but who do not wish to lose control over the company they are creating. The fact that you can put almost anything you like in the constitution means that you have to be very careful how you draw it up. Evidently this can only be done using a specialised *avocat*.

## SASU

If you are starting out a one-person business and are looking for substantial investment as well, you can set up a SASU: *Société par Actions Simplifiée Unipersonnelle*, a SAS for sole traders. The SASU requires an initial capital of €37,000, of which half can immediately be used for investment, as long as it is paid back within 5 years. As with the SAS, the SASU has a chairman, but no other directors. There is only one shareholder. Anyone who creates a SASU would be working from the assumption that their turnover was going to exceed €500,000 soon after starting up. As a SASU you can also become a SAS without any formalities, by simply selling shares, or dividing shares between inheritors if the owner dies.

# OTHER BUSINESS STRUCTURES

The following are rarely used by foreigners. You will nonetheless often come across them, and they may be your customers.

## SNC

The *Société en Nom Collectif* is a partnership, usually made up of family members, who have joint unlimited liability for the company's debts. If the company folds then individuals can be pursued by creditors for the entirety of the debt. The advantage of the SNC is that there is no capital to be paid up. Borrowing funds is relatively easy since the partners have unlimited liability. The SNC can be used for any type of activity; this type of construction should be avoided for obvious reasons.

## SEL

The *Société d'Exercice Libérale* is specifically limited to regulated liberal professions, and is popularly used by doctors, architects, lawyers, surveyors, etc. The income of the directors is the income of the company. Running costs of the business are tax-deductible. The company can opt to pay corporation tax (IS) which is lower than the marginal rate for individual income tax payers. The SEL can also employ salaried staff who do not need to have shares in the company. Dividends are also paid out to shareholding members. Usually all partners have the same number of shares.

A popular scheme now is for a group of professionals to get together and 'sell' their list of clients (particularly medical) to the newly constituted SEL which borrows money to buy the list. This raises funds for the partnership, while the SEL can deduct the interest from its tax bill. It is becoming popular to transform SCMs into SELs. A SEL can be started with only one partner, in which case it is a *Société d'Exercice Libérale Unipersonelle* (SELU). There are also SELARLs, SELAFAs, and SELCAs, the equivalent of SARLs, SAs and SCAs for liberal professions.

## SCS/SCA

Another business structure is the *Société en Commandite Simple*. This corresponds to a Limited Partnership in the UK. There are at least two partners, the *commanditaire* – the sleeping partner – and the *commandité* – the acting partner. Sleeping partners are only liable up to the limit of their share capital, while acting partners have joint unlimited liability. There is no minimum capital. This is an inconvenient form of company because of the difficulties of managing the sleeping partner/acting partner relationship.

A larger type of SCS is the *Société en Commandite par Actions*. The minimum share capital is the same as for SAs – €37,000. This type of set-up cannot be recommended given the complexity of the administration. The main attraction is the ability to raise funds easily.

## SCM/SCP

The *Société Civile de Moyens* is used almost exclusively by doctors, midwives and other paramedical professionals who need to invest in expensive equipment, and who operate from a building owned or rented by one of the members. There are at least two partners, and shares can be bought and sold. The individual members continue to be taxed as self-employed persons. The company does not exercise any commercial activity; it is purely intended to facilitate the purchase of equipment and to save taxes.

A more sophisticated SCM is the *Société Civile Professionnelle* (SCP) which is mainly used by physiotherapists and similar professionals. The fees earned are paid into the SCP and then divided up between the partners according to the amount of shares they hold. Partners are jointly and indefinitely liable.

## SCI

The SCI or *Société Civile Immobilière* has recently become well-known abroad as a convenient vehicle for owning and managing properties or land while making it easy to transfer the property in the form of shares. It is now widely used where unrelated persons or common-law partners want to buy a property. The SCI's capital consists of cash or property (including land). There is a transfer tax on the sale of a property to an SCI of 4.89%, except under certain conditions. Where the SCI buys a brand-new property then TVA is payable at 19.6% unless the property is less than 25% inhabited by surface area, or if TVA is charged on the letting of the property.

The SCI is a company like any other, in that there are partners and directors, and the company can only be set up for 99 years. There are considerable costs involved; setting up the SCI costs on average €2,500. One typical activity for a SCI is to rent out unfurnished property, offices, factories, etc. The SCI is not ideal if you are planning to run *gîtes*, or *chambres d'hôtes*. By definition an SCI is meant to be non-trading as it only owns property, not furniture. You will therefore need to rent the property out to another business such as a SARL. There are also certain implications from the point of view of UK tax authorities, which concern directors' benefits-in-kind. If the authorities are aware that as a director you have the free use of a property in France for holidays then you can become liable for income tax on the assessed benefits-in-kind. The way around this is to ensure that shareholders are not directors – *gérants* – of the company.

**Tax and Social Security Implications**. The profits generated by SCIs are basically taxed as private income on the scale of the *impôt sur le revenu*. Individual partners are taxed separately. Capital gains realised from the sale of property are also taxed according to IR scales in force at the time of the sale, as private capital gains. If the SCI rents out property then its income is liable to corporation tax or IS. Once the SCI is liable for IS then transfer tax has to paid on properties that it acquires at 4.89%. The SCI can have salaried employees. For further information on SCIs see chapter 5, *Acquiring a Business*.

# ASSOCIATION LOI 1901

An *Association Loi 1901* is a non-profit making organisation, intended to promote a cause in the public interest. The French call *associations* 'the third sector', next to the public and private sectors. They are popularly used to run charitable organisations, sporting clubs, and other organisations that are supposedly of benefit to the public. While they do not have any capital as such, for practical reasons there has to be an initial input of capital so that the company can function. It is essential to state clearly whether the funds that are put into the *association* can be withdrawn again (*apports avec droit de reprise*), otherwise they belong to the *association* for good.

Generally, they have at least a president and a treasurer, and usually a secretary as well. They are required to hold an Annual General Meeting. The directors of the association are considered to be working voluntarily, although there is some scope for paying them. If you are a director of the association and also receiving a salary then there is a risk that the French tax authorities will rescind your status as a non-profit organisation, so you are better off employing a third party. Dividends or profits cannot in any case be paid to the directors or anyone else, as there is no share capital. Whatever money the association makes goes back into the 'business'. The association must still present audited accounts at its AGM.

One of the main objectives of the *association* is to try to obtain state-sponsored subsidies for your particular pet project. This type of business form is also useful for obtaining subsidies in order to employ young people under the age of 25. In other cases the whole thing is based on pure idealism. If you want to start a charitable enterprise then you are obliged to take on this kind of legal structure. The constitution of your *association* is deposited with the *Bureau des Associations* at the *préfecture* in your department. You will also have to register with the local *Centre des Impôts* (tax office) if you are buying and selling goods.

## SCOP

The *Société Coopérative Ouvrière de Production* is a business form that can be translated as a 'production co-operative'. The co-operative movement goes back to the 19th century. Legally SCOPs are either SARLs or SAs. At least 51% of the shares are owned by the workers, who also have 65% of the voting rights. The salaried workers are also the partners in the company. They elect the chairperson/managing director and the board of management. The members decide on the distribution of the profits, which can go back to into the company's reserves or are paid out to the workers. Workers are required to buy a share in the company when they join which they can sell when they leave.

## GIE

The *Groupement d'Intérêt Economique* is another form of business used mainly by affiliated retailing companies, industries and sometimes by regulated liberal professions. The GIE is set up for a definite period of time, and is an independent legal entity from the companies that join together to set it up. It does not issue shares but is allowed to raise capital by issuing bonds or securities. Decisions are taken at General Meetings by majority voting. The functioning depends to some extent on the type of companies that make up the GIE. Member companies have unlimited liability.

Since the GIE is a grouping of existing companies – usually on a large scale – they have no relevance to small start-ups by foreigners. You will come into contact with them since your suppliers, supermarkets, etc. will probably be part of one. There is an even bigger type, the GEIE – the *Groupement Européen d'Intérêt Economique*, a multinational grouping of companies.

## SOCIETE DE FAIT

This means 'de facto company', or to be more precise, 'elements of a company'. The term is used by the authorities where two or more persons act as partners in a company without being legally registered. This can happen when two or more people buy a property together where they are in an *indivision* – the partners own an indivisible asset, which can only be sold with the agreement of all the partners. An *indivision* comes about automatically if a couple married under the common ownership of assets regime buy property together, or partners in a civil partnership or PACS, and also where property is inherited by two or more people.

If the partners in the *indivision* rent out or make money from a property then they can be considered to constitute a *société de fait* by the tax authorities, and the de facto company (not the partners) will then have to pay corporation tax (*impôt sur les sociétés*) on the profits. If the partners have declared their income to the tax authorities then the *société de fait* can continue undisturbed, but if profits have not been declared then there will be heavy penalties and the *société de fait* has to be dissolved. Perhaps more worryingly, partners in a *société de fait* are fully and indefinitely liable, but they can regain any assets left over after liquidation.

## STARTING A COMPANY WHILE REMAINING IN A SALARIED JOB

You can start up a company while remaining a salaried worker. Your registered company is then a sideline until you can give up your salaried job, but you have all the liabilities that are involved in owning a company. You continue to benefit from the social protection given to salaried workers, including unemployment insurance.

Another possible way to try out running a business without deciding on a particular structure is to use a *Société de Portage* (short for *Société de Portage Salarial*) – an 'umbrella company' – which enables you to be independent but remain a salaried worker. Your salary is paid by the company, who collect fees from your customers, deal with VAT, social security and tax, and then pay you a salary after deducting a percentage of your revenues. There is no risk involved in this, and you can give up the business when you want.

## FOREIGN-REGISTERED COMPANIES

There is yet another possibility, beyond what has been listed above, and that is to set up your company in the UK (or wherever you happen to come from) and operate your business in France. The advantage is that you continue to remain in a familiar system, pay your taxes in the UK (if you are not tax-resident in France) and avoid the burden of French social security payments. French residents also have the option of starting a company in the UK. Up till now the French authorities have accepted this kind of scheme since there is nothing in it that contravenes European law, but the implications could be serious for the French social security system if it was widely adopted.

## The Ski Chalet

Kate and Andrew Thorley have run Chaletgroup.com, a fully catered ski chalet in Méribel in the Alps, since 2000.

*We both had jobs that we enjoyed in London, Andrew as a facilities manager, and Kate as a telecoms consultant – but we did start to think hard about our lifestyle and whether we should go on with the rat race. The first idea was to take a year off and sail all year, but we ended up buying the ski chalet and started Chalet Group. We have just one chalet, where we provide a complete service to skiers, with minibuses to the ski-lifts, rental of equipment delivered to the chalet, everything the guests need. We provide meals in the restaurant which is for the chalet guests alone.*

*We sat down and drew up a business plan and a proper financial model on paper. In particular, we considered the location of the chalet and how large it would need to be. We also had an adviser to chalet businesses, Ed Mannix of London Overseas Consultancy. The conclusion was that we should set up a UK-based company, which we called the Chalet Group, but Companies House objected to the name as we are a bit small to be a 'group', so officially we are Head for the Hills Ltd, but the website is www.chaletgroup.com. We rent the property to the company, and draw our salary from the company. We remain tax resident in the UK, and make our social security contributions in the UK. The chalet runs for four and a half months of the year. The rest of the year the company occupies the chalet, which means us of course.*

*Although the business structure may appear a bit strange, it is used by a lot of people in this type of business. It means that you do not have to deal with the French system very much. The most we have had to do was to get a French restaurant and drinks licence. The money we earn in France is taxed in the UK as foreign earned income.*

*This is not a way to get rich, but a lifestyle choice. We have seen people come here at the start of the season, rent a chalet, and then find at the end they have less money than when they started with, because they didn't make a business plan. To make a lot of money, you need more chalets, or a very large multi-million pound operation employing lots of people. Or you have to come up with some quirky idea that grabs people's imaginations. We do all the work ourselves, with our seasonal staff, who are mostly British.*

## DISSOLVING YOUR COMPANY

Companies dissolve for a variety of reasons. Their lifespan has run out, or the partners voluntarily decide to dissolve the company, or the reason for the company's existence no longer exists. A company is not dissolved by decease, bankruptcy or liquidation, however dissolution entails liquidation. If you are unable to meet your debts then you can go into administration, which is known as *redressement judiciaire* or *RJ*. Only 10% of companies in RJ emerge the other side and carry on.

The closure of the company entails distributing the assets back to the shareholders, if there is any surplus left after debts have been paid off. Once the company has been liquidated the following steps have to be taken:

○ final accounts are deposited with the Commercial Court
○ a notice of closure is put in a *journal d'annonces légales*
○ the company is removed from the Registre du Commerce
○ a notice is placed in BODACC

A company can be compulsorily wound up at the request of its creditors if it cannot meet its obligations. Removal from the Registre du Commerce is known as *radiation*. There is the possibility of starting up again at some future time, assuming that you were not made bankrupt. Further details are given in the chapter *Selling On*.

# Acquiring a Business or Property

## CHAPTER SUMMARY

O Properties can be found through agencies in the UK, or in France.

O **Agents and Estate Agents.** Be clear whether you are dealing with an estate agent, or a property agent acting as an intermediary.

O **Finding a Business.** Many businesses are advertised privately on French websites.

O **Prices.** Always ask whether prices include fees and commission or not.

O **Pre-contracts.** These are binding and should not be signed lightly.

O *Conditions Suspensives.* Insert get-out clauses to allow you to escape from a contract.

O **Inheritance.** Take legal advice from a UK-trained lawyer about whose name should go on the title deeds.

O **Capital Gains Tax.** French Capital Gains Tax affects businesses as well as properties.

O **Planning Permission.** Make sure that you can obtain permission to carry out any necessary alterations.

O **Commercial Leases.** These are generally favourable to the lessee.

O *Fonds de Commerce.* The business goodwill can be bought and sold just as property.

For those in the commercial sector, the location and cost of their property will have a crucial role to play in whether their business survives or not. The cheapness of property in France is a main factor in bringing foreigners here; certain kinds of business can be run from a residential property, at least to start with. When you take over an existing business, you buy the goodwill or customer base of the business as well as renting or buying the property. In most cases you buy the business, and take over the lease of the property. It must be said, nevertheless, that very few foreigners take over a business and continue to operate in the same sector.

Generally the French buy the business, or *fonds de commerce,* and rent the building that houses it. If the building is for sale then it will be advertised as murs commerciaux. There is a strict distinction between *les murs* or *les locaux* (premises), and the *fonds*. The subject of *fonds de commerce* is dealt with in more detail below.

## WHERE TO FIND PROPERTIES/ BUSINESSES

Before turning to French *immobiliers* it is worth consulting some French property magazines published in the UK, and contacting some UK-based estate agents to see what they have available. Some UK national publications list a few businesses for sale, e.g. *Dalton's Weekly, Exchange & Mart, Daily Telegraph*. If you have little time to spare on looking then you may need to engage the services of a property search agent; French property magazines have a lot listed. As with residential property, it is always preferable to rent a place in the area you are interested in and look round for businesses that are for sale, or whose owners might be willing to sell to you.

The first question is whether you are looking for a building to convert into a business or to buy an existing business, with or without the building that goes with it. The bigger and more expensive properties are dealt with by *immobiliers commerciaux*, who are in the business of renting business premises rather than selling them. French *agents immobiliers* usually have a few commerces for sale. Some have specialised sections dealing only with *commerces*: they are easy to find by simply searching on the internet sites of some of the larger chains of *immobiliers*. Otherwise it is a matter of looking for specialised agents, who can be found under *commerces* or *spécialistes du fonds de commerce* through internet sites given below, or in the on-line yellow pages: www.annu.fr. There are also weekly magazines with suitable commercial property; every département has its own free weekly. Many newspapers list properties on their websites. There is a more or less complete list of newspapers in France on the site: http://hoppa.com/eu/fr/ – under 'Media'. The best national weekly for finding businesses is *ICF L'Argus de Commerce*.

On the internet look under *immobilier d'entreprise, commerce à vendre, commerce à céder, fonds de commerce, reprise de commerce, affaire à vendre, acquisition d'entreprise* and similar permutations.

## UK-based Estate Agents

The following is only a small selection of estate agents; the number dealing with France is growing all the time. They generally deal with residential property, but will also from time to time have commercial properties. If you are looking to buy a *fonds de commerce* (the business without the property), then you will need to look at the internet sites suggested below.

## List of Agents

The following agents are listed with the areas that they cover. Unless otherwise stated, they will mainly deal with properties in the western half of France, where most English-speaking expatriates are located, outside of the big towns. You should check to see if they belong to a professional organisation such as the NAEA or FOPDAC in the UK, or FNAIM in France. UK-based organisations are not necessarily estate agents. Some act as intermediaries between clients and French *immobiliers*.

## UK-based

*A Home in France:* The Old Anchor, Moat Lane, Wingrave, Bucks HP22 4PQ; ☎01296-688727; fax 01296-681433; e-mail info@ahomeinfrance.com. Contact Danielle Seabrook. **All areas**.

*Beaches International Property Ltd:* 3-4 Hagley Mews, Hagley Hall, Hagley, Stourbridge, W. Midlands DY9 9LQ; ☎01562-885181; 01562-886724; e-mail info@beachesint.co.uk; www.beachesint.com.

*Brittany Property Shop:* 95 Farm Rd, Abingdon, Oxfordshire OX14 1NB; ☎00 33 2 96 86 61 06; fax 00 33 2 96 86 61 07; www.brittanypropertyshop.com. **Some businesses.**

*Capital Mover Ltd:* 20 Second Avenue, London W3 7RX; ☎07971-902 853; fax 020-8749 1077; www.capitalmover.com. New-build.

*Currie French Properties:* 2 Fulbrooke Rd, Cambridge CB3 9EE;

☎01223 576084; fax 01223 570332; email cfps@ntlworld.com; www.french-property.com/currie.

*David King Associates:* ☎020-8673 6800; www.dkassociates.co.uk. **Paris, West, South; over £150,000.**

*Domus Abroad:* Maurice Lazarus, 4 Gardner Rd, Hampstead, London NW3 1HA; ☎020-7431 4692; fax 020-7794 4822; www.Domusabroad.com. Services for both buyers and sellers.

*Eclipse Overseas:* 29 Stuart Rd, Highcliffe-on-Sea, Christchurch, Dorset BH23 5JS; ☎01425-275984; fax 01425-277137; www.french-property.com/eclipse. **Normandy, Charente, Loire, Vendée, Brittany.**

*European Property Search:* 9-11 St Cross Rd, Winchester, Hants SO23 9JB; ☎01962-853568; fax 01962-870008; www.overseaspropertyonline.com.

*Fourways French Properties:* The Green, Morcombelake, nr Bridport, Dorset DT6 6EA; tel/fax 01297-489366.

*The French Property Shop:*The Clergyhouse, Churchyard, Ashford, Kent TN23 1QG; ☎01233-666902; fax 01233-666903; e-mail sales@frenchpropertyshop.com; www.frenchpropertyshop.com. **Southwest.**

*Francophiles Ltd:* Barker Chambers, Barker Rd, Maidstone, Kent ME16 8SF; ☎01622-688165; fax 01622-671840; e-mail Fphiles@aol.com; www.francophiles.co.uk. Property searches in **Normandy, Brittany, Pas de Calais, Southwest.**

*Gascony Property:* 12 Royal Terrace, Southend-on-Sea, Essex SS1 1DY; ☎01702-390382; fax 01702-390415; www.gascony-property.com.

*Hamptons International:* 168 Brompton Rd, Knightsbridge, London SW3 1HW; ☎ 020-7589 8844; e-mail international@hamptons-int.com; www.hamptons-int.com. **Côte d'Azur.** Branch in Nice.

*A House in France Ltd:* John Hart, 11 Mountview, Mill Hill, London NW7 3HT; ☎020-8959 5182; fax 020-8906 8749; e-mail john.hart@virgin.net; www.french-property-news.com/ahif.htm.

*Hexagone France Ltd:* Webster House, 24 Jesmond Street, Folkestone, Kent CT19 5QW; ☎01303-221077; fax 01303-244409; e-mail gwen@hexagonefrance.com; www.hexagonefrance.com. **Normandy, Picardy, Brittany.**

*La Résidence:* St Martin's House, 17 St Martin's St, Wallingford,

Oxon OX10 0EA; ☎01491-838485; fax 01491-839977; e-mail sales@laresidence.co.uk; www.laresidence.co.uk.

*Latitudes:* Penny Zoldan, Grosvenor House, 1 High St, Edgware, Middx HA8 7TA; ☎020-8951 5155; fax 020-8951 5156; www.latitudes.co.uk.

*Leisure & Land*: Grosvenor House, 1 High St, Edgware, Middx HA8 7TA; ☎020-8951 5152; fax 020-8951 5156; e-mail sales@leisure andland.co.uk; www.leisureandland.co.uk. **Specialises in income-producing properties.**

*Maison France:* Lincolnshire; ☎01427-628537; fax 01427-628855; e-mail info@maisonfrance.com; www.agence-maisonfrance.com.

*North & West France Properties:* Park Lodge, Park Rd, East Twickenham, Middx TW1 2PT; ☎020-8891 1750; fax 020-8891 1760; e-mail sales@all-france-properties.com; www.all-france-properties.com.

*Propriétés Roussillon:* Roussillon House, 29 Aversley Rd, Kings Norton, Birmingham B38 8PD; ☎021-459 9058; fax 021-608 8884; e-mail Props.Rouss@btinternet.com; www.proprietes-roussillon.com. **All areas**.

*Sifex Ltd:* 1 Doneraile St, Fulham, London SW6 6EL; ☎020-7384 1200; fax 020-7384 2001; e-mail info@sifex.co.uk; www.sifex.co.uk. Exclusive properties in **Southern France. Châteaux in all regions of France.**

*Sinclair Overseas Property Network:* The Business Centre, P.O. Box 492, Leighton Buzzard, Beds LU7 7WG; ☎01525-375319; fax 01525-851418; www.sinclair-frenchprops.com. Associate offices throughout France.

*Spratley & Co Ltd, International Property Consultants:* 60 St Martin's Lane, London WC2N 4JS; ☎020-7240 2445; fax 020-7240 2469.

*Villas Abroad Ltd:* Lacey House, St Clare Business Park, Holly Rd, Hampton Hill, Middx TW12 1QQ; ☎020-8941 4499; fax 020-8941 0202; e-mail villas abroad@fopdac.com; www.villasabroad properties.com. **Côte d'Azur. Mostly new-build.**

*Waterside Properties:* ☎01892-750011; fax 01892-750033. **Properties with waterside location**.

*G.A.K. Williamson & Assoc.:* 28 Broad St, Alresford, Hampshire SO24 9AQ; ☎01862-734633; fax 01862-734929; e-mail gakwfrance@aol.com.

## France-based

*ABC Immobilier:* 41 ave Clémenceau, 34500 Béziers; 04 67 93 51 66; fax 04 67 49 26 92; e-mail abc-*immobilier*3@wanadoo.fr; www.abc-immo.fr. **Béziers.**

*Agence Hamilton:* 30 rue Armagnac, 11000 Carcassonne; ☎04 68 72 48 38; fax 04 68 72 62 26; e-mail info@agence-hamilton.com; www.agence-hamilton.com. **Languedoc, Midi-Pyrénées.**

*Agence Hermann de Graaf:* Le Bourg, 24800 St Jean de Côle; ☎05 53 62 38 03; fax 05 53 55 08 03; e-mail agence@*immobilier*-dordogne.com; www.*immobilier*-dordogne.com. **Dordogne.**

*Agence Langlois:* 234 rue de Périgueux, 16000 Angoulême; ☎05 45 95 08 51; fax 05 45 69 77 12; e-mail agence.lgh@laposte.net; www.lghfrance.com. **Charente.**

*Agence L'Union:* Charles Smallwood, Place de la Halle, 82140 St Antonin-Noble-Val; ☎05 63 30 60 24; fax 05 63 68 24 67; e-mail info@agencelunion.com; www.agencelunion.com. **Tarn, Tarn-et-Garonne, Lot, Aveyron.**

*Agence Tredinnick:* 12 rue Dupuy, 16100 Cognac; tel/fax 05 45 82 42 93; e-mail props@charente-properties.com; www.charente-properties.com. **Charente.**

*Celtic Immobilier:* 4 Av Foch, 19100 Brive; 0825 07 00 50; e-mail alan-walker@wanadoo.fr; www.celtic-*immobilier*.com. **Lot,Corrèze, Dordogne.**

*Coast & Country:* 'La Palombière', 71 ave de Tournamy, 06250 Mougins; ☎04 92 92 47 50; fax 04 93 90 02 36; e-mail info@coast-country.com; http://coast-country.com.

*Conseil Patrimoine:* 52 bvd Victor Hugo, 06600 Nice; ☎04 97 03 03 33; fax 04 97 03 03 34. **Paris, Riviera.**

*Janssens Immobilier:* 2 rue de la République, Bonnieux; ☎04 90 75 96 98; e-mail janssens.*immobilier*@wanadoo.fr. **Luberon.**

*France Limousin Immobilier:* 1 rue Fosse du Trech, 1900 Tulle; ☎05 55 20 01 97; fax 05 55 26 16 17. **Limousin.**

*L'Affaire Française:* 25 Grand Rue, Jarnac 16200; ☎05 45 81 76 79; fax 05 45 35 09 52; e-mail FrenchProperties@aol.com; www.French-Property-Net.com. **Charente, Dordogne, Limousin.**

*Privilège Immobilier:* Gestion Privée et Patrimoine, 13 rue du Maréchal

Clauzel, 09500 Mirepoix; ☎05 61 69 79 56; fax 05 61 69 79 76; e-mail gp.p@net-up.com. **Ariège.**

*Properties in France Sarl PIF:* 6 allée de la Croix de Noël, 49390 Mouliherne; 02 41 52 02 18; fax 02 41 52 02 47; e-mail pif@compuserve.com. **Loire Valley.**

*Propriétés et Domaines:* Rue de l'Eglise, 83420, La Croix Valmer; ☎06 07 37 41 63; fax 04 94 54 39 58; www.proprietesetdomaines.com. **Var and Provence. Vineyards and character properties.**

*Snow and Sea:* Kingsland House, 1st Floor, 122-124 Regent St, London W1B 5SA; ☎020 7494 0706; fax 020-7734 9462; e-mail pascal@snowandsea.com; www.snowandsea.com. **PACA.**

### Property Consultants

While it is sometimes difficult to separate them from property agents, there are some consultants who offer wide-ranging services covering all aspects of property purchase:

*A Home in France:* The Old Anchor, Moat Lane, Wingrave, Bucks HP22 4PQ; ☎01296-688727; fax 01296-681433; e-mail info@ahomeinfrance.com. Contact Danielle Seabrook.

*Anglo-French Homes:* 9 rue 14 juin 1944, 61120 Vimoutiers; ☎02 33 39 80 55; http://anglo-french-homes.co.uk. **Calvados, Orne.**

*Sam Crabb:* ☎01935-851155; www.samcrabb.com. Independent consultant since 1993.

## INTERNET

### Property Websites in English

http://salut-france.com.
http://united-residence.com/france.
www.bluehomes.de/blue-en.
www.christies.com.
www.efmag.co.uk.
www.overseaspropertyonline.com.
www.focusonfrance.co.uk.

www.francebypost.com.
www.francemag.com.
www.francophiles.co.uk
www.frenchconnections.co.uk.
www.french-property.com.
www.french-property.co.uk.
www.french-property-news.com.
www.knightfrank.co.uk.
www.livingfrance.com.

www.ukproprietesdefrance.com.

## Commercial Property Websites

http://ca.tpe-pme.com.
www.acquisitions-
entreprises.com.
www.actcontact.net.
www.actinbusiness.com/
Offrescommerces.htm.
www.avendrealouer.fr.
www.bnoa.net.
www.bureaux-commerces.com.
www.buroscopie.com.
www.century21commerce.fr.
www.cessionaffaires.com.
www.cession-commerce.com.
http://cessionpme.com.
www.commerces-a-vendre.com.
www.cra.asso.fr.
www.entreprises-a-vendre.fr.
http://escap-immo.com.
www.guy-hoquet.com.
www.observatoiredelafranchise.fr.
www.pmicontact.net.
www.repreneur.fr.
www.restaurants-a-vendre.fr.
www.toutcommerce.com.
www.transcommercecom.
www.vendez-votre-
commerce.com.
www.vendez-votre-affaire.com.

## Farms/Vineyards

http://we136.lerelaisinternet.com.
www.domaines-en-

provence.com.
www.gard-immobilier.com.
www.jurisvin.fr.
www.leisureandland.co.uk.
www.proprietesetdomaines.com.

## Private Advertisers

www.appelimmo.fr.
www.bonjour.fr.
www.e-immo.biz.
www.entreparticuliers.fr.
www.explorimmo.com.
www.immobilier-particulier.net.
www.journaldesparticuliers.fr.
www.kitrouve.com.
www.lacentrale.fr.
www.lannonce.com.
www.lesiteimmobilier.com.
www.mister-annonces.com.
www.pap.fr.
www.petite-annonces.net.
www.pointimmo.com.

## General Property Websites

www.123immo.fr.
www.3d-immo.com.
www.abonim.com.
www.century21.fr.
www.europropertysearch.com.
www.fnaim.fr. National estate
agents organisation.
www.immo-web.net.
www.lesiteimmobilier.com.
www.letuc.com.
www.logic-immo.com.

www.nexdom.com.
www.orpi.com.
www.panorimmo.com.
www.partenaire-europeen.fr.
www.proprietesdefrance.com.

### Regional Commercial Property Websites

www.acheterlouer.fr. Ile-de-France, Loiret, Eure, Eure-et-Loire, Aisne.
www.agencedelabourse.fr. Normandy.
www.bankimmo.com. Côte d'Azur.
www.commerces-bretagne.com. Southern Brittany.
www.fonbailcom. Paris area.
www.*fonds*commerce.com. Provence.
http://immo34.ifrance.com. Gard, Hérault, Aveyron.
http://immobilier.region-bretagne.net. Brittany.
www.immodumidi.com. South.
www.immoest.com. Alsace.
www.immo-sgi.fr. Paris region. Hospitality.
www.imogroupstmarcellin.com. Isère.
www.jouzel-immobilier.com. Nantes.
www.leman-transactions.com/listcommerces.htm. Savoie.
www.marce44.com. Western France.

www.negocia-transactions.fr. Western France.
www.normandie-commerces.net. Normandy.
www.vendee-immobilier.com. Vendée.

### French Magazines

*Artisans Mag.* www.info-presse.fr.
*A Vendre et Louer.*
www.avendrealouer.fr.
*Franchise Magazine.*
www.franchise-magazine.com.
*L'Hôtellerie.* www.lhotellerie.fr.
*ICF L'Argus des Commerces.*
www.argus-commerce.com.
*L'Officiel de la Franchise.*
www.info-presse.fr.
*L'Officiel des Commerciaux.*
www.info-presse.fr.
*Pic International.* www.pic-inter.com.
*PME-Acquisitions d'Entreprises.*
www.acquisitions-entreprises.com.
*Repreneur.* www.repreneur.fr.
*Reprendre et Transmettre:*
www.acquisition-cession.com.
www.immobilierenfrance.com.

### General Information Sites

www.acfci.cci.fr. National chambers of commerce site.
www.ajinfo.org. Businesses in difficulties up for sale.

www.cession-commerce.com.
General information on buying a
business.
www.entreprendre-en-france.fr.
General information.
www.immoprix.com. Prices of
property and land by areas.
www.immostreet.com. General
information.
www.infologement.fr. Mortgage
advice.
www.juri-logement.org. Legal
information.
www.lesiteimmobilier.com.
Useful for calculating fees and
costs.
www.logement.equipment.go
uv.fr. Ministry of Housing and
Urban Planning.
www.logement.org. General
information.
www.panoranet.com. Information on mortgages and insurance.
www.portailpme.fr. State-sponsored website.
www.snpi.fr. Estate agents
organisation.
http://universimmo.servicesalac
arte.wanadoo.fr/argus. Estimates
of property values.

## PROPERTY ADVERTS AND PRICES

It is the usual practice in France to give the habitable or usable surface
area of a property in square metres. It is compulsory in the case of
apartments. The following gives some current examples of properties
with commercial potential, or actual businesses without the property.
Add on 20% for fees:

€1,220,000 – 3 hectares land, 18 chalets, holiday centre, Dordogne.
Includes property and *fonds de commerce.*
€785,000 – 85 hectares of forested land, with fishing, horse-riding,
and *gîtes,* near Limoges.
€375,000 – 28-bedroom hotel on Brittany coast.
€262,000 – Hotel-restaurant, with Category 4 licence, Bergerac, Dordogne.
€245,000 – 3-star camping with tennis and fishing, central Lot.
€213,000 – Restaurant with seating for 150, and 6 bedrooms, in
Nord-Picardie. *Fonds de commerce* only.
€196,000 – 310 sq.m. commercial property, Nice.
€183,000 – 13,000 sq.m. land and 3,000 sq.m. greenhouses, for

hydroponic cultivation of flowers, Dordogne.

€183,000 – 400 sq.m. shop with Category 3 drinks licence, Nerac, Lot-et-Garonne.

€140,000 – 600 sq.m. disused car repair workshop with land and parking, Castelnaudary, Aude.

€130,000 – 600 sq.m. warehouse, Côtes-d'Armor, Brittany.

€120,000 – Former *crêperie* on Brittany coast, with 4 bedrooms, overlooking sea.

€110,000 – Butchers in Auvergne. *Fonds de commerce* only.

€100,000 – Restaurant Cap d'Agde, Hérault.

€90,000 – 4-bed village house with shop, Mayenne.

€60,000 – Small hairdressers, central Montpellier. *Fonds de commerce* + €585 monthly rental.

€40,000 – 12-bed hotel and restaurant, Baraqueville, Aveyron.

€30,000 – Right to lease (*droit au bail*) of a small shop in new block of flats, Toulouse.

€2,200 per month –  rental of 1,100 sq.m commercial premises in Sarlat, Dordogne.

# PURCHASING A BUSINESS OR PROPERTY

The French sometimes say that you do not need a notaire to buy a property. This is true in as far as you can transfer the title of a property by private treaty – *sous seing privé* – but such a transfer is only binding on the parties who enter into it and is inferior to an authentic act drawn up and witnessed by a notaire. If someone tries to sell you a property or business by private treaty, or asks you to hand over a cash deposit, you would be best advised to refuse. It is illegal to give a deposit on a property to anyone other than an *immobilier* with a *carte professionnelle*, a notaire or an *avocat*.

A notaire is the only person who can register the sale with the land registry – the *bureau des hypothèques* – so in that sense it is mandatory to use his services. If he does nothing more than register the sale of the property he still gets his 1% or so of the sale price. A notaire is a public official, appointed by the state, whose main function, as far as property transfers are concerned, is to ensure that everything is done correctly, and that all taxes have been paid. It is normal for the notaire appointed by the seller to handle the transaction. They may have handled previous sales of the property. The buyer is entitled to appoint their own notaire without paying any additional costs; the two notaires share the fees between them. The buyer pays the fee in any case.

The most important thing to understand is that the notaire does not look out for your interests. One of the biggest mistakes that Britons make in France is to imagine that a notaire is the equivalent of a solicitor. If you want impartial legal advice it is best to approach a bilingual lawyer or *avocat*, most likely one based in the UK; some are listed below. If you are concerned about inheritance issues, or whose names should be on the title deeds, then the services of a UK-based lawyer can save a lot of problems. Few notaires speak good English, and they will be doubly cautious about giving advice in a foreign language. The main thing is to get an estimate of the notaire's fees in advance. You may be required to pay fees in advance; an adjustment is then made at the end. It is not unknown for notaires to send bills for unspecified 'additional work' which the buyer then feels they have no choice but to pay.

Notaires also act as tax collectors, so be on your guard about what you tell them. Their activities are supervised by the departmental *chambre des notaires*. Notaires also have professional liability insurance. Websites of notaire organisations can be found through www.immonot.com or www.notaire.fr. There is also a convenient list on: www.day-tripper.net/propertyxnotaires.html.

**Functions of a Notaire.** Whether you are buying a property or a business, it is best to use the services of a notaire. For a fully valid deed of transfer the services of a notaire are absolutely necessary. Only an act that has been drawn up and witnessed by a notaire – an *acte authentique* – can be made binding on third parties. The notaire can also, amongst other things:
o  Conduct a search in the land registry to see whether any third parties have any claim on the property, e.g. because of unpaid debts by the owner.

○ Check on 'easements', such as rights of way, etc.
○ Transfer your money via a blocked account to the seller, while ensuring that all fees and taxes have been paid in full.
○ Ensure that any pre-emptive rights on the property are 'purged'.
○ Check on planning permissions that could affect your property.

## PRE-CONTRACTS

Once you find a property that you like, the next step is to make an offer. Sellers in areas where there are a great many foreigners looking for property may ask for rather more than the property is worth. You can try to ask what you consider a reasonable price, but where there are a lot of foreign buyers you will not have much scope for bargaining. Knowing how long a property has been on the market is a useful guide to bidding. The offer is made to the estate agent, or the vendor if it is a private sale. You can make a formal written offer, an *offre d'achat*, or *promesse d'achat* – promise to buy – which the seller can consider. It only becomes legally binding on the seller if he or she accepts it. You are not allowed to make any deposits accompanying an *offre d'achat*. The *promesse d'achat* is not particularly recommended; it is better to make a verbal offer, and then ask for a pre-contract to be drawn up.

If your offer is accepted, a pre-contract – an *avant-contrat* – will be drawn up which will be forwarded by the agent *immobilier* to the notaire handling the sale. Although there is no legal obligation to use a preliminary contract, it is universally used. There are two main types of contract commonly used: the *compromis de vente* which is binding on both parties, and the *promesse de vente* (promise to sell), which is binding on the seller. The latter is commonly used north of the River Loire, including Paris. It is normal to pay 5-10% of the sale price as a deposit.

Results of inspections for asbestos, termites and lead paint can appear in the pre-contract, or in the final contract.

## Before Signing the Pre-Sale Contract...

Because of the binding nature of pre-contracts, it is vital to go through the following points before you sign anything:

O Are you sure that you can use the property for your intended purpose?

O Have you obtained preliminary planning permission for any building work you want to do?

O How long will existing planning permission be valid for?

O Does the sale include all the outbuildings and attached land, without reservation?

O Are the boundaries of the property clearly marked out?

O Are there any rights of way over the land?

O Do any third parties have any rights relating to the property?

O Will you share property rights over boundary walls with neighbours?

O If the property is recent, have you seen the handing-over report: the *procès verbal réception des travaux*?

O Has planning permission been obtained in the past for any work?

O Has the contract been checked by a qualified person?

You have the right to obtain an extract from the land registry (*extrait de matrice cadastrale*) from the *mairie* to verify the above points.

## *The Promesse de Vente*

With the 'promise to sell' the seller commits himself to selling within at least one month, or more usually within two to three months. In return the potential buyer will pay an *indemnité d'immobilisation*, a sum that compensates the seller for temporarily taking his property off the market. The usual amount is 10% of the sale price. The *promesse de vente* can be signed in front of a notaire, or can be signed privately. The seller pays the notaire a fee of €300-400. If the *promesse* is signed privately, it is to be signed in triplicate, and one copy is deposited with the *recette des impôts*. It is in the buyer's interests to sign the *promesse* in front of a notaire.

It is strongly recommended that the *indemnité d'immobilisation* be paid into a blocked account held by a notaire, and not directly to the seller. If you exercise your option to purchase, the *indemnité* will be deducted from the sale price. If the deal falls through the *indemnité* will be returned to you if one of the get-out clauses can be invoked within the allotted time; otherwise you will lose it outright.

***Pacte de Préférence.*** This is a variation on a *promesse de vente,* whereby the seller promises to sell the property to the potential buyer if they choose to exercise their option on it. Essentially, it is a right of first refusal. This type of contract is becoming less popular, but it is still used a lot for rental properties.

## The Compromis de Vente

The more common type of pre-contract also goes under the name of *promesse synallagmatique,* since it binds both seller and buyer. It is usual to pay 5-10% of the sale price as a deposit or *indemnité;* this is not the same as the *indemnité d'immobilisation* mentioned above. The deposit should be paid into a blocked account – *compte séquestre* – held by a notaire or by the estate agent.

The nature of the deposit is vitally important. If it is an *arrhes,* then the buyer can withdraw from the agreement but will forfeit the deposit. If the seller decides not to sell, then they are required to pay the buyer twice the amount of the *arrhes* as compensation. A variation on this type of deposit is a *dédit,* a specified sum that is forfeited if the buyer pulls out of the deal.

The other type of deposit, the *acompte* – which can be translated as 'down-payment' or 'instalment' – has more serious implications. In this case the sale is legally enforceable on both buyer and seller. There is no way to prevent the sale from going ahead.

The *compromis de vente* can be signed in front of a notaire, for which there is a charge. It can also be done privately – *sous seing privé* – in duplicate, and no copy has to be registered. In the first case, you have a week's cooling-off period after receiving the draft *compromis de vente* by registered post, during which you can decide not to go ahead with the deal. With the private contract, you have a week after signing during which you can withdraw without penalties.

All payments should be made by bank transfer or banker's draft through the estate agent or notaire's blocked account. Cash sales of properties will not be registered in some parts of the south of France, as a measure against money laundering. Using a banker's draft gives you greater freedom to withhold payment if you are not happy with the terms of the final contract.

## The Contents of the Compromis de Vente

It is important to understand that signing the *compromis de vente* virtually makes you the owner of the property you are promising to buy. If you sign a *promesse de vente* the seller remains the owner of the property. Getting out of a *compromis de vente* will be expensive and difficult, so you must be entirely satisfied that the contract is worded the way that you want. You may be asked to sign a standard printed contract which will not contain the get-out clauses that you need. While there are no standardised requirements as to the content, the contract should at least contain the following:

- A full copy of the entry in the population register (*copie intégrale de l'état civil*) of the buyer if they are already living in France.
- Legalised copies of passports, birth certificates, marriage certificates, divorce certificates.
- Official declaration of marriage regime, or civil partnership contract (PACS) from *mairie.*
- A description of the property, including outbuildings.
- The surface area of the land.
- The habitable surface area of the property (compulsory in the case of *copropriétés*).
- Proof that the seller is the rightful owner of the property, i.e. an authentic copy of the previous *acte de vente,* along with copies of previous *actes de vente* and other significant documents relating to the property.
- The agreed selling price of the property.
- Name of the notaire handling the sale.
- Who is to pay the notaire's fees.
- Who is to pay the estate agent's commission.
- The property's unique number in the *Plan Cadastral* – land registry.
- Any equipment or fixtures included in the sale: e.g. fitted kitchens,

burglar alarms.
- Results of reports on termites, lead and asbestos.
- Details of guarantees with newer properties.
- Date by which the *acte de vente* is to be signed.
- Receipt for any deposit.
- Date on which you will have the use of the property.
- Penalties if one of the parties withdraws from the deal.
- Get-out clauses: *conditions suspensives.*
- Guarantees against *vices cachés* or 'hidden defects'.

The last point is very important. It is necessary to determine who will pay the costs of repairs if hidden defects are later discovered. Any clause that frees the seller from having to make good hidden defects can be challenged if they have not followed the proper procedures in relation to termites, asbestos and lead. If the property is less than 10 years old, it will be covered by a *garantie décennale* – a 10-year insurance policy against major construction defects taken out by the builder. The person who bought the new property originally should also have insurance for 10 years, the *assurance dommage ouvrage*. Evidently, once a buyer agrees to take responsibility for hidden defects, then there is no further room for negotiation if any are found. Another solution is for either the seller or the buyer to take out an insurance policy against the discovery or appearance of major faults in the building.

### Get-Out Clauses

The negotiation of *conditions suspensives* is an area where expert legal help can be very useful. The most usual one is that the signature of the final deed is dependent on obtaining mortgage finance. This get-out clause should not be treated lightly. If you do not make reasonable efforts to obtain mortgage finance, and you are shown to be acting in bad faith, then you could lose your deposit. Other clauses can be inserted, e.g. you can make the purchase dependent on being able to sell your existing property, or on obtaining planning permission to make alterations to the property. A variation on the term *condition suspensive* is *condition résolutoire:* a clause that nullifies the contract automatically if its conditions are met.

## Rights and Obligations/Servitudes

In between the signing of the *compromis de vente* and the *acte de vente*, the notaire has some time in which to make enquiries about the status of the property. Between one and three months can elapse between the preliminary and final contract signings; two months is a normal interval. During this time he will be able to obtain a declaration from any bodies – such as SAFER – that might have pre-emptive rights over the property, that they do not intend to exercise them. He should establish that there are no mortgages still applying to the property. The seller should have made the necessary arrangements for the purging of the mortgage from the mortgage register. In the case of property that has been completed recently the seller will have to supply a *certificat de conformité* from the *mairie* certifying that all the necessary building permits were obtained when the property was constructed, and no regulations regarding urban planning have been broken. There are many cases where properties have been built or extended without planning permission, so it pays to be on your guard.

The matter of *servitudes*, that is rights and obligations or 'easements' in legal parlance, is particularly important. The most common type of *servitude* is where a farmer has the right to use part of your land, or allow animals to roam on it, or to draw water from your well. Your neighbour may have obtained the right to make windows in a wall overlooking your property, a *servitude de vue*. The biggest headache can be rights of passage – *droits de passage* – which allow locals to walk over your grounds on their way to go hunting or whatever. It is quite possible that your notaire will ask everyone in a village to sign a document agreeing that they have no right of way over your land.

Any *servitudes* that the previous owner of a property has entered into will have been drawn up in an *acte authentique*, signed by a notaire, and registered with the land registry. *Servitudes* can be registered for a limited number of years, or for as long as the property exists. They come with a property, and are not attached to the owner. They can work in your favour if they give you the right to use someone else's land. The seller of the property should inform you of *servitudes*; the notaire will find the details in previous title deeds and the *conservation des hypothèques*. If you are worried about *servitudes* and other claims by third parties, it is possible to take out an insurance policy guaranteeing good title to the property for a small sum. One company offering title insurance is Towergate: see www.towergate.co.uk.

## The Acte Final

After a period stated in the preliminary contract the parties will proceed to signing the final deed of sale, known as the *acte authentique de vente*. The *acte de vente* is signed by the buyer, the seller and one notaire. If there are two notaires involved, one acting for the buyer and one for the seller, only one of them will witness the *acte de vente*. Which one depends on local custom. You will be sent a *projet de l'acte* – a draft of the *acte de vente* – well in advance: a month is normal. This will contain much the same information as the original *compromis de vente*. You will be asked to produce originals of your birth/marriage/ divorce certificates, and they may have to be translated and notarised; enquire well in advance. At this point you should have made arrangements for payment of all the sums involved in the purchase, including the taxes and notaire's fees. The notaire will in any case require advance payments to cover his expenses. If a mortgage is involved, the notaire will draw down the money from your bank account.

## Power of Attorney

A date will be fixed for the signing. Very often there are last-minute hitches and the date may be put off. For this reason it is highly desirable to arrange to give a trusted person a power of attorney – a *mandat* – to act on your behalf if you are unable to attend the actual signing. For practical reasons, the power of attorney is best made up in the French form. It should be witnessed by a notaire, or at a French consulate. If it is witnessed by a British notary public, it will have to be legalised by the Foreign and Commonwealth Office (www.fco.gov.uk) to make it valid in France. The document should state what powers you are giving to your representative. The power of attorney allows your representative to do virtually anything you wish, and should only be given to a reliable person; preferably a close relative.

## The Actual Signing

Assuming that all the loose ends are tied up, you will be invited to the signing of the *acte de vente*. This will be an interesting experience, or perhaps nerve-racking if there are last-minute hitches. Apart from yourself, the seller and the notaire, and their clerk, there may be other interested parties present. The signing has to take place on French soil, but you can use an authorised representative to sign for you, a normal practice. By this point, all the necessary funds should have been transferred to your notaire's blocked bank account, or you should have your banker's draft ready. There are various taxes and fees to be paid at the last minute, and you should be prepared for this. It is highly embarrassing to find that the sale cannot go ahead because you haven't left any money in your French bank account. You should also have paid the first insurance premium on the property, *before* signing the *acte de vente*. Subsequent payment dates are based on the date of the signing.

Certain items will often be mentioned in or attached to the *acte de vente* that will not have appeared in the *compromis de vente*, such as:

o Details of mortgage loans.
o Full description of the property, with details of previous sales.
o Details of the insurance policy on the property.
o The amount of Capital Gains Tax payable by the seller; or exemption.

## COSTS OF PROPERTY PURCHASE

The high level of costs involved with property purchase is one of the main reasons that property prices do not go up very fast in France. The fees and taxes that have to be paid to the notaire and to the state are inaccurately referred to as *frais de notaire*, when only a part of them go to the notaire. One part of the notaire's fees are based on a sliding scale between 5% and 0.825% + TVA at 19.6%, depending on the value of the property. Additional services, such as searches in the land registry, do not have fixed fees. If you buy a commercial property, then the fees are the same as for residential property. The intangible part of the business, the *fonds de commerce*, is subject to slightly lower stamp duty than residential property (see below). There are fees to be paid to the notaire for registering a mortgage.

The stamp duty on transfers of so-called 'new' property (less than 5 years old) is much lower: basically the cost of entering the sale in the land registry. TVA at 19.6% has to be paid on the first transfer of a new property, which represents a large disincentive to buying new. A second transfer within 5 years (or after) only attracts 4.89% transfer tax. The notaire's fees are identical on the sale of both new and old properties; the difference is in the transfer taxes.

## Notaire's Fees

| | |
|---|---|
| up to €3,049 | 5% |
| €3,049-€6,098 | 3.3% |
| €6,098-16,769 | 1.65% |
| €16,769 and above | 0.825% |

## Example Calculations

| Value | €100,000 | €100,000 (new) | €100,000 (50% mortgage) | €150,000 (50% mortgage) | €200,000 (50% mortgage) |
|---|---|---|---|---|---|
| Notaire's fee | 1,115.78 | 1,115.78 | 1,115.78 | 1,528.28 | 1,940.78 |
| Notaire mortgage fee | 0 | 0 | 1,546.00 | 0 | 1,821.00 |
| TVA | 218.69 | 218.69 | 521.71 | 299.54 | 737.31 |
| Transfer taxes | 4,890.00 | 509.84 | 4,890.00 | 7,335.00 | 9,780.00 |
| Tax on mortgage | 0 | 0 | 307.50 | 0 | 615.00 |
| Registration fees | 304.88 | 304.88 | 304.88 | 304.88 | 304.88 |
| Various costs | 381.10 | 381.10 | 762.20 | 381.10 | 762.20 |
| Conservateur hypothèque | 100.00 | 100.00 | 125.00 | 150.00 | 250.00 |
| Total | 7,010.45 | 2,630.28 | 9,573.00 | 9,998.80 | 16,211.16 |

It follows that the total fees for a typical property transfer without a mortgage come to an average of 7.2% of the sale price. The *droits de mutation* – transfer taxes – are made up of:

| | |
|---|---|
| *taxe départementale* | 3.60% |
| *frais de recouvrement* | 0.09% (2.5% of the above) |
| *taxe communale* | <u>1.20%</u> |
| | 4.89% |

The *frais de recouvrement* are the expenses involved in collecting the *taxe départementale.* TVA (Valued Added Tax) is levied at 19.6% on new properties, as well as extensions, garages and outbuildings added on by the seller in the last 10 years, which could come to a substantial amount.

Another substantial expense is the commission payable to the estate agent or *immobilier,* which can range from 3% to 10% or even more with very cheap properties. It is becoming more usual for the seller to pay the estate agent's fees. In many areas where Britons like to buy it is still normal for the buyer to pay the fees. Advertisements do not always make this clear, so ask first.

## After the Sale

Once the *acte de vente* has been signed, the notaire has to pay all the taxes and commissions (unless you are paying the *immobilier* directly) out of the sums that you have passed over to him. The title is registered with the *Bureau des Hypothèques* – the register of deeds and mortgages, as well as the mortgage, if any. Eventually you will receive a certificate informing you that the title has been registered. The whole process will take some months. The original title deed – *la minute* – remains with the notaire. He is authorised to make authentic copies if necessary.

## Under-Declaring the Sale Price

It was once common practice to under-declare the sale price so as to save on taxes and fees, while paying a part 'under the table', or *sous la table.* There is no advantage in the long run to the buyer, since they will be penalised with higher Capital Gains Tax in the future when they resell. The penalties for under-declaring are serious. The one way around this is for the seller to leave some furniture or other moveable goods in the property which can then be given an inflated value, thus reducing taxes payable. This is acceptable to the authorities, as long as you do not go too far.

### Special Procedures in Relation to Copropriétés

The same surveys for asbestos and lead paint have to be done with *copropriétés* or co-ownership properties as with other residential property. You should also ask to see the *carnet d'entretien*, or log-book of the building, to see what kind of repairs have been carried out in recent years. The manager of the *copropriété* will most likely be present at the signing of the *acte de vente*. This must contain details of what percentage of the communal areas belong to you – your *quote part* – and what percentage of the communal charges you will be required to pay.

### Notaires as Estate Agents

It might come as a surprise to find that notaires also act as estate agents, especially in western France and in rural areas. Notaires keep databases on property prices and may have competitively-priced properties to sell. They are more likely to give an honest description of the property than an *immobilier*. The notaire will require a commission on the sale, but not as much as an *immobilier;* the commission is on a sliding of scale of 5% on the first €50,000 and then 2.5% above, plus TVA, and may or may not be paid by the seller. Reckon on 3% of the sale price. The main disadvantage of using notaires is that you need to be able to go to see them in person. They are notoriously slow to reply to letters or phone calls. As a rule, the secretary cannot make appointments for you; you have to speak with the notaire himself.

# INHERITANCE

Planning for inheritance should start before you buy a property in France. It can be advantageous to have separate wills in the UK and France. If you were tax-resident in France, then after your decease there can be a conflict between the French and UK authorities, since the latter are hard to convince that you were no longer domiciled in the UK at the time of decease. Remember that domicile in UK tax terms means the country where you have your longest-lasting ties, or the country you intend to return to at the end of your life. If you have continued to vote in UK elections, have kept property or investments in the UK, or been a frequent visitor, then the UK authorities can argue that you retained your UK domicile. One solution is to give away your assets in good time, or put them in someone else's name, but all this must be done as early on as possible. It is also vital to think about whose name is to go on the title deeds. For this reason it cannot be overemphasised that the advice of a British lawyer who has training in French law is absolutely essential.

French inheritance laws mean that you cannot choose to leave your property to anyone you like. Children have first priority, followed by parents, grandchildren and grandparents. Only where there are no surviving direct descendants or ascendants does your partner become a reserved heir (*héritier réservataire*). Since 2002, spouses take priority over grandparents and brothers and sisters of the deceased. Further details are given below on the rights of surviving spouses. A more detailed explanation of French inheritance taxes and ways of dealing with them is given in the author's *Buying a House in France* (publ. Vacation Work).

### French Succession Taxes

The crucial concept in French inheritance law is the reserved heir, or *héritier réservataire*. Inheritance taxes are known as *droits de succession*, hence they are generally referred to as succession taxes in English. They form part of the system of transfer taxes or *droits de mutation*.

Under French law, one part of your assets has to be left to specified members of your family (*la réserve légale*), while the rest is yours to do with as you please (*la quotité disponible*). Blood relatives are entitled to inherit in descending order:

## RESERVED HEIRS

*Children:* 50% for the first child; 66.6% between two children; 75% between three and above. No distinction is made between children from a first and subsequent marriage.

*Parents:* Where there are no children, parents receive 25% each. A single surviving parent can only receive 25%.

*Spouses:* Only become reserved heirs if there are no direct ascendants or descendants.

The grandchildren become reserved heirs if the children are no longer living. Brothers and sisters can be disinherited. They only inherit automatically if there are no descendants, ascendants or spouse. Children of the current marriage are treated equally with children of previous marriages, and children born outside marriage, including half-siblings of the deceased's children. The principle that children born from adultery have equal rights with their half-siblings is also now accepted in France. In the absence of the above then relatives take precedence over strangers, depending on their relationship to the deceased, up to the fourth degree. Relatives beyond the fourth degree are considered to be unrelated for the purpose of succession tax.

**Inheritance and Gift Taxes.** These are levied at the following rates. Children and parents benefit from a tax-free sum of €46,000; spouses from €76,000:

| Tax percentage | Spouse | Children/Parents |
| --- | --- | --- |
| 5 | the first 7,600 | the first 7,600 |
| 10 | 7,600-15,000 | 7,600-11,400 |
| 15 | 15,000-30,000 | 11,400-15,000 |
| 20 | 30,000-520,000 | 15,000-520,000 |
| 30 | 520,000-850,000 | 520,000-850,000 |
| 35 | 850,000-1,700,000 | 850,000-1,700,000 |
| 40 | 1,700,000 and over | 1,700,000 and over |

Brothers, sisters and grandchildren pay at rates of 35% (0-€30,000) and 45% on the excess. More distant relatives up to the fourth degree pay at 55%. Anyone else pays at 60%.

### Protecting your Partner

French law is far less favourable to partners than British law; to improve the partner's situation the law was changed in 2002. As a minimum, the surviving partner should receive either 25% of the full property or the *usufruit* of the property for their lifetime. The surviving partner has an absolute right to remain in the marital home for one year from the decease, even when the home is rented. The partner can move out of the property, and receive their part of the assets of the deceased.

The law distinguishes between three types of partner: a marriage partner; a common-law partner or *concubin* with whom you live without entering into a legally recognised partnership, known as a *union libre*; and a partner with whom you have entered into an official notarised civil contract, the PACS (*Pacte Civil de Solidarité*). The PACS law was enacted in 1999 to improve the lot of gay couples; the contractants make themselves liable for each other's debts and agree to support each other; after three years they can file joint tax returns. Any two people who are not closely related can enter into one, whether they are couples or just live together. The PACS can be dissolved as well.

| | Common-law partner | PACS partner | Spouse |
|---|---|---|---|
| The following is an example of what a partner might expect to inherit on assets of €300,000, where there are no other heirs whatsoever, and no provisions have been made to reduce succession taxes: | | | |
| Tax-free sum | 1,500 | 57,000 | 76,000 |
| Taxable sum | 298,500 | 243,000 | 224,000 |
| Rate of tax | 60% | 50% (-1,500) | 20% (-2,630) |
| Actual tax | 179,100 | 120,000 | 42,170 |
| Inheritance after tax | 120,900 | 180,000 | 257,830 |

A common way to improve the marriage partner's lot is to make a *donation entre époux* (gift between spouses), an act which can be registered with a notaire for a minimal cost (see below).

## Régime Matrimonial

When you buy property or a business in France, it is important to consider the type of marriage regime that you want to adopt. If you go for the *communauté universelle avec clause d'attribution intégrale* your partner acquires all your assets on your death; your children will receive the entire inheritance when your partner dies. This is the option chosen by most French couples until recently. Another option is the *communauté de biens réduite aux acquêts* where the partners retain the assets they had upon marriage and those acquired by gift or inheritance during the marriage, but jointly own those acquired during the course of the marriage. Partners can be made liable for each other's debts in relation to assets acquired jointly. In the case of divorce there is the matter of dividing up the assets. A simpler solution is the *régime de séparation des biens* – separation of estates – where the marriage partners' assets remain separate. Another variant of the separate estates regime is the *régime de participation aux acquêts,* where the partners share in the increase in value of each other's assets during the marriage. Naturally any regime which involves sharing of assets leads to complications when the assets have to be divided up. They presuppose that one has precise records of what the partners owned before they married, and what they acquired during it.

Marriages contracted in the UK, Ireland and in most US states, are assumed to come under the regime of separation of estates in France. Some US states which formerly came under French or Spanish law use the *communauté de biens réduite aux acquêts* régime, which is becoming popular with the French.

It is worth considering the opinion of the leading British expert on French property and inheritance, Henry Dyson, who states that the *communauté universelle* may be the best option if there are no children from previous marriages, but that it is best to acquire the property/ business before changing one's marriage regime. Using this regime the partner will receive their inheritance virtually tax-free and the children will have to wait until the surviving partner dies before they receive their share. Changes in the marriage regime must be entered in your will.

---

**Marriage Regime Change**

Patrick Delas, a French *avocat* presently practising in London with Russell-Cooke Solicitors, has some advice on changing your regime:
*British people are surprised to learn that they are not free to leave their assets to their partner under French law. A solution is to change the marriage regime to communauté universelle or* communauté des biens réduite aux acquêts. *Otherwise under French law British citizens are presumed to have been married under the* régime de séparation des biens *which means that your assets go to your children*

*(if you have any) while your partner has a lifetime usufruit or 25% of the whole. In France a marital contract has to be witnessed by a notaire **and** validated by a court, but EU law allows non-French citizens to change their marriage regime just by having it witnessed by a notaire, and we have a qualified notaire in my office who can carry this out. It is not, however, advisable to change your marriage regime if there are children from a first marriage, because they have the right to enter an opposition to the change, as it would reduce their inheritance. Of course if you change your marriage regime to the* communauté universelle *or the* communauté des biens réduite aux acquêts *and you then get divorced, then you will have to go through the process of valuing the assets so as to share them out between the couple.*

## Reducing Transfer and Succession Taxes

In the case of buying property, there are a couple of well-known methods of reducing transfer taxes, namely the SCI and the *tontine*. The SCI or *société civile immobilière* is a company specifically set up to own property. There are at least two *associés* or partners who own the shares. There are considerable costs involved; setting up the SCI costs on average €2,500. You will moreover have to hold an annual general meeting. Decisions about the running of the company are made by majority shareholder voting. Shares can be transferred with minimal tax liability. Capital Gains Tax still has to be paid when the property is sold. The usefulness of the SCI for inheritance purposes is mainly limited to a situation where the shareholders are domiciled and resident in the UK, which makes it possible to avoid French inheritance rules.

If you are interested in setting up an SCI, it is best to do so at the same time as buying the property, otherwise the SCI will pay transfer taxes on the purchase. The SCI is not ideal if you are planning to run *gîtes*, or *chambres d'hôtes*. By definition an SCI is meant to be non-trading, and it only owns property, not furniture. The solution is to rent the property out to another business structure, a SARL. There are also issues with the British tax authorities. If shareholders are actively involved in managing the company and use the property for holidays then they can be taxed on benefits in kind if they are tax-resident in the UK. A possible solution is for shareholders to have no role in running the company.

You should seek expert legal assistance if you are thinking of setting up an SCI. If you engage a lawyer then they should be fully conversant with UK and French law, and should have practised in both countries. The SCI is worth considering for expensive properties. It is also very useful where unrelated people wish to buy a property together, such as in the case of co-ownership.

***Tontine.*** The *tontine* was thought up by an Italian banker, Lorenzo Tonti, in the 18th century. It is more correctly called a *clause d'accroissement.* This is where two or more people whether married or not, acquire assets, on the understanding that the one who lives the longest acquires the whole, thus entirely cutting out the inheritors of the other members of the *tontine.* For legal purposes deceased members of a *tontine* – and, by extension, their inheritors – are treated as though they never had any share in the assets. The survivor is treated as though they owned the property from the day that it was bought. Acquiring property with a *tontine* clause was once fiscally very advantageous but these days it is much less so, unless you start a *Société Civile* (registered company) with a *tontine* element. Where the partners are unrelated, or *concubins,* the 'winner' of the *tontine* is subject to succession tax at 60% on half the value of the property, unless the property is worth less than €76,000 and it is their principal residence, in which case the survivor only pays 4.89% transfer taxes. If there is a PACS between them, the succession tax is only 50%. Surviving spouses pay the succession tax that applies to them.

Partners cannot enter into a *tontine* unless they have roughly the same life expectancy and can therefore profit equally from the *tontine.* They should also contribute equal amounts to the purchase. It is not allowed to buy *en tontine* with your children as partners, or with someone who is likely to die soon. Only marriage partners married under the common assets can enter into a *tontine,* but there could be difficulties if they fall out or get divorced. It is also virtually impossible to sell your part of the *tontine* since the buyer will lose everything if the person they bought their share from dies before the other members.

The advantage of the *tontine* is that it allows you to decide who will inherit your property. It is very effective in cutting out the family of the partner who dies first out of the will. It is not actually tax-efficient (except for very cheap properties), since there is only one heir in this situation, and no flexibility as to who inherits. The *tontine* clause has to be put into the *acte de vente* before it is signed; afterwards is too late.

***Société Civile Tontinière.*** The best way to maximise the benefit of a *tontine* is to start a company for this purpose. The company owns the property, which can be bought and sold. The shares in the company cannot be sold for the reason outlined above. The advantage of the *Société Civile Tontinière* is that the transfer of the shares to the surviving member(s) is only subject to transfer taxes (4.89%), and not to gift tax. The value of the property is irrelevant. There is a very high likelihood, however, that sooner or later the French tax authorities will clamp down on this loophole, but this will not be retroactive.

## Using Gifts to Lessen Succession Taxes

One classic method of reducing succession taxes is to make gifts during your lifetime. Depending on your age. Gift tax – *droits de donation* – is payable at the same rates as succession tax. It has to be paid immediately, but the donor can pay the tax on behalf of the donee. Lifetime gifts enjoy two rates of reduction:

50% if the donor is under 65.
30% if the donor is between 65 and 75.
From 75 and above there is no reduction in tax.

Tax is also reduced if the donor dies more than 10 years after the gift is made. If you make a gift in the UK, it is tax-exempt if the donor dies more than 7 years after making the gift.

Grandparents can give grandchildren €30,000 tax-free every 10 years (as of 2003). Gifts that are not revealed to the tax office will not be subject to gift tax, but if their existence becomes known after the donor's decease then they will be treated as part of the inheritance and will be subject to full succession tax. The gift can be witnessed by a notaire, who will make up an acte authentique, a document which has legal force and which is recognised by third parties.

***Donation Entre Époux/Donation au Dernier Vivant.*** These are two names for one type of gift. The gift can be written into the marriage contract in which case it is irrevocable; otherwise it can be revoked without informing the partner. The *donation au dernier vivant* means 'gift to the survivor'. The survivor only receives the assets on the death of their partner. Succession tax is payable above the basic allowance of €76,000.

The *donation entre époux* is of benefit to the spouse when the deceased leaves family members who are reserved heirs. Without the *donation entre époux* the surviving partner will receive less than they would have if their partner had made the donation. On the death of the partner the survivor can opt to continue to have the *usufruit* or benefits of the spouse's entire assets for the rest of their lives, while the children have the *nue propriété*, i.e. they own the assets without having the use or profit of them. The surviving partner can manage the deceased's portfolio of investments, but they can be challenged by the deceased's blood relatives if they appear to be mismanaging the assets. The survivor can also opt to receive the part of the inheritance that they are allowed as pleine propriété, without the *usufruit*, or to have 25% *pleine propriété* and 75% *usufruit*. This regime is particularly useful where there are children from previous marriages.

The *donation entre époux* is not an effective method of avoiding succession taxes; it is simpler and cheaper to put the provisions you want in your will. It is advisable to take legal advice before making a gift to ensure that this is best for you. This type of gift must be registered with a notaire. It is doubtful whether non-residents can enter into a *donation entre époux*.

***Donation-Partage.*** One or both parents can make a gift to their children during their lifetime, and thus reduce the amount of taxes payable on transferring assets to their children or grandchildren. This is a method of dividing up and giving away your assets early. If the parents make the gift jointly – the *donation-partage conjonctive* – it is assumed for fiscal purposes that half the gift came from the father and the other half from the mother. Gift tax is payable on the *donation partage*. There is a reduction of 50% if the donor was aged under 65 at the time they made the gift, and 30% if they were between 65 and 75.

If both parents make a gift jointly to their children, the children are allowed up to €46,000 per parent – i.e. €92,000 in total – free of tax.

It is possible for the donor to give away just the *nue propriété* of the property and retain the *usufruit*, and this can generate substantial tax savings.

The gift made under *donation partage* does not form part of the inheritance; ordinary gifts – *donations simples* – are reintegrated into the inheritance and evaluated for succession tax. The parents do not have to divide up their gifts equally between the children; normally the children agree that the gifts should be apportioned in a certain way. Children are not legally obliged to accept a gift, and this has no effect on their legal rights. They can challenge the distribution of the gifts after the parent's decease, if they believe that the gift has reduced their inheritance, e.g. they were not born when the gift was made.

## Succession Taxes and Businesses

Once all the business assets have been valued then succession taxes are payable as they would be on any assets. There are certain measures in place to lessen the effects of the death of the founder of a business on the spouse. As a general principle the intangible elements of a business – the *fonds de commerce* – need to be valued unless the business is simply to disappear. This might appear to pose a problem since a *fonds de commerce* is not a physical object, however lawyers and *immobiliers* have standardised tables for valuing *fonds de commerce* (see example below). Assuming that the *fonds* can be passed on, then the inheritors will find themselves in a situation known as *indivision*, co-owners of an indivisible asset, a situation which requires the unanimity of all the *indivisaires* (partners in the *indivision*) regarding decisions on what to do with the asset. The inheritors can apply to a court – the *tribunal de grande instance* – to have the *fonds* sold. Creditors can also apply to have a business sold.

Another scenario is that the surviving partner or one of the inheritors applies to be allowed to continue running the business. Only inheritors who have been co-owners and who have actually contributed to the development of the business can apply to run it. Since most French people until recently were married under the regime of common assets (*communauté universelle*), it has been usual for the surviving spouse to carry on and not have to pay succession taxes. This will not apply to Britons or US citizens, unless they have specifically chosen the regime of common assets (see above).

If your spouse was also a partner in the business then he/she can carry on the business undisturbed. For this purpose the spouse has to have been officially registered as a *conjoint associé*. Where the spouse has been working for the partner without being paid a salary for more than 10 years, then they receive a tax-free lump-sum of up to €43,000 (but not more than 25% of the value of the business), in which case they need to have been registered as a *conjoint collaborateur* in order to qualify.

**Capital Gains Tax and Inheriting a Business.** The sale of a business involves Paying Capital Gains tax (*Impôt sur les Plus Values/IPV*) on the difference between the purchase price and the selling price. If you inherit a *fonds de commerce* with a market value, you are faced with the choice of carrying on the business, or paying IPV if you sell on the business. Exemption from IPV is only granted if the spouse or an inheritor in direct line carries on the business using the deceased owner's most recent valuation as a starting point. If the business is sold then IPV is payable, but an exemption is granted if the business turnover did not exceed twice the maximum turnover of a *micro-entreprise*, namely €250,000 for a *commerce* and €90,000 for other businesses. As regards those who have made their living letting out property, the exemption from IPV only applies if the owner was considered a professional landlord, i.e. earned more than 50% of his/her income or more than €23,000 per year from lettings. Further information about IPV is given in the chapter *Selling On*.

Note that if your business was not properly registered, then there cannot be any exemption from IPV. You will be treated as a private person who has made a capital gain.

# TYPES OF WILL

There are three types of will:

**Holographic** (*testament olographe*): entirely in the person's handwriting, it is best done in French, and is generally not witnessed. If you choose, you can register it with the central register of testaments, the Fichier des Dernières Volontés. Most wills in France are in this form.
**Authentic** (*testament authentique*): can be printed or written and has to be witnessed by two notaries or one notaire and two other persons. Automatically registered with the Fichier des Dernières Volontés.
**Secret** (*testament mystique*): a will made up or dictated by a person who then hands it over in a sealed and signed envelope to a notaire in the presence of two witnesses. The notaire writes on it 'sealed document' or other comments. The testator either leaves it with the notaire or keeps it himself.

The holographic testament is generally the best, with the proviso that someone needs to know where it is kept. The secret testament has virtually fallen out of use.

## *Inheritance Procedures*

In the first instance you will need to go to within 24 hours to the nearest *mairie* with the death certificate issued by a doctor and all the available indentity papers of the deceased, in order to obtain the official form stating the person has died – *fiche d'état civil*. You need several copies to send to different organisations, such as the deceased's pension fund, insurer and banks.

The family and/or partner will then visit the notaire who dealt with the deceased's will as soon as is practically possible after registering the death. The surviving partner, potential inheritors, the executor or creditors can request a *greffier en chef* (chief clerk) from the local civil court to put seals on the deceased's property (*pose de scellés*) if they believe there is a risk of theft or fraud. The *greffier* can make up a list of the goods and conduct a search for a will.

Legally, the reserved heirs, and anyone with a power of attorney, have the right and duty – known as *saisine* – to use the deceased's assets from the moment of death, to pay debts or bills as they arise (up to a limit). The deceased's bank account is automatically blocked, but money can still be taken out for bills, the funeral, and standing orders.

The names of the heirs are listed on the *acte de notoriété*, a legal document made up by the notaire or by a chief clerk of the court. This does not mean that heirs can immediately take their part of the inheritance, or that they are bound to accept an inheritance encumbered with debts. An heir can register the deceased's car in their name, with the right documents, and the agreement of the other heirs, before the estate is finally divided up.

A number of documents are required to start the inheritance process:

- The death certificate.
- A copy of the French will.
- A copy of the British will, translated into French.
- The names of all the potential inheritors.
- Marriage/divorce certificates.
- Death certificates of deceased former inheritors still mentioned in the will, if any.

In the course of time, you will need to produce documents relating to all of the deceased's bank accounts, investments and properties. The inheritors, and anyone who has received gifts from the deceased subject to gift tax, are required to file a *déclaration de succession* within a year. Interest is payable on the succession tax after six months if the deceased died in France, or 12 months if abroad. The *déclaration* is a form obtained from the French tax office, to be filled in in duplicate if the assets are worth over €15,000. Foreigners will find it convenient to appoint a notaire to make the *déclaration*. The succession tax has to be worked out by the person filling in the *déclaration*. The tax authorities can challenge the value you place on a property, by comparing it with similar properties in the area. A small undervaluation is acceptable, but you can't go too far.

The tax does not come out of the inheritance; the inheritors are required to pay it together before they can receive the inheritance. It is possible to ask for a delay in payment of up to 10 years; you can also ask to pay in instalments.

It is possible to use an executor (*exécuteur testamentaire*) named in your will in France, but this is probably best avoided, unless you have reason to believe that your next of kin are untrustworthy or incompetent. Unless the executor is a notaire, the French authorities may assume that the executor is actually an heir and charge them the maximum rate of tax: 60%. The executor is charged with filing the *déclaration de succession* correctly. They are entitled to payment for the work they do, which can come to a substantial sum, another reason to avoid using them.

**Further Reading.** For a detailed study of French succession law, see Henry Dyson's *French Property and Inheritance Law,* published by OUP in 2003. This is a technical work written for lawyers. The author is an international legal consultant who can advise on property purchase and company formation; ☎00 33 04 93 62 70 70; fax 00 39 0184 67 24 79. For a general summary of inheritance in the UK and France, see Bill Blevins and David Franks' *Living in France.*

## Law Firms Dealing with French Commercial Property

Ideally, one will want to use the services of a UK law firm, with lawyers qualified in both UK and French law. Some firms have French lawyers working for them in the UK, or have offices in France. Such lawyers can advise one on whose name to put the property in, and what measures to take to minimise succession taxes. The *acte de vente* still has to be signed in front of a French notaire and registered in France.

*A Home in France:* The Old Granary, Low Lane, Cuddington, Bucks HP18 0AA; ☎0870-748 6161; fax 0870-748 6162; www.ahomeinfrance.com. Run by Danielle Seabrook, this company offers complete bilingual legal assistance to British residents to manage their risk in buying in a foreign jurisdiction.
*Bennett & Co Solicitors:* 144 Knutsford Rd, Wilmslow, Cheshire SK9 6JP; ☎01625-586937; fax 01625-585362; www.bennett-and-

co.com.

*Blake Lapthorn Solicitors:* Holbrook House, 14 Great Queen St, London WC2B 5DG; ☎020-7430 1709; fax 020-7831 4441; www.bllaw.co.uk. Has an in-house team of three French lawyers.

*Henry Dyson,* ☎00 33 4 93 62 70 70; fax 00 39 0184 67 24 79. International legal consultant who can advise on inheritance and SCIs.

*Fox Hayes Solicitors:* Bank House, 150 Rounday Rd, Leeds LS8 5LD; ☎0113-249 6496; fax 0113-248 0466; www.foxhayes.co.uk. Contact Graham Platt: qualified both in Britain as a solicitor, and admitted to practise as an Avocat in France. Deals with property, company, litigation and probate.

*John Howell & Co*: The Old Glassworks, 22 Endell Street, Covent Garden, London WC2H 9AD; ☎020 7420 0400; fax 020 7836 3626; e-mail info @europelaw.com; www.europelaw.com. A team of English, French and Dual Qualified lawyers working in a Law Firm specialising purely in 'foreign' work.

*Howard Kennedy Solicitors:* ☎020-7636 1616; www.howard-

kennedy.com. Large London firm dealing with the top end of the market. Ask for Anthony Slingsby.

*The International Property Law Centre:* The International Property Law Centre, Unit 2, Waterside Park, Livingstone Rd, Hessle HU13 0EG; ☎01482 350850; fax 01482 642799; e-mail internationalpr operty@maxgold.com; www.maxgold.com. Contact senior partner and solicitor Stefano Lucatello, an expert in the purchase and sale of French, Italian, Portuguese and Spanish property and businesses, and the formation of offshore tax vehicles and trusts.

*Kingsfords Solicitors:* 5/7 Bank St, Ashford, Kent TN23 1BZ; ☎01233-665544; fax 01233-645836; e-mail jdc@kingsfords-solicitors.com; www.kingsfords-solicitors.com. British lawyers with expertise in French conveyancing. Fixed-price property buyer's package and other services.

*Liliane Levasseur-Hills:* 69 Pullman Lane, Godalming, Surrey GU7 1YB. Fully qualified French notaire offering assistance with buying and selling French property, French inheritance law, and French wills.

*Pannone & Partners:* 123 Deansgate, Manchester M3 2BU; ☎0161-909 3000; fax 0161-909 4444; www.pannone.com. Contact: Lindsay Kennealy.

*Penningtons Solicitors:* Bucklersbury House, 83 Cannon St, London EC4N 8PE; ☎020-7457 3000; fax 020-7457 3240; www.penningtons.co.uk. Paris office: 23 rue d'Anjou, 75008 Paris; ☎01 44 51 59 70; fax 01 44 51 59 71.

*Prettys Solicitors:* Elm House, 25 Elm St, Ipswich, Suffolk IP1 2AD; ☎01473-232121; fax 01473-230002; www.prettys.co.uk.

*Riddell Croft & Co Solicitors:* 27 St Helen's St, Ipswich, Suffolk IP14 1HH; ☎01473-384870; fax 01473-384878; www.riddellcroft.com. Experienced, bilingual practitioners offer help with buying and selling property in France, rentals, tax and estate planning and wills. Can also help with property search.

*Russell-Cooke:* 2 Putney Hill, Putney, London SW15 6AB; ☎020-8789 9111; fax 020-8780 1679; e-mail Delasp@russell-cooke.co.uk; www.russell-cooke.co.uk. Large firm with French law and property department, headed by Dawn Alderson, qualified in both English and French law and member of the Bordeaux bar. Bordeaux office: 42 place Gambetta, 33000 Bordeaux; ☎05 56 90 83 10; fax 05 56 90 83 11.

*Sean O'Connor & Co:* Bilingual Solicitors, 2 River Walk, Tonbridge, Kent TN9 1DT; ☎01732-365378; fax 01732-360144; e-mail seanoconnorco@aol.com.

*Stephen Smith (France) Ltd:* 161 Cemetery Rd, Ipswich, Suffolk IP4 2HL; ☎01473-437186; fax 01473-436573; e-mail stephen@step hensmithfranceltd.com; www.stephensmithfranceltd.com. Stephen Smith is the author of *Letting Your French Property Successfully,* published by PKF Guernsey.

*Taylors Solicitors and Notaries Public:* The Red Brick House, 28-32 Trippet Lane, Sheffield S1 4EL; ☎0114-276 67 67; fax 0114-273 1287; www.taylorssolicitors.co.uk.

*Turner and Co Solicitors:* 94 New Hall St, Birmingham B3 1PB; 0121-200 1612; fax 0121-200 1613; e-mail turneranco@aol.com; www.french-property-news.com/turnerandco.htm.

# PLANNING PERMISSION

Anyone intending to use a property for the purposes of running a business needs to be doubly careful about ensuring that they have permission to make changes to their property.

Many communes have a PLU – *Plan Local d'Urbanisme* – which states which pieces of land may be built on; the PLU is still popularly referred to by its old name: POS or *Plan d'Occupation des Sols.* Linked to this is the COS – *Coéfficient d'Occupation des Sols* – a figure giving the maximum amount of square metres of surface area that can be built on each square metre of land. The implication is that if you want to increase the surface area of a property over the limit given in the PLU then you will have to pay a charge, if permission is granted at all. If the commune has no PLU, then the use of the land is decided by central government, via the *Règlement Nationale d'Urbanisation* (RNU).

Outline planning permission – a *Certificat d'Urbanisme* – is only compulsory if you are selling a piece of land for building on (except for housing estates or *lotissements*). Otherwise the CU is an opinion on whether something can be built or extended on a piece of land in relation to the town planning laws. If it is positive it more or less guarantees a *permis de construire* (actual planning permission) for a period of a year from the time you are given the decision. For buyers of property there is an element of risk in that the CU may expire before they get around to applying for a *permis de construire*. Some foreigners have been caught out by French sellers showing them an out-of-date CU and assuring them that they would be able build their extension or new building. If you apply for a new CU it takes about two months to receive a decision.

Once you have decided on your precise plans, you will then apply for the *permis de construire* (PC). Where the surface area of the property is increased by less than 20 sq.m. no PC is required, but a *déclaration de travaux exempts de PC* is. If the surface is increased by over 20 sq.m, a PC is required. The main point of the PC is to do with changes to the external appearance of the property that could affect the rights of other people. This means that if you change the rendering on your house, or the appearance of the frontage, then a PC is certainly required.

All PCs are granted *sous réserve du droit des tiers* – with the reservation that third parties' rights are not affected. Having a CU or PC does not mean that your neighbours cannot raise objections if you are building something that will overlook their property, or for that matter if you infringe on some 'easement' or *servitude* that burdens your property. These are matters of private civil law where the *mairie* has no say. The *mairie* will not necessarily be aware of all the easements affecting your property, unless they are mentioned in the land registry, i.e. the *conservation des hypothèques*.

You can still be taken to court after construction work has been completed if the alteration to the property has a real effect on your neighbours' rights to the peaceful enjoyment of their property. The best advice is to talk to your neighbours at the planning stage and get their agreement before you start any actual work. If they do not give their agreement then you will need to engage the services of an *avocat*. Your *avocat* can go as far as to ask all the neighbours to sign a document that they renounce any rights of way over your land, etc.

**Planning Permission and Shops, etc.** The regulations are basically the same for shops as for residential properties. If you plan to change the appearance of your shop-front, or your sign, then you enter a *déclaration de travaux exempts de permis de construire,* i.e. the work is exempt from a PC. For a change of use or increase in the size of the premises of more than 20 sq.m. then a PC is required, as it is with residential property. A shop with a surface area of more than 300 sq.m. requires an authorisation from the *préfecture* to start business.

# BUSINESS LEASES

The nature of the lease you can enter into will depend on what sort of activity you are going to carry on. It is not related to the type of legal structure that you choose. The ideal lease for businesses is the *bail commercial.*

## *Bail Commercial*

The *bail commercial* was thought up in order to give businesses stability and protection from eviction. The main body of the legislation dates back to 1953, a time of political instability and high inflation. The government has been considering scrapping some of the clauses which particularly penalise property owners, in particular those linking rent increases to the construction price index, and the ban on renting out rooms in a businesses property for habitation.

A *bail commercial* cannot be for less than 9 years. There are shorter commercial contracts, but they should be avoided (see below). The lease must state what the premises are to be used for. The ideal lease is a *bail tous commerces* – you can use the premises for anything kind of business you like – but this would require paying a higher rent. The usual type of lease is a *bail exclusif* which specifies the type of business you can carry on. You are in theory allowed to carry out similar activities if these are necessary for your business to develop, but changing the use of the premises, known as *déspécialisation*, can entail a lot of difficulties. You can ask for a clause allowing *déspécialisation plénière* so that you can entirely change the nature of your business if there are compelling reasons for doing so. You can also have a clause allowing you to change to a similar type of business, the *déspécialisation partielle* or *restreinte*. If the owner of the premises prevents you from changing the use without good reason, then you can apply for a court order to force him to allow you to change your business. The level of rent may be increased or you may have to pay compensation to the owner, if he/she can show that their interests are prejudiced in some way by the change in your business.

The amount of rent and payment dates (*échéances*) are fixed in the contract. With a 9-year lease, the rent will be revised every three years – *révision triennale*. The amount will increase, or decrease, in relation to the change in the *indice du coût de la construction*, an index published every three months by the French statistical institute, INSEE, giving the cost of constructing new buildings. If building costs go down then your rent could also decrease. The owner can demand a rent increase if the nominal rental value of the property used for calculating property taxes – *valeur locative* – has gone up more than 10%, or if you have changed the nature of your business. You may have to agree to the use of another index that could allow the owner to put up the rent more often, a so-called *clause d'échelle mobile*. This could be connected with the profitability of the business.

A rent that is controlled is called *plafonné* – i.e. it has a ceiling. The rent becomes 'unceilinged' or *déplafonné* after a period of 12 years has passed since the initial contract was signed without any explicit renewal having taken place, or if the initial contract was for more than 9 years. The ordinary 9-year contract is still *plafonné* when renewed, in relation to the INSEE index, unless the value of the property has changed significantly because of a change in the building, or changed circumstances in the area. The rent can also be *déplafonnée* if you are renting an office, a piece of land, or a building which can only be used for one purpose, such as a hotel.

Other elements in the commercial lease include:

***Description des locaux.*** This is an inspection report on the premises, similar to an *état des lieux* with residential accommodation. You should not accept a property in bad condition without making it clear who is to pay for repairs, even though this is governed by the Code Civil. The report may require you to return the premises to their original condition when you leave.

***Clause de non-concurrence/Clause d'exclusivité.*** These are clauses preventing the owner from starting a competing business, or renting part of the same building to a competing business.

***Répartition des travaux.*** Who has to pay for repairs can be specified in the contract, but is in any case subject to the provisions of the Code Civil. According to Art.1755 of the Code Civil commercial lessees cannot be made to pay for repairs caused by wear and tear or *force majeure* to a property. The usual regime is that the owner pays for major repairs, and the lessee for minor ones, as with a residential lease. The items that fall to the lessee (*réparations locatives*) are stated in Art.606 of the Code Civil. There should also be a clause in your lease specifying whether the lessee can carry out repairs themselves.

***Prestations et taxes.*** It is quite normal for lessees to be made liable for the service charges and local taxes for their part of the building. You will therefore have to pay the *impôt foncier* (land taxes) and the municipal rubbish collection charges, etc.

***Garantie des vices cachés.*** As with a normal lease you can ask for a clause stating that there are no hidden faults that would prevent you from enjoying the use of the premises.

***Pas de porte.*** This is a premium paid on entry to the premises which makes up for the ban on raising the rent by more than the rise in the construction index. The *pas de porte* is a disincentive to the less well-off starting businesses, but it is entirely legal. The amount is negotiated between the contracting parties. The *pas de porte* is not likely to be abolished until rents on commercial property are liberalised.

The lessee always has the right to renew the contract if they have carried on a business on the premises for 3 years. It can be written into the contract that they have to make an express request to do so. Negotiating a commercial lease in French is no piece of *gâteau*; the owner can try to insert clauses that are to your disadvantage. By all means ask for help from a qualified lawyer or other person, as mistakes here could be very costly.

Do not assume that you can rent out rooms above your business premises to a tenant. It is unusual for rooms to be rented out for residential purposes above businesses, but regulations may soon be changed to make this easier.

# OTHER TYPES OF LEASES

*Bail dérogatoire.* This is popularly known as a *bail précaire,* or sometimes a *bail de courte durée* or *bail américain.* It assumes that the lessee is only remaining in the premises for up to 24 months at most. It is up to the owner to prove why a *bail précaire* is justified, otherwise the lessee can apply for a regular *bail commercial.* The usual reasons are the imminent demolition of the building, a compulsory purchase order or the lessor's family circumstances. A clause can be written into the lease allowing the lessor to retake possession of the premises at very short notice, the *convention d'occupation à titre précaire.* According to the law a *bail précaire* cannot be renewed, although it may be extended if some external event justifies it, i.e. the event that would have brought the lease to an end has not occurred. The longer the lessee remains on the premises the less likely it is that the lease can remain a *bail précaire.*

As a general principle, if the lessee is still occupying the premises after 24 months then the lease is automatically transformed into a regular *bail commercial* governed by the 1953 law, and the lessee can apply for the status of a *bail commercial.* The *bail précaire* can be renewed on the understanding that the lessee agrees to renounce their right to a *bail commercial.* The lessee can only renounce the *bail commercial* when they are actually entitled to it, i.e. when the 24 months are up. The lease can be for 23 months only, to exclude any chance of the lessee applying for a *bail commercial.* Some *fonds de commerce* are advertised giving a choice between a *bail précaire* with a low rent along with the payment of a *pas de porte* or premium, or choosing for a normal *bail commercial.*

It can also happen that after 3 years has passed (at least) that circumstances arise whereby the owner has to offer a lessee a *bail de courte durée.* This can be because the building is to be demolished or sold, or for other reasons. In this case the *bail* will be for at least 1 year and not longer than 3 years.

*Location saisonnière.* This is a seasonal lease, e.g. for the summer only. The lessee is bound to leave at the end of the season.

*Bail professionnel.* A lease that may only be used by regulated liberal professions, e.g. doctors, accountants, architects, lawyers and the like.

There is more freedom for the owners than with a *bail commercial.* Legally, it has to run for at least 6 years, with 6 months' notice required on both sides to cancel the contract. The owner is not required to renew the contract. It can be renewed tacitly (*reconduction tacite*), and the owner can raise the rent after 6 years by whatever amount he wishes. You are not allowed to live on the premises. The contract must be drawn up in writing, and all correspondence is by registered letter with confirmation of receipt. The lease is subject to the Code Civil, and in addition Article 57A of the law of 23 December 1986 on leases.

**Bail de droit commun.** This is a type of lease based on the Code Civil that offers more protection for owners than tenants. It applies where a business rents part of a building without using the premises for professional activities. Usually this type of lease will only be used for nonprofit organisations called *Associations Loi de 1901.*

**Bail mixte.** To give it its full name, *bail mixte professionnel et habitation,* this can only apply if you carry on a liberal profession in a basically residential property, or are running a non-profit organisation from the premises. There are two minimum lengths of contract: 3 years if the owner is a natural person (*personne physique*) or family SCI, and 6 years if they are a company (*personne morale*). In many ways it is similar to a residential lease. You are not legally required to actually live on the premises, but the lease will not be renewed in the same form if you are not living there when it comes to an end.

The *bail mixte* can be agreed verbally, or written out by hand, or using a pre-printed contract. The best contract is one drawn up by a notaire. Unless your contract is witnessed by a notaire it cannot be made binding on third parties.

### Running a Business from Rented Property

Hugo Nuyts has run the popular Hôtel Mimosas in Nice since 1999, with his partner. He has also been an electrical engineer and is still a tour director with Trafalgar Tours.

*We came to Nice thinking to buy a villa, and ended up buying a hotel, which is in a large block of flats near the promenade. We took over the lease from the previous owner; there are two other hotels in the same building. It's a standard 3-6-9* bail commercial *that is used by the local property-owners' syndicate. As we were taking over an existing business we just needed to inform the Chambre de Commerce, and we received our* Extrait K *from the* Greffe du Tribunal de Commerce. *This was handled by the notaire.*

*To rent out rooms you need insurance, a* contrat multirisque professionnelle. *It is best to get your insurance through a bank, rather than an insurance company. You are also required to install modern electrical safety equipment. Old porcelain fuses are not allowed; they have to be the up-to-date circuit breakers approved by EDF. You are also registered with the* Centre des Impôts, *the tax office. Before you can rent any rooms out you require an attestation from an* avocat *saying that you have registered with all the right offices. To serve breakfasts or drinks you have to have a basic drinks licence from the* Douanes et Droits Indirects. *As a self-employed person, I'm required to make pension payments to* ORGANIC, *contributions to a sickness fund, and payments to* URSSAF *if I employ people.*

*We pay charges to a* syndic *as we are in a* copropriété. *The* syndic *didn't do what he was supposed to: he wasn't cleaning the corridors, or painting the hallways, and the intercom and alarm system didn't work. Moreover, there was lead piping which had been illegal for 10 years, and there was water leaking all over the place. I offered to replace it myself with plastic piping, but the* syndic *refused. Obviously, you couldn't run a hotel in this kind of environment. In the end I stopped paying rent along with the two other hotels in the building. We paid the rent into a blocked account – a* compte CARSAN – *while the case was going on; then the owners took us to court for non-payment of rent. The judge agreed that the water pipes had to be replaced and a lot of other work had to be done. He also said that the actual constitution of the* copropriété *was illegal because it didn't mention the* syndic. *The court sent an inspector to see all the work had been done; finally we each got €1,500 compensation.*

*Things in the South of France work slowly; it's an Italian system. The best advice I can give is to get a good accountant, because they will save you money. A good lawyer is also essential.*

## *Working from Home*

Laws on starting a business from home have changed. The Loi Dutreil of 2003 eased restrictions on registering a business at rented accommodation. You now have an absolute right to register your company at your home address for five years without having to ask your landlord's permission. The only requirement is to inform the landlord of your plans by registered letter. Company directors have the right to work from home under the same conditions as self-employed people, given below. Unless there is a clause in your lease preventing this, then you can continue to work from home indefinitely, and have your company registered at your home.

If you are self-employed, and you have registered as an *entreprise individuelle*, you do not require a *siège social* (registered office) in any case; you only need an *adresse d'entreprise*. If there is nothing in your rental contract or in the regulations of your *copropriété* preventing you, then you can carry on your professional activity from home as long as you:

- do not receive customers at home
- there are no deliveries of goods
- you are working from your principal residence.

For a long time the law prevented you from carrying on a self-employed profession from home without permission from the *préfecture* in towns with more than 10,000 inhabitants and in Paris, because every building is registered as having a specific use. Since 2003 it has been possible to work from home as long as you fulfil the three conditions above. If you cannot observe these conditions then an application for change of use will still have to be made to the *préfecture*. If there are difficulties with working from home then you could also try to obtain a *bail mixte* (see above), which allows you to carry on your business and live in the same premises.

When your business is registered at your home address, then you must effectively live there. From the point of view of taxation, one-third of your costs (electricity, telephone, etc.) can be deducted from your taxable profits. You will need to keep a clear separation between your private and business costs, e.g. by having two telephone lines. You may be able to deduct more if you can show that the nature of your job requires you to use more than one-third of your living space.

According to a survey carried out in 1999, 61% of businesses are started from home, and 29% from another address. The other 10% are started in so-called 'business nurseries' or *pépinières d'entreprise*.

A further improvement to the status of those working from home concerns a new measure to protect your principal residence from creditors, which is intended to come into force at the start of 2004. According to Article 8 of the Loi Dutreil you can now make a declaration of non-seizability (*déclaration d'insaisissabilité*) in front of a notaire that renders your home safe from creditors. The declaration is registered with the *bureau des hypothèques* (land registry) and has to be published in the local official journal. It is advisable but not compulsory to inform your partner about this action.

## BUYING AN EXISTING BUSINESS

Taking over an existing business in another country is undoubtedly a risky proposition, most of all if you have not run a similar business in your own country. Few foreigners take over a business in France and continue with it uninterrupted. Buying the shares in an existing business (e.g. a SARL) has disadvantages from the point of view of problems with existing debts, so it is generally preferable to start from scratch with something new. If one is taking over a business as a going concern then it is essential to have it valued by a professional. For any type of new enterprise a good *avocat* (lawyer) and an accountant (*expert-comptable*) are essential.

As a preliminary it is possible to find information on a company's capital, turnover and annual profit by entering the 9-figure SIREN number on the website: www.infogreffe.fr, or the name and address if you do not have the SIREN. It is also possible to have a report prepared through the same website on the company's future prospects. Some information is only given to other registered French businesses.

## *Fonds de Commerce*

A *fonds de commerce* is generally a shop selling goods or services. The French make a clear distinction between the building – *les murs* – that houses a businesses, and the more or less intangible elements that make up a business, known as the *fonds de commerce*. The basis of the business is the clientele that has been built up, which would not exist without the work that the owner has put in. It follows that if you are operating a franchise, then the clientèle are attracted by the brand name under which you operate. If you can prove that the shop has been successful because of your own efforts then you can make a case for selling it on as a *fonds de commerce*.

Because of the intangible nature of the *fonds de commerce*, its value is not that easy to assess. Apart from your customer base, there are other important elements included in the *fonds de commerce*, primarily the name of the business – *le nom commercial* – and the shop sign – *l'enseigne*. There may be other elements, such as the right to continue a lease – *droit au bail* – or contracts of various types with customers and suppliers. Even the guarantee that no one is going to set up a similar business in your area has a value to the buyer. The equipment – *le matériel* – needed to run the business, and the stock – *les marchandises* – is generally sold separately from the intangibles. They may be included if there are doubts about the seller's solvency, but as a rule a *fonds de commerce* is valued on the basis of the intangible elements. The movable equipment for running the business is usually included when you buy it. It is a principle that a *fonds de commerce* has a positive value; it only concerns assets, not liabilities.

A shop's value depends very much on its location. A greengrocer's has little future if it is next door to a supermarket. There is also a distinction between potential customers (*achalandise*) and the actual customer base (*clientèle*). Evidently, it would be advisable to use the services of an expert to make a valuation of a business's real value. There is a calculator available on: www.cession-commerce.fr to assess the value of businesses, which takes into account factors such as location, equipment, parking etc.

Because a *fonds de commerce* is something quite intangible, if the business does badly then your investment could simply disappear into thin air. The valuation of a shop is based on the assumption that the shop is open 300 days and 50 weeks a year. Turnover is calculated TTC (all taxes and TVA included).

| Percentages used to value *fonds de commerce* | |
| --- | --- |
| Animal beauty parlour | 60-90% x annual turnover |
| Antique shop (*brocante*) | 60-90% x annual turnover |
| Café-tabac | 90-100% x annual turnover |
| Delicatessen | 100-300 x daily receipts |
| Hotel | 80-400% x annual turnover |
| Restaurant | 50-200% x annual turnover |
| Small grocery | 80-130 x daily receipts |
| Wine bar | 200-300 x daily receipts |

A further way of checking on your potential income is to look at the average incomes of small businesses, information that is issued by the Fédération des Centres de Gestion Agréés every October. Figures are available for each département as well from the local Centre de Documentation at the Chambre de Commerce. The monthly incomes given below can refer to a couple rather than a single person.

| | |
| --- | --- |
| Campsite | 470 |
| Hôtel-restaurant | 1,150 |
| Small grocery | 1,400 |
| Bookshop/stationers | 1,700 |
| Restaurant | 1,820 |
| Carpenter | 1,900 |
| Boulangerie/pâtisserie | 2,030 |
| Electrician | 2,280 |
| Café-tabac | 2,340 |
| Plumber | 2,500 |
| Estate agent | 3,350 |
| Pharmacist | 7,800 |

## Income as a Percentage of Turnover After Costs

The following are figures for average incomes after the costs of raw materials and goods have been subtracted. All taxes, wages, rentals and remaining costs have to come out of these percentages. These relate to the Nord-Pas de Calais area, but can be applied to the whole of France. Note that if your percentage is less than half the average then your business is probably not going to prosper.

| | |
|---|---|
| Men's hairdresser | 63.6% |
| Animal beauty parlour | 53.4% |
| Painter & decorator | 42.8% |
| Roofer | 31.4% |
| Electrician | 31.2% |
| Builder | 30% |
| Plumber | 29.1% |
| Boulangerie/pâtisserie | 25.4% |
| Café | 23.1% |
| Florist | 21.2% |
| Restaurant | 19.7% |
| Antique shop | 18.1% |
| DIY shop | 16.7% |
| Greengrocer | 15.1% |
| Grocery | 12.6% |

## *Checklist on Assessing a Fonds de Commerce*

- O cost of lease, and likely rises in cost
- O previous three years of accounts
- O running costs
- O insurance
- O employees' contracts
- O stocks
- O credit to customers
- O working capital requirement

**It is most important to verify that the rent paid for the premises of the** *fonds* **is not about to be raised substantially.** If the rent appears low then this drives up the value of the *fonds,* but it also often means that the lessee has been paying the owner undeclared amounts.

## *Formalities of Purchase*

As far as French law goes, buying a *fonds de commerce* is much the same as buying a property. The seller will choose a notaire to handle the sale. The notaire can set their own level of fees; they are not fixed by the state. Their fees will generally add up to 2-3% (+TVA) of the sale price. You are required to nominate someone to hold the funds in a blocked account, i.e. a notaire or *avocat* or an *immobilier.* The pre-contract may be called a *compromis de cession* rather than a *compromis de vente.* The same types of pre-contracts exist as with immovable property: *promesse synallagmatique, promesse de vente, promesse d'achat.* There are complications if the *fonds de commerce* is run from a rented property. You will pay a certain amount for the right to the lease, the *droit au bail,* but the actual owner of the property may have put clauses in the lease restricting its transfer, or what kind of business can be run from the premises. There are always difficulties involved in changing the type of business that you run.

The *fonds de commerce* can also be subject to *vices cachés,* or non-apparent faults. An example could be a ban on altering the appearance of the property, or restrictions on licences. These are all matters that have to be looked at very carefully.

There are always clauses in the *compromis de vente* which allow the seller to retake possession of the *fonds de commerce* if the buyer does not pay the full price within a certain period of time. This is known as the *privilège du vendeur.* Equally, the seller is not permitted to start a similar business, or act as a manager, director, administrator or even investor in a business similar to the one he is selling within the same town. It is also illegal for the seller to use customer data for the benefit of a competitor. The seller's immediate family are also subject to the same rules.

Debts that affect the *fonds* must also be considered. You will need to be sure that the seller does not owe money to the tax or social security authorities, and that third parties do not have a lien (*nantissement*) on the equipment in the building. Liens have to be registered with the *conservation des hypothèques.* They can be checked on-line via www.infogreffe.fr for a small amount.

Once the actual *acte de cession de fonds de commerce* has been signed, it is registered with the nearest *centre des impôts* or tax office. The act has to be published in a local newspaper which carries such advertisements (known as a *journal d'annonces légales*) within 15 days. Both buyer and seller have to inform the local Registre des Commerces et Sociétés of the change to the status of the business, using the form *Mutation de Fonds de Commerce ou de Clientèle*. The clerk of the commercial court will have the details published in the national BODACC journal at the buyer's expense within one month. There is then 10 days for anyone who has a claim on the *fonds de commerce* to enter an opposition to the sale. The notaire or *avocat* will not release the blocked funds until all creditors have been paid off. Anybody can enter an opposition to a sale from the time the *fonds* or property is put on the market, and this has to be investigated by the lawyer. As a rule only the Trésor Public (tax receipt office) is likely to be fast enough to enforce payment of taxes owed to it (both *impôt sur le revenu* and *impôt sur les sociétés*). Other parties may not be aware that the business is being sold.

Transfer taxes are generally payable at a rate of 4.80%. No transfer tax is payable on sales of *fonds* for less than €23,000, but only a small tax of 15 euros. The *droit au bail* (right to the lease), lists of clients and sales of brands or patents that are actually being used, also attract 4.80% transfer tax, whether they are sold separately from the *fonds* or not. TVA of 19.6% is payable on the sale of equipment or merchandise pertaining to a *fonds*.

The transfer tax on a *fonds* breaks down somewhat differently from a normal property transaction:

|  | 0>€23,000 | €23,000-€107,000 | >€107,000 |
|---|---|---|---|
| National tax | €15 | 3.80% | 2.40% |
| Departmental tax |  | 0.60% | 1.40% |
| Communal tax |  | 0.40% | 1% |

There are possible reductions in transfer taxes if the business is located in a priority development area, i.e. a ZRU or ZFU in a town or a ZRR in the countryside, and in certain other situations. If you are taking over a bar or restaurant and reduce the drinks licence from Category 3 or 4 to Category 1 or 2, then you can benefit from a reduction.

# RENTING AN EXISTING BUSINESS

There is a further possibility, which is to rent an existing business and manage it for your own account while paying rent to the owner, known as a *contrat de location-gérance*. The person letting the business has to have been registered as a *commerçant* or *artisan* for at least 7 years, as well as having run the business they are letting for at least 2 years. The lessee registers as a business in the usual manner, and enjoys all the profits from the business. He has to continue any employment contracts that exist. The lessor is not permitted to set up a competing business.

The downside to this arrangement is that the Tribunal de Commerce can demand immediate payment of all debts relating to the business if it has reason to believe that there is risk of non-payment. In this respect the lessor and the lessee remain jointly liable until all debts have been paid off within a period of 6 months. The lessor remains the owner of the *fonds de commerce*, and is responsible for renegotiating the lease on the property, if it is rented.

# FRANCHISES

Franchise businesses exist as anywhere else. The idea is to sell a product or service according to a model that has been laid down by the creator of the product or service. The advantage is that you have a well-known product and you receive logistical support and training. You pay a sum on entry to the franchiser or an annual percentage of your profits. There are a lot of pros and cons with franchises and you would be best advised to make a comparison between how your business would fare without the franchise and with it. There is a national French federation of franchisers, the Fédération Française de la Franchise. You should first check that your prospective franchiser is a member of this organisation. See the website www.franchise-fff.com.

# Financing your Business

# BUYING FOREIGN CURRENCY FOR YOUR BUSINESS ABROAD

If you're starting a business abroad for the first time, you've probably got enough to do without worrying about exchange rates. You've found your ideal location and secured the price of your property, and now all you have to do is look forward to making a successful start. Right? Well, partly. Somewhere along the line you will have to change your pounds into euros, and that's where even the best business plan can fall apart if you don't plan ahead. Whether you're importing and exporting goods, buying a property outright or buying from plan in installments, protecting yourself against exchange rate fluctuations can save you hundreds, if not thousands of pounds.

As you are no doubt aware, foreign exchange markets are by nature extremely volatile and can be subject to dramatic movements over a very short space of time. In some ways it's all too easy to leave your currency exchange to the last minute and hope that the exchange rates fall in your favour. But it makes good business sense to protect your capital and save yourself paying a lot more than you bargained for.

As a matter of course, many people will approach their banks to sort out their currency, without realising that there are more cost-effective alternatives in the marketplace. There are a number of independent commercial foreign exchange brokers who can offer better rates and a more personal, tailored service. Their dealers will explain the various options open to you and keep you informed of any significant changes in the market. They will also guide you through every step of the transaction so that you are ultimately in control and able to make the most of your money.

If you're still not convinced of how planning ahead can help you, take a look at the following example.

In recent history the euro stood at 1.54 and within six months had fallen to 1.38. Therefore, in just 6 months the cost of a €200,000 office location would have increased by over £15,000!

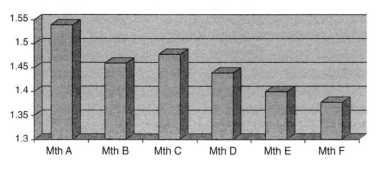

Although changes in the economic climate may be beyond your control, protecting your capital against the effect of these changes isn't.

There are a number of options available to you:

- **Spot Transactions – Buy now, pay now.** These are ideal for anyone who needs their currency straight away as the currency is purchased today at the current rate. However, if you have time to spare before your payments are due, it may be wiser to consider a Forward Transaction.

- **Forward Transactions – Buy now, pay later.** These allow you to secure a rate for up to 18 months in advance to protect yourself against any movements in the market. A small deposit holds the rate until the balance becomes due when the currency contract matures. This option not only protects against possible drops in the exchange rate but also gives you the security of the currency you need at a guaranteed cost, regardless of fluctuations in the market.

- **Limit Orders** allow you to place an order in the market for a desired exchange rate. This has the advantage of protecting you against negative exchange movements whilst still allowing you to gain from a positive movement. Your request is entered into the system and an automatic currency purchase is triggered once the market hits your specified rate.

With the stress of organising your business abroad you may find that you simply don't have the time to shop around for the best exchange rate, but that's where a reputable currency company can really come into its own. With specialists in the field ready to explain all the pitfalls and possibilities to you in layman's terms and guide you through each stage of the transaction, you can be sure that your currency solutions will be perfectly tailored to your needs.

*Currencies Direct* has been helping people to understand the overseas property markets since 1996. Specialising in providing foreign exchange solutions tailored to clients' individual financial situations, they offer a cost-effective and user-friendly alternative to the high-street banks.

With offices in the UK, Australia and Spain, *Currencies Direct* is always on hand to help you. For more information on how you can benefit from their commercial rates of exchange and friendly, professional service, call the *Currencies Direct* office in London on 020-7813 0332 or visit their website at www.currenciesdirect.com.

## CHAPTER SUMMARY

- **French Banks.** The banking system is rather backward by UK or US standards, and banks are not so keen to lend money.
- **Non-resident Accounts.** You can open an account from the UK.
- **Credit Cards.** There are no credit cards as such in France, but deferred debit cards.
- **Overdrafts.** Be very careful never to go overdrawn without the agreement of your bank.
- **Importing Currency.** You can save a lot on exchange costs by using a specialised company to import currency.
- **Grants.** There are only limited grants available for starting a business, and they are counted towards business profit.
- **Loans.** There are numerous soft loans available handed out by local bodies but controlled by central government.
- **Incentives.** There are special incentives if you start a business in an economically backward area.
- **Mortgages.** French properties can generally only be mortgaged with French lenders.
- **Using Mortgages to Raise Capital.** The French authority discourage mortgaging of property to finance business. You can protect your home from creditors as a sole trader.
- **Mortgage Fees.** Mortgage arrangement fees are relatively high in France – up to 6%. Both the lender and the notaire will charge fees.
- **Mortgage Insurance.** Insurance is not officially compulsory but is taken out in almost all cases.

# BANKING

There are several types of bank in France: clearing banks such as *Crédit Lyonnais*; co-operative banks such as *Crédit Agricole*; corporate banks, e.g. *BNP Paribas;* and savings banks or *Caisses d'Epargne.* The *Crédit Agricole* has an immense advantage in that it has the largest number of branches, 7,500 in France alone. The departmental branches of CA function as separate banks and issue their own shares. Other co-operative banks include the *Crédit Mutuel* and *Banque Populaire*; if you want to take out a mortgage with a co-operative bank you are usually required to buy shares in the bank, but not if you just want a cheque account. The post office, *La Poste*, has 17,000 branches in France and longer opening hours than banks, so it could be convenient to have a post office account, or *Compte Courant Postal (CCP)*.

The French bank you choose will depend a lot on whether there is a branch near you, and whether you need specialised services. It is worth finding out if there is anyone who speaks English in your branch; where there are large concentrations of English-speakers some banks are trying to recruit English-speaking staff.

The Calvados region of Crédit Agricole has now started a service called Britline (with offices in Caen, Normandy), which allows you to open a non-resident bank account in France by post (☎ 02 31 55 67 89; fax 02 31 55 63 99; e-mail vincent.gray@ca-calvados.fr; www.britline.com). Britline sometimes has a stall at French property fairs in the UK. Britline cannot open a business account for you. The only exception is an account for a Société Civile Immobilière, a type of company specifically set up to own property.

Below is a list of the major French banks with their websites:

Barclays Bank SA: www.barclays.fr
Banque Populaire: www.banquepopulaire.fr
BNP Paribas: www.bnpparibas.fr
Britline: www.britline.com
Caixa Bank: www.caixabank.fr
Crédit Agricole: www.credit-agricole.fr; http://www.ca-[name of department].fr
Crédit Commercial de France: www.ccf.com
Crédit du Nord: www.credit-du-nord.fr
Crédit Lyonnais: www.creditlyonnais.com
Lloyds Bank SA: www.lloydstsbiwm.com
Société Générale: www.socgen.com

It is best to wait until you know where you are going to live before you open a bank account. Opening an account prematurely can influence your judgement if you are looking for property.

While you are still looking for property, you can use a cashpoint or credit card. Credit cards in France operate with a chip rather than a magnetic strip. You need to know your PIN code otherwise you may not be able to use your card in shops.

If you are staying in one of the major cities you may be able to open an account with a branch of a British bank. Barclays is the best represented. Lloyds has branches in Paris, Lyon, Cannes and Marseille; HSBC owns Crédit Commercial de France. NatWest has no branches in France. British banks in France have to operate under French law; they mainly target wealthy expats with a lot of money to invest. The exception is Crédit Commercial de France owned by HSBC.

## Credit Cards

Strictly speaking, there is no such thing as a credit card in France because of the laws against usury, rather there are charge cards with a deferred debit. Every 30 days the amount you owe is automatically debited from your bank account, meaning that you may pay for something the day after you bought it. In the UK, credit is for 30-60 days, in France for 0-30 days. If you want to defer payment you will need to open a sub-account which allows you to borrow money at a lower interest rate than you would pay in the UK on a credit card. There is an annual charge for credit cards in France. A Gold Card costs about €90 a year.

The national French debit card, the Carte Bleue (CB) can only be used in France. If you need a credit card that functions abroad, you can ask for Carte Bleue/Visa or Mastercard. You are expected to clear your bill at the end of each month, unless you have arranged to borrow money.

## Bank Accounts

Opening a bank account is not difficult. If you are resident in France then you simply take along your passport, *carte de séjour* (or equivalent) and proof of your fiscal address in France. For non-residents the bank will ask to see your last three months' salary slips. The basic form of bank account is the *compte de chèque* which comes with a cheque book. If the bank thinks that you are not a good bet because of some previous misdemeanour, or because you cannot prove your income, they may only give you a *compte de dépôt*, an inconvenient form of account that only allows you to take out cash and has no cheque book or cashpoint card. If at the end of the day you cannot find a bank to open an account for you, then you can go to the Banque de France (there are branches in big towns) who will assign a bank to you.

When you open a bank account you will be offered a Carte Bleue, originally conceived as a substitute for writing cheques. The CB is a cashpoint card which can also function as either a debit card or credit card; you choose one of the two. CB also stands for *carte bancaire*, i.e. any kind of credit card. CBs work with a chip rather than magnetic strip; you key in your PIN number when making transactions in shops, so you need to remember it.

As well as the bank's own number, there is one central number for reporting lost bank cards: 01 45 67 84 84.

**Resident and Non-Resident Accounts.** Whether you are considered resident or non-resident from the bank's point of view, depends on where you are fiscally resident, i.e. where your centre of interests lies. If you spend more than 183 days a year in France you will normally pay your taxes there, so you are fiscally resident. As a non-resident you can only open a *compte non-résident*. Correspondence will be sent to you in your home country. It is also possible to open an account by post through a French bank branch in the UK (mainly in London). After choosing your branch in France, you need to supply a reference from your UK bank, a legalised copy of your signature, photocopies of the main pages of your passport, and a draft in euros to start you off. It is generally far simpler to open an account in person in France after talking to the local bank staff.

## Banking Practices

Banking services are not as sophisticated or as liberal in France as in the UK or US; banks are not at all keen to lend money in a hurry. The main rule to remember is that you must never go into the red without prior arrangement, otherwise you risk becoming an *interdit bancaire*. It is also worth bearing in mind that if you go into the red any standing orders that you have will automatically be stopped, so your telephone and electricity could suddenly be cut off.

When you open your account you opt for monthly or fortnightly bank statements, or whatever arrangement suits you. There are charges for most transactions, apart from statements. You can authorise utility companies to debit your account automatically (*prélèvement automatique*) for bill payment, but this is not obligatory. This is not the same as a standing order (*ordre permanent/virement automatique*). With the internet you can see what is going on with your account. The antiquated French version of internet, Minitel, is still used for some on-line banking services.

Bank opening hours are a favourite gripe with foreigners in France; there is a law that prevents banks opening more than five days a week, so your bank may close on Mondays. Very small branches (*permanences*) in country areas may only open one morning a week. The internet is making things easier.

## Cheques

Cheques are used for half of all financial transactions in France; there are no cheque guarantee cards, but you can be asked for other identification. Cheques are written out in a similar way to those in the UK or USA, with the information positioned differently. Your bank will send you your first cheque book once there are funds in your account. French cheques are not negotiable to a third person. The basic form of cheque is the *chèque barré*, which is only payable to the payee (*destinataire*); the bank has to inform the tax inspectors if you want to use open cheques. When you pay a cheque into your account or cash it then you sign it on the back (*endosser le chèque*).

**Bouncing Cheques.** If you write a 'wooden cheque' (*chèque de bois*) you will be given 30 days to rectify the situation. The Banque de France is informed immediately, and you are not allowed to write any further cheques until matters are resolved. You not only have to pay money into the account to cover it, but also a fine of 15% of the amount that goes to the French treasury. There is also a form to fill in, declaring that you have dealt with the problem or '*incident*'. If the money is not paid you are put on a Banque de France blacklist, and are barred from writing any cheques in France for five years. Bank cards and cheques have to be surrendered.

A cheque is considered the equivalent of cash and cannot be cancelled, unless it has been lost or stolen or is deemed to be fraudulent by the bank. A police report has to be submitted to the bank in such cases.

## Business Accounts

Everyone agrees that you should have a separate business account – *compte d'entreprise* – from your personal account. If you are self-employed you require a *compte professionnelle*. Actually persuading the bank to let you open one may be less simple than you might expect. You need to show your creditworthiness, and try to get the backing of a chamber of commerce. A further consideration is that charges are higher on business accounts than on current accounts, and the more money that goes through your account the more you pay. There are risks in mixing private and business finances, so there is no alternative to opening a separate account.

## Bank Loans

Obtaining a loan is not an easy process. French banks lend less readily than British ones, and require a great deal of supporting information before they will consider you. As a basic principle, banks will only lend up to 70% of the cost of a *fonds de commerce* or building. You will need to find the other 30% yourself. The greater your *apport personnel* – the amount you can put up front – the more readily the bank will lend. This is not all, because you will also have to pay all the taxes, fees and costs associated with the purchase of a property or business, as well as for any stock. You should therefore budget on putting up 50% of the total cost yourself.

To approach the bank you need to put together a *dossier de demande de prêt*, a request for a loan, something that has to be done using an accountant, lawyer or other professional. You should also by all means use the services of an organisation such as Entreprendre en France (www.entreprendre-en-france.fr) to back you up. If you have been unemployed in France you can call on the Association pour le Droit à l'Initiative Economique (ADIE – www.adie.org). You can also get backing from a Boutique de Gestion, whether you have been unemployed or not (see in phone book). Your dossier will include:

○ 3-year provisional accounts
○ plan for financing your business over 3 years
○ cash-flow projections for 3 years
○ projections for working capital requirement
○ your CV with your skills and experience
○ market study
○ type of business structure

At the end of the day, your financial projections have to show that you are going to generate enough profit to pay yourself a salary and repay your creditors. Naturally, your bank will want to know everything about your prospective business. They will be happier to lend you money if you can show a list of customers who have said they are going to do business with you. The banks also like to see that you have done some market research, an *étude de marché*. One popular way to do this is to hand out little questionnaires, asking whether you would be interested in buying such-and-such a product. Bringing in a market research company is not really worth the money. You can ask at the Chambre de Commerce if they have existing market studies. The DTI in London is another place where one can find information on French consumer trends; see www.uktradeinvest.gov.uk.

Bank loans are granted for the period of time that it takes to pay off, or write off an item of equipment. Therefore, for a computer the loan is for 3 years, for furniture 10 years, for buildings 20 years. For more information it is worth obtaining a brochure from the Fédération des Centres de Gestion Agréés, entitled *Obtenez de l'Argent de Votre Banquier* ('Get Money from your Bank' – see www.fcga.fr). It pays to stay on good terms with your bank. From time to time you should sound them out about extending further credit, but at the same time open an account with another bank just in case things go sour.

# THREE-YEAR CASH-FLOW PROJECTION

The document that your prospective lender will need to see is the *prévisionnel financier*, which should state in detail how you are going to finance your business, and what profits you expect to make. You will need to demonstrate your Working Capital Requirement or *Besoin de Fonds Roulement*. The profitability of your business can be shown by comparing your requirements with your resources.

|  | Year 1 | Year 2 | Year 3 |
|---|---|---|---|
| **Long-Term Requirements** | | | |
| Start-up Costs | | | |
| Investments | | | |
| Working Capital Requirement | | | |
| Distribution of Profits | | | |
| Loan Repayments | | | |
| | | | |
| **Total Requirements** | | | |
| | | | |
| **Long-Term Resources** | | | |
| Own Funds | | | |
| Net Profits | | | |
| Depreciation | | | |
| Grants/Subsidies | | | |
| Loans | | | |
| | | | |
| **Total Resources** | | | |

It is generally suggested that you make three different financial projections: a worst-case, average and best-case scenario. If you cannot survive the worst-case scenario then the plan is probably not going to work.

# IMPORTING CURRENCY

When buying property or a business in France, you will under normal circumstances have to pay in euros, the local currency. In the days of foreign exchange controls, before 1974, it was usual to take a suitcase full of pound notes over to France to pay for your property. Thanks to the Single Market, you can take as much cash as you like with you, but there is no advantage in doing so, and it is certainly risky. If you take more than €8,000 in cash with you into France you are required to declare it. Taking a large amount of cash with you is not only risky; the French customs authorities might also become suspicious of you.

Nowadays currency is normally sent using electronic transfer; the SWIFT system is the most well-known. There are charges involved at both ends, so you need to know who is paying for them, and how much the receiving bank in France is likely to charge. The receiving bank charge should be nominal.

Since the UK has not yet joined the Euro, anyone buying property or business abroad is confronted with the possibility that a percentage of their money is going to disappear into the pockets of a high street bank. Fortunately, this need not be the case, since a number of specialist foreign exchange companies offer services that rival those of the high street banks in terms of price and service.

A specialised company such as *Currencies Direct* (Hanover House, 73-74 High Holborn, London WC1V 6LR; ☎ 020-7813 0332; fax 020-7419 7753; www.currenciesdirect.com) can help in a number of ways, by offering better exchange rates than banks, without charging commission, and giving you the possibility of 'forward buying', i.e. agreeing on the rate that you will pay at a fixed date in the future, or with a 'limit order', i.e. waiting until the rate you want is reached before making the transaction. For those who prefer to know exactly how much money they will need for their property purchase, forward buying is the best solution, since you no longer have to worry about the movements of the pound against the euro working against you. Payments can be made in one lump sum or on a regular basis. For example, it is usual when purchasing a new-build property to pay in four instalments, so-called 'stage payments'.

There is a further possibility, which is to use the services of a law firm in the UK to transfer the money. They can hold the money for you until the exact time that you need it. However, remember that law firms will also use the services of a foreign currency exchange service themselves, so you may be better off going to a company like *Currencies Direct* yourself to avoid excess legal fees.

## WHERE TO FIND CAPITAL

The bank will need to know where your contribution to the capital is going to come from. Naturally, it cannot come from other bank loans. The first place to look is your own immediate family. The expression 'love money' has now entered the French language; banks will be favourably impressed if your nearest and dearest are willing to stake their assets on your business.

The state has various schemes in place to guarantee bank loans up to a certain amount (65% is typical). Local organisations have their own schemes in place as well as offering so-called *prêts d'honneur* – a loan you swear to pay back. In Paris, for example, Paris Initiatives Entreprises will lend 4,000 to 30,000 euros at zero interest without requiring guarantees. Regional bodies generally do not lend more than €30,500 without guarantees. There are also *prêts bonifiés*, loans at a low interest rate backed by the state, that are offered by a number of organisations (see box below).

An important organisation that can advise you on where to look for loans and other assistance is *France Initiative Réseau* (www.fir.asso.fr) which runs 275 *Plates-Formes d'Initiative Locale* (PFIL). If you are more ambitious and want to invest on a larger scale, then you could consider using the services of a specialised company, such as Subsidies in France (www.subsidies-in-france.com), which helps businesses obtain all the subsidies and loans that are available, including those from the European Union.

For general information about grants and loans, look at the DATAR website: www.datar.gouv.fr, through which you can find the organisation relevant to you. French chambers of commerce in other countries will have some information on business incentives, although they mainly deal with big investors; addresses are given in chapter 3, Procedures.

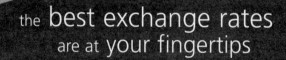

**BDPME.** The French state provides loans through the organisation *Banque du Développement des Petites et Moyennes Entreprises* (www.bdpme.fr). There is a variety of loans, all of them come with the condition attached that you have to raise the equivalent sum yourself from banks. The main loan is the *Prêt à la Création d'Entreprise* (PCE), which is worth €3,000 to €8,000. Your own resources that you bring to the business cannot exceed €45,000. The loan is given to new businesses for the first three years of their life and is intended to be spent on financing intangible parts of a business, such as the requirement for working capital. It cannot be used to buy a building, but could be used to acquire a *fonds de commerce* (business goodwill). It is repayable within 5 years.

If you are more ambitious you can apply for a *Contrat de Développement Création et Reprise* (i.e. to create or develop your business) from the BDPME. In this case you can obtain between 15,000 and 76,000 euros, to be paid back over 6 years. The amount is not more than the money you have already raised yourself, including bank loans. If you are taking over a business, there is more money available: 38,000 to 228,000 euros but the amount is no more than 40% of the loans you have obtained. It is a condition of bigger loans that you have already been approved for a bank loan, or that you have other investors backing you. The loan is repayable within the same timescale as your bank loan, which could be 7 years.

**Women entrepreneurs.** There are initiatives to help women start up a business. France has a Minister for Women (www.droits-femmes.gouv.fr). Information is available from *Initielles,* which assists with start-ups in the Midi-Pyrénées region; see http://initielles.f2g.net. The state guarantees loans made to female entrepreneurs through the *Fonds de Garantie à l'Initiative des Femmes (FGIF).* The loans range form €5,000 to €38,112 and run for 2-7 years. FGIF only guarantees up to 70% of the loan. The loan has to be applied for at the time of start-up and covers requirements for the first 5 years of operation. To find out more go to the websites: www.franceactive.org and www.fir.asso.fr.

# GRANTS

Finding out-and-out grants for your business is not that easy, unless you are going to create jobs in an area of high unemployment. The first person to ask is the local *maire* and the Chambre de Commerce. Grants are generally handled by the Conseil Régional – the Regional Council – via various local organisations. It is a matter of finding out which one to approach.

The best-known grants are the ones given to prospective owners of *gîtes* and *chambres d'hôtes*. Grants for both are distributed by the Conseil Général through Gîtes de France, which is organised on a regional basis. The amounts available vary considerably. If you are lucky Gîtes de France may match the amount you spend. One British owner in Normandy who had spent €3,600 on conversion work was told by Gîtes de France that the work couldn't possibly have cost that little and was given €4,500 in matching funds. In other areas, the département may have little money to hand out.

There are conditions attached: you have to agree to allow Gîtes de France to handle the letting and publicity for 10 years during the summer in return for a cut of your takings of some 15%. It has the final say in what kind of facilities your *gîtes* will have, and grades your premises in its catalogue with one to three *épis* or wheatears. If you sell the property within 10 years then the grant will be repayable.

The first person to approach when looking for grants is the local mayor. The local Chambre de Commerce/Métiers/Agricole will also be helpful. If your initiative concerns tourism, then you should go to the *Syndicat d'Initiative* in rural areas. Their function is to promote all kinds of small businesses and investments as well as tourism. There are grants available for renovating listed buildings or buildings with special historical associations, but any renovations will be subject to stringent requirements. Whatever kind of renovation you plan to do, all the plans and estimates must be approved first before any work is started, otherwise you will not receive the grant. Grants cannot be taken into account in your financial projections because of the length of time that they take to come through. There are loans from ADEME if you do work on your property to make it more energy-efficient. See www.ademe.fr.

# SOURCES OF GRANTS, LOANS AND INFORMATION

**This is a list of bodies that can help you find grants and soft loans.**

| | |
|---|---|
| ADEME – www.ademe.fr | Loans and advice for efficient energy use |
| AGEFIPH – www.agefiph.asso.fr | Loans for handicapped business creators |
| Association des Banques Populaires pour la Création d'Entreprise | Soft loans |
| Association Love Money – www.love-money.org | Investors clubs |
| Association pour Favoriser la Création d'Entreprise (AFACE) | Loans; contact Chambre de Commerce |
| Banque de Développement des PME – www.bdpme.fr | Loans |
| CIGALES – www.cigales.asso.fr | Local investors clubs |
| Conseil Général | Departmental government |
| Conseil Régional | Regional government |
| Crédit Coopératif – www.credit-cooperatif.fr | Loans to cooperatives and similar |
| DRIRE – www.drire.gouv.fr | Gives assistance to businesses at local level. |
| Euro-Info Centre – www.industrie.gouv.fr/eic | European grants information |
| France Active – www.francactive.org | If you create jobs for the disadvantaged |
| France Initiative Réseau – www.fir.asso.fr | Loans and assistance |
| Micro Credits – www.adie.org | EU-backed loans to very small businesses |
| Réseau Entreprendre – www.reseau-entreprendre.org | Loans |
| Société Financière de la NEF – www.lanef.com | Loans for socially useful businesses. |

**Free advice.** The French regions control funds known as FRAC (*Fonds Régional d'Aide aux Conseils*) which are intended to encourage small businesses to use the services of professional advisers. The long-term FRAC grants cover 50% of the cost of the advisers, up to a limit of €30,000. The short-term grant covers 80% of the costs up to a limit of €3,800. Enquire at the Chambre de Commerce.

*Small local grants.* The different departments and regions have small grants available for business start-ups. If yours is the first shop of its kind in a village with fewer than 2,000 people then you can apply for a grant to help with interest payments on a loan; this is the *aide à l'installation des commerçants en zone rurale.* The amount can be as little as £100. There are also grants for artisans, such as the *aide à la creation des bâtiments artisanaux.* It is a general condition of grants that you are starting your first business.

Even if you do not qualify there may still be hope for you. The Conseil Régional of Aquitaine will give outright grants to new businesses if no other grant or loan can be found, known as a *Bourse d'Initiative à la Création d'Entreprise* which comes to a lump sum of €1,524. There is a lot of paperwork involved, and **the grant is treated as part of your business profits**, so you will have to pay social security charges and tax on the amount.

There is no guarantee that you will get a grant; it depends on how much money Paris has made available to the local distributing body, but with luck you should get something.

## SPECIAL DEVELOPMENT ZONES

Certain areas qualify for tax-breaks and other incentives to new business. In the first instance it is worth finding out whether your region is considered to be 'lagging behind' or 'in difficulty' as regards the European Social Fund. France is the biggest beneficiary of the ESF, in particular Objective 2 (zones that are in decline) which covers most of the country. However, EU funds are only available to legally registered companies, not to individuals or sole traders. The local Euro Info office can help you find out if you could qualify. See www.travail.gouv.fr/fse and www.industrie.gouv.fr/eic.

France has a whole range of zones beginning with Z where favourable tax regimes exist to encourage businesses to set up. The modalities are complex, and can only be summarised here. Some of them include:

**Zone Franche Urbaine.** Exemption from employer's part of social security charges for 5 years, if you employ at least one full-time salaried employee, on the part of salary below 1.5 times the minimum wage. Exemption from *taxe foncière* (land tax) on buildings and from *taxe professionnelle* for 5 years. Exemption from income tax/corporation tax up to a limit of €61,000 per taxpayer.

**Zone de Redynamisation Urbaine** and **Zone de Revitalisation Rurale.** Exemption from employer's part of social security charges on 1.5 times minimum wage for 12 months.

## FINDING INVESTORS

If you start out with a limited company, a SARL/EURL and other companies mentioned in chapter 4 (but not an *entreprise individuelle*), then you are in a position to sell shares in your company to investors. There are tax incentives for investors, and tax write-offs if they lose their money. There are also venture capital companies (*sociétés capital-risque*), who are prepared to back particularly promising business ideas. Private investors can agree to guarantee a certain amount in loans and then only liable up the amount they have guaranteed. You can also consider 'Business Angels', groups of private investors looking for opportunities. See www.franceangels.org. Note, however, that private investors are not that interested in rural businesses, but rather in cutting-edge hi-tech and internet firms.

A further possibility is to open a *compte courant d'associés*. This is a bank account opened in the name of a shareholder or partner in a company, into which partners pay money to fund the company. They can charge interest. These are loans that can be called in at any time, unless the statutes of the company state otherwise. Such an account cannot be opened for an *entreprise individuelle*.

As in the UK, there are also local clubs of investors who may be willing to support your enterprise. There are over 100 clubs

called *Cigales* which make small investments in new businesses
(www.cigales.asso.fr). Many départements also have *Clubs des Créateurs
d'Entreprises* who will give you support if not actual investment. There
is a directory of organisations that invest in small businesses, the
*Annuaire des Investisseurs Régionaux,* which should be available in your
local Centre de Documentation or public library. It can be ordered via
www.annuaire-des-investisseurs-regionaux.com.

# MORTGAGES

The French authorities discourage home-owners from mortgaging their property in order to raise finance to run a business. Since
2004 **sole traders only** can register an act of unseizability – *acte
d'insaissabilité* – with the land registry which makes it impossible for
creditors to seize your principal residence. This may not help you to
borrow money against your home if there is no way for the lenders to
get their hands on it if you default.

The following is a brief summary of French mortgages. For a more
detailed explanation see *Buying a House in France* (publ. Vacation
Work). It is highly advisable to have an offer of a loan before you look
for a property in France, whether you are buying something new or
planning to borrow money to renovate. A French mortgage lender can
provide you with a statement guaranteeing you a loan (*certificat de
garantie*) for which there may be a charge. You don't have to take up
the offer, but you will at least be ready to sign a preliminary purchase
agreement if you see a property you like.

The only type of mortgage – *hypothèque* – available in France is
the repayment mortgage. Fixed-rate mortgages are by far the most
common; it is also possible to mix fixed and variable rates. The
mortgage lender does not hold the deeds to your property as security;
these remain with the notaire. Your mortgage is registered with the
local *bureau des hypothèques,* and there is a fee to have the mortgage
removed once you have paid it off.

## *UK and French Mortgages*

There are two possibilities: one is to remortgage your UK property, the other is to take out a mortgage with a French bank using a French property as security. UK-based banks will not lend money on foreign properties; the French branches of UK banks operating under French law in France will, as well as one or two other specialised UK lenders.

Remortgaging or taking out a mortgage in the UK has advantages; fewer questions will be asked, and you will be able to borrow more than you would in France. Since UK properties are likely to go up in value faster than those in France, there is rather less of a risk for the bank. If your income is in sterling, then it makes sense to have a UK mortgage. It is equally possible to borrow a smaller sum for a short period to cover the cost of buying your French property.

The charges involved with setting up a French mortgage (*frais d'hypothèque*) are high, but you can benefit from French mortgage interest relief if you pay taxes in France. French banks rarely lend more than 80% of the value of a property; 70% is a realistic amount. The maximum term is normally 15 years.

### *The Loi Scrivener and Protection for Borrowers*

Borrowers are generally well protected, but in spite of the strict rules defaults among foreigners are common, mainly because the borrower has spent too much doing up a dilapidated property, or hasn't worked out their business plan well. In the case of default, the property is compulsorily sold at auction and will probably fetch considerably less than if you had sold it yourself.

The lending organisation must first state in writing: the lender's name and address, the type of loan, the property that is to be acquired, the rate of interest, total repayment and the time period of the loan, and also that the property purchase is dependent on obtaining the loan. In the case of variable rate mortgages, the interest rate taken as a reference point, and the actual repayment rate, are stated. There is a *délai de réflexion* (cooling-off period) of 10 days before the offer of the loan can be accepted and any funds transferred. The acceptance can be sent by ordinary post. The offer of credit remains open for 30 days, during which time the borrower can look at other offers.

There is a useful French mortgage calculator on www.french-property.com (in English). Most of the general property sites mentioned in chapter 5 have mortgage calculators, but these are entirely in French. French regulations mean that your monthly repayments cannot exceed 33% of your net income; if you are already repaying other loans these have to be subtracted first. At the same time, the costs and taxes associated with the property purchase – 12% to 15% of the purchase price – will also be taken into account. Mortgage lenders' websites will give you a rough idea of how much you can afford to pay (see www.adomos.com; www.guideducredit.fr; www.patrimoine.com).

## Charges and Procedures Involved with French Mortgages

The lender will charge approximately 1% of the loan as a fee for arranging the mortgage (*frais de dossier*). There are further fees for valuing the property, arranging insurance, and then the notaire's own fees which add up to 1-2% of the value of the mortgage. All in all you can expect to pay some 5.9% on a loan of €50,000, or 3.5% on €200,000.

There is another type of loan, the *privilège de prêteur de deniers* (PPD) – a lender's guarantee – that is not subject to 0.615% registration tax. The PPD cannot be used to borrow money for construction or renovation costs, or for anything other than buying an existing property.

## Mortgage Insurance

Mortgage lenders generally insist that you take out death/disability insurance – *assurance décès/invalidité*. The type of insurance is *assurance décès temporaire,* running for the lifetime of the mortgage contract. If you die or are incapitated the mortgage is paid off. These are not life insurance contracts: the premiums are lost and there is no payout at the end.

## Mortgage Brokers/Advisors

*Abbey National France:* 70 rue Saint Sauveur, 59046 Lille Cedex; ☎03 20 18 18 89; fax 03 20 18 19 20; www.abbey-national.fr. Call themselves 'gentlemen-prêteurs'. Branches in Bordeaux, Grenoble,

Marseille, Montpellier, Paris, Toulouse.

*Axa-Baud:* 5 rue d'Auray, 56150 Baud, Morbihan; ☎02 97 51 01 45; e-mail agence.herrmann@axa.fr. Mortgages, loans and insurance. Based in Brittany.

*Banque Woolwich:* 9 rue Boudreau, 75009 Paris; 01 42 68 44 33; e-mail mortgage.abroad@woolwich.tm.fr. Or call UK hotline: 020-8298 4400, and ask for brochure *Helpful Hints on Housebuying in France.*

*Barclays France:* Champs Elysées International Branch, 6 rond-point des Champs Elysées, 75008 Paris; ☎01 44 95 13 80; fax 01 42 25 73 60; e-mail champsint.france@barclays.co.uk.

*Barclays France:* Côte d'Azur International Centre, 2 rue Alphonse Karr, 06000 Nice; ☎04 93 82 68 02; fax 04 93 88 58 95; e-mail cotedazur.int@barclays.co.uk.

*Charles Hamer:* Independent advisors on French mortgage finance since 1998. 87 Park St, Thame, Oxon OX9 3HX; ☎01844-218956; fax 01844-261886.

*Conti Financial Services:* 204 Church Rd, Hove, Sussex BN3 2DJ; ☎0800-970 0985 *or* 01273-772811; fax 01273-321269; e-mail enquiries@conti-financial.com; www.overseasandukfinance.com. Well-established independent mortgage brokers.

*Michael Hackney:* Independent mortgage broker who was MD of Abbey National France for four years; tel/fax 01869-277314.

*Mortgage France:* La Fraye Touarte, Rte de Gréolières CD6, 06480 La Colle sur Loup; ☎04 93 32 13 95; e-mail info@mortgagefrance.com; www.mortgagefrance.com. See interview opn p. 65.

*Templeton Associates:* French mortgage and finance experts, with offices in UK and France; ☎01225-42282; www.templeton-france.com.

### Foreign Currency Exchange Service

*Currencies Direct:* Hanover House, 73-74 High Holborn, London WC1V 6LR; ☎020-7813 0332; fax 020-7419 7753; www.currenciesdirect.com

# Part II

## Running a Business in France

BUSINESS ETIQUETTE AND CORRESPONDENCE

TAX, SOCIAL SECURITY AND OTHER MATTERS

EMPLOYING STAFF

MARKETING YOUR BUSINESS

SELLING ON

# Business Etiquette and Correspondence

## CHAPTER SUMMARY

- **Assume Nothing.** Be prepared to adjust to a different social and business environment.
- **French Formality.** French society is rather formal and respectful behaviour is the norm.
- **Language is Key.** Make every effort to learn to speak French correctly. Your success may depend on it.
- **Meeting and Greeting.** Learn how to address people, and when to shake hands or kiss.
- **Negotiations.** You must prepare your arguments very carefully but be prepared to be flexible.
- **Conversation.** Say what you think, and don't joke too much.
- **Chauvinism.** Try to understand the reasons for French nationalism and do not take offence if the French criticise your country.
- **Writing Letters.** Acquire a book on writing letters in French and pay very careful attention to opening and closing letters and e-mails.

One of the more intimidating aspects of moving to France is knowing how to behave socially and what to talk about. A good knowledge of the French language is of fundamental importance, and will take you a long way into being accepted by your social circle. French society is generally more formal than in Britain and the US. The French in particular draw a very clear distinction between people whom they already know and those whom they have not been introduced to. They are generally wary of strangers. This may not be very apparent on the surface, but it is important to understand that you are in an environment unlike the one you have been used to. There are regional variations; as a general rule, people are less formal in the south of France, and also in the northwest, where there has been a lot of Flemish influence.

# ETIQUETTE

## *The French Language*

The French are exceedingly proud and possessive about their language, which is the primary vehicle for spreading French culture around the world. The 20th century saw French lose its predominant position as the international language of diplomacy. The younger generation of French have given up some of their feelings of snobbery about their language; they are happy to use British and American expressions, which are creeping into the media more and more, while the Académie Française regularly issues edicts banning these linguistic intruders.

The prospective Anglo-Saxon resident should not imagine that this is a language that is about to throw in the towel in the face of English language imperialism. Many visitors are irritated or puzzled to find that when they address the locals in their own language they will often reply in English, flatly refusing to carry on a conversation in French with you. They are just trying to be helpful: they reason that the conversation will be clearer if they speak in English, because clarity in expressing oneself is of primary importance here. Some French are proud of their English and want to practise it on you. Others feel that their English is hopelessly bad and will avoid speaking it at all costs. In any case, it is best to let them speak English if they want to.

On the whole, the average Brit or American tends to overestimate their own French-speaking abilities. French is more approachable than, say, German, because English is full of French loanwords which came in from 1066 onwards, but in many cases the commonly used French words used in English don't actually mean the same in French as they do in English and there are whole dictionaries devoted to explaining these 'false friends'. The same holds true for French. One is reminded of a current tourist brochure that describes southwest France as 'a land of evasions'.

Most foreigners do not have the time to study French in depth, even though it can pay enormous dividends in getting on with the French. Do by all means try to sign up for an evening class before you leave for France, and keep on improving your grammar while you are there. There are plenty of subsidised courses run by local governments in

France, where you can meet other foreigners in the same boat as you. Once you can read French novels and newspapers, and can discuss more interesting topics in French, you will earn respect as someone who is *'cultivé'*. One's status in life is largely determined by how educated you are; the term 'intellectual' is a term of praise rather than an abuse, as it often is in the UK. A refreshing aspect of French society is that everyone is interested in discussing philosophy or literature, even down to the humblest worker. There are no barriers when it comes to talking about ideas.

## *Language Manners*

As has already been said, the French take their language very seriously. They will quickly put you in your place if you try to make out that your French is better than it really is. In order not to offend people, there are certain ground rules to observe. In the first place, you should address anyone you don't know as *Monsieur* or *Madame*, even if you are talking to the local drunk in the park. *Mademoiselle* is quite OK for someone under 16, but otherwise stick to *Madame*. On initial acquaintance, you should always start with the formal *vous* rather than *tu* (meaning 'you') unless everyone around is using *tu*. With people of your own age and social grouping, the transition to *tu* should happen quite quickly. If everyone around you is addressing each other as *tu* it will seem odd if you don't do the same. With people who are a lot older than you it is not unusual for them to address you as *tu* and for you to reply with *vous*. As a rule older people whom you do not know well are always addressed with *vous*.

The use of the more respectful *vous* – the verb is *vouvoyer* – is also rather loaded. With strangers you must use *vous*. If you continue to use *vous* with social acquaintances then you are keeping your distance. In business situations one would not normally use *tu* except among young people. It is perfectly normal to use *tu* in an office amongst colleagues. In any case you should take your lead from the French. They will let you know when it is time to start using *tu*.

**Meeting and Greeting.** Knowing how to greet people is a must. At the very least you should shake people's hands when you meet them, and that means **shaking everyone's hand in the room**, starting from the left and going around clockwise. This includes men and women if you are not on close terms. In a work situation you will shake hands with male colleagues (if you are male) and kiss the women when you meet in the morning, and when you leave in the evening. Women naturally kiss both men and women.

If you are dealing with an official or someone from whom you are seeking a favour, then the 'superior' takes the initiative in shaking hands. If they do not extend their hand on meeting they will usually do so when you leave. There is no need to shake hands with tradesmen or cleaners, but you should shake hands with notaries, architects and other professional people. It is very important to use people's titles *Monsieur, Madame* (or *Mademoiselle* for girls under 16) but not with their surname. If they have a professional title, then you should use it: *Monsieur/Madame le Professeur/le Docteur* and so on. In the workplace you will not be on first-name terms with superiors unless you are working for a foreign-based company. The boss will always remain *Monsieur le Directeur.*

Kissing is a subject to be familiar with. It is customary to give women two pecks – *deux bises* – one on each cheek on leaving a party, or once one is on friendly terms. For a man to give a woman three pecks – *trois bises* – implies something more than just being casual friends; to do so may give offence. For family and close friends it is expected, but you should take your lead from other people. One kiss on the cheek is also over-familiar. Rather confusingly, some women give four pecks to their good friends. In the South of France, three pecks is more acceptable between casual friends. When work colleagues meet for the first time in the morning, it is normal to kiss twice; foreigners should follow the lead of the locals. It is also usual for men to kiss each other twice if they are close friends. No one will be too offended if you find this awkward; it is a matter of whether you feel comfortable with it.

## BUSINESS PRACTICES

Hierarchies are strictly observed in organisations. The boss or *président directeur général (PDG)* is a sort of demi-god who is expected to know everything about every aspect of the business. While taking the decisions he/she is also supposed to take a paternalistic interest in the employees' welfare. French managers do not socialise with subordinates, but only with their own class. When making appointments you may well deal with the person you are meeting themselves. Secretaries are not generally given the authority to make appointments on behalf of their bosses. French managers do not necessarily stick to strict time schedules. If something comes up they will change appointments at short notice. They are also not as punctual as northern Europeans; being 15 minutes late is not considered that serious. While dress is formal in offices it is not necessarily that smart. The French are less obsessed with their appearance than, say, the Italians.

## Business Meetings and Entertaining

When you present a case for obtaining a loan or going into a business partnership with someone there are certain ground rules to follow. The French generally like everything to be clearly presented and logically argued. You need to consider all the possible objections someone could make to your plans and have arguments ready to counter them. Be careful not to smile too much or make irrelevant jokes. There is no scope for appealing to emotions or trust in a negotiating situation. The French do not generally follow a consensus model of negotiation; there is a winner and a loser. If your listeners gesticulate or shout that is a positive sign, it means that they are interested in what you are saying. You should be more concerned if there is no reaction on their part. You should not look for a quick conclusion; the French like discussion and time to reflect; they appreciate flexible thinking. At the end of the day, you should not be put off if they say something is impossible. No does not mean no. Everything is possible in France if you are prepared to discuss things.

France is also a fairly corrupt country, and ranks 13th on the world corruption scale, slightly worse than Spain, but better than Italy. Outsiders are amazed to hear that well-known politicians are involved in bribery, handing out fictitious jobs, influence-peddling and other dubious practices, and nobody seems to care. Giving backhanders is an accepted part of doing business. Unless you are looking to join the French underworld – *la pègre* – you will not be expected to get involved.

**Entertaining.** It is usual to invite prospective clients out for a meal. It is not usual to invite anyone from your working environment to your home unless you are close friends. The culinary arts and dining out are subjects that are taken very seriously in France. It is rather important to know what to do in a restaurant, especially if you are taking out a prospective client or trying to gain some influence with someone. It should be clear at the outset who is inviting whom; just by saying '*je vous invite*' then it is clear who is paying. If you are trying to close a business deal then you are the one who pays. The French are always conscious of who is *le demandeur* – the one who wants something out of a situation. In informal situations between friends then it is quite normal to share the bill, a practice called *faire suisse* (going Swiss), which is about as pejorative as 'going Dutch'. Everything on the bill will be precisely calculated and each will pay their precise share.

It is still normal to take longish lunch breaks, which can include going to a restaurant if there is the time. Lunch hours are traditionally 1½ hours in northern France and 2 hours in the south, but they are getting shorter everywhere, especially in Paris. The French generally like to have a full meal at lunchtime if they can, particularly in the countryside. This can affect the afternoon's work if wine is consumed as well and leads to a lot of frustration for foreign employers.

Discussing business matters during a meal is acceptable, as long as it is done after the cheese course. Before this time you should stick to other topics. By the time the fruit course comes round everyone should be in a good mood, and you may be able to clinch a good deal. It is also a fact that conversation may be flagging towards the end of the meal, so introducing a more controversial subject can get everyone worked up again.

The etiquette of eating in a high-class restaurant in France is not that different from what you would expect anywhere else. It is considered good manners to eat off the back of the fork, and to keep your hands on the table when you are not eating. You should make sure that your fellow diners' glasses are kept topped up. If you are eating out with French friends, they will know which wines go with different courses, otherwise the wine-waiter – *le sommelier* – can advise you. Your dining companions will appreciate it if you ask them about the local cuisine and their views on how it should be cooked.

## Keeping Your End Up

The French generally tend to make fun of everybody and everything, and especially foreigners, but in a light-hearted way. Trying to do the same if you are not French may not work too well if you appear to be making personal remarks about people. From time to time you may be told to your face that the British, for example, are cold and uptight, or even worse. A habit that grates with the French is evasiveness, i.e. not saying what you really think. Remember that the word 'French' means 'frank' or 'free'. The French are generally straight-talking and don't shrink from telling the truth. People can be very rude to each other, and still be the best of friends. Quarrels are quickly forgotten. At the same time French are generally respectful of other people's privacy and gossiping is strongly disapproved of.

The French do not, however, like to be criticised or made fun of, partly because they live in a very competitive society and also because of their wounded national pride following three German invasions. Some older French still resent the fact that the British and Americans had to rescue France in two world wars. There is also a further factor, which is the importance of frivolity in French culture. Being light-hearted and not taking things too seriously is another French value which can be difficult to take on board if you come from a northern European culture, especially when it intrudes into business matters.

One should joke by all means, but not at the expense of the French, and certainly not too much. Try not to take one-sided jokes at your expense too personally. Criticising your own country is also best avoided. The French respect people who are self-confident and proud of their country; they dislike the kind of self-disparagement practised by the British. It can be taken literally, and makes for an uncomfortable atmosphere. The French in general like to be right; they react badly to criticism, and will not appreciate it if you expose their ignorance on some matter.

Needless to say there are topics of conversation that should be avoided in social contexts where you do not know the other person well. Anything relating to the Catholic Church, the Second World War, former French colonies or foreign immigration are potentially hazardous topics. It is absolutely taboo ask too many personal questions. On the other hand, French men will be delighted to discuss the latest electronic gadgets, or football or cars (as everywhere).

## FRENCH BUSINESS LETTERS

It would be dishonest to say that writing letters in French is easy. Even graduates in French approach the subject with some trepidation. It is strongly advised to buy a book on writing formal letters. There are three that can be recommended: *500 Lettres pour Tous les Jours* (publ. Larousse), *330 Modèles de Lettres et de Contrats* (publ. Prat), and *250 Modèles de Lettres* (publ. Jeunes Editions) The latter has the advantage of having some English translations, as well as a CD-Rom with the texts. Also see www.voslitiges.com for examples of letters.

As one might expect, letters are somewhat more formal in French than in English. Things need to be said using the right phrases, and in a polite way. Generally, the worse the news you are communicating the more polite you have to be. Bluntly telling someone they owe you money or that they are getting the sack is not the done thing. The language should be soft and elegant, so as not to upset the other person.

**The Salutation.** The salutation with officials and business people is *Monsieur* or *Madame*. If they have a title it is best to use it, so you can start: *Monsieur le Directeur*. One of the oddities of titles is that some of them remain masculine even when used for women: thus *Madame le Professeur, Madame le Notaire, Madame le Docteur*. On the other hand, you can say *la secrétaire* as well as *le secrétaire,* and *la ministre* or *le ministre*. Some titles have feminine forms: *Madame la Directrice* (managing director/chairman of the board). A female manager is *la gérante.*

You should never begin a letter *Cher Monsieur* or *Chère Madame,* unless you are on friendly terms with the addressee. Never use combinations such as *Cher Monsieur Dupont* or *Chère Madame Dupont,* which include the person's surname, even if that would appear natural in English. The only acceptable combination is *Mon cher Dupont,* which is too familiar. You never write *Mon cher Monsieur* or *Ma chère Madame* either.

**The Close.** Ending the letter correctly poses even more difficulties. There are literally dozens of permutations of endings which can run to a whole tortuous sentence. A list is given below. There is a crucial convention in writing letters, namely that the close includes the salutation within commas, as a kind of echo: If you addressed someone as '*Monsieur*' or '*Madame*', then the ending would be '*Recevez, Monsieur (or Madame), l'assurance de mes salutations distinguées.*' Generally women should not use formulas which substitute '*sentiments*' for '*salutations*' when writing to men they do not know. It is common to use the word '*sincère*' in business closes if you want to show how sincere you are. The first time you write to someone you need to use formulas with *considération* or *distingué*. Unless you have built up some rapport with the other person, then even *Meilleures salutations* is too familiar.

You can use the more informal ending '*Cordialement*' in a more relaxed business context, or in an e-mail. It would not be usual in a formal business context, but if you are in a partnership with someone it would be entirely appropriate.

**Writing e-mails.** Writing a '*mel*' or '*courrier électronique*' is not quite as difficult as a formal letter. Generally you will use the same salutation and close as in a letter, but the more convoluted closes should be avoided. If you are writing informally to a person you are on close terms with, you can start with *Bonjour* (name). The informal ending is generally *Cordialement* or *Salutations*.

---

## ALL-PURPOSE CLOSES

**The following are more or less in order of formality. The longer the close the more polite in general.**

*Je vous prie d'agréer, Monsieur/Madame, l'expression de ma considération distinguée.* Suitable for all formal or official letters.

*Je vous prie d'agréer, Monsieur/Madame, l'expression de mes salutations respectueuses.* Respectful.

*Veuillez agréer, Monsieur/Madame, l'assurance de ma considération distinguée.* Formal.

*Veuillez agréer, Monsieur/Madame, l'expression de mes salutations distinguées.* Polite.

*Recevez, Monsieur/Madame, l'expression de mes salutations distinguées.* Neutral; private letters when making a complaint.

*Salutations distinguées.* Suitable for formal e-mails or short letters.

*Sincères salutations.* Suitable for someone in a long-term business relationship.

*Meilleures salutations.* Suitable for business colleagues one knows well.

*Cordialement.* Suitable for informal letters and e-mails.

*Bises/Je t'embrasse/Gros bisous/Bons baisers,* etc. Kisses, and so forth. Use with caution.

## *Potential Misunderstandings*

Because of the superficial resemblance of much French and English vocabulary, there are numerous potential pitfalls one has to watch out for. One point is apologies; one should never write *Je m'excuse de ....* or *Nous nous excusons de ....* since you then appear to be excusing yourself, rather than asking the other person to excuse you. The correct formula is '*Je vous prie de bien vouloir m'excuser de .....*' or '*Nous vous prions de bien vouloir nous excuser de ....*' Awareness of this point will win you a more positive reaction.

One only needs to read English written by French people to understand that some words do not mean what you might expect. As a general rule of thumb, French prefers a more exaggerated expression than English. Some examples include:

| | |
|---|---|
| *actuellement* | at the moment; not 'actually' |
| *le chariot* | a shopping trolley or cart |
| *les coordonnées* | your personal details, i.e. name, address, telephone etc. |
| *les coordonnées bancaires* | bank details, otherwise called RIB. |
| *déception* | disappointment |
| *désolé* | means 'sorry' not 'desolate' |

| | |
|---|---|
| *le diplôme* | a higher education degree, but not only from a university |
| *une évasion* | an excursion, or tourist trip |
| *éventuellement* | means 'possibly' or 'if necessary', not 'in the end' |
| *important* | means 'big' as well as 'significant' |
| *une réclamation* | a complaint |
| *un tampon* | a business stamp |

The list is endless and there are whole books on the subject.

### Presentation

There is one major difference in the way a letter is laid out in French compared with the English style, namely, the sender's details appear at the top left or centre, higher than the addressee's details at the top right. You may need to put '*A l'attention de*' (For the attention of). The date appears on the right, below the addressee's details. Below this, as in an English letter, you will have '*Objet*' (Ref. or Re:),

The presentation is also slightly more conservative than in English in that commas are used after the salutation and close, where they have long since disappeared in English. There is no need to indent every paragraph, however. The signature followed by the printed name can appear on the left, in the centre or even on the right. The latter seems to be the most usual.

## EXAMPLES OF LETTERS

While it would be outside the scope of this book to give a full guide to business correspondence, and there are many excellent French books on the subject, the following are some examples of letters that one might have to write:

### Request to Open a Bank Account in Case of Refusal

If you are refused a bank account, then you can ask the Banque de France to intervene on your behalf.

*Messieurs,*
Dear Sirs

*Je me suis adressé à plusieurs banques afin d'ouvrir un compte, toutes ont refusé.*
I have been in touch with several banks with a view to opening an account, but they have all turned me down.

*Vous trouverez ci-jointes leurs lettres de refus.*
Please find enclosed their letters of refusal.

*Je vous serais donc reconnaissant de bien vouloir me désigner, le plus rapidement possible, une banque auprès de laquelle je puisse ouvrir un compte.*
I would therefore be grateful if you would assign me a bank, as soon as possible, where I could open an account.

*Dans l'attente de votre réponse, je vous prie d'agréer, Messieurs, l'expression de ma considération distinguée.*
In anticipation of your reply, I remain....

(Example from *500 Lettres Pour Tous les Jours,* publ. Larousse).

### Letter Requesting a Loan from a Bank

*Souhaitant procéder à l'agencement de mon nouveau commerce, situé ........ ........ j'aurais besoin d'emprunter une somme de 5,000 euros.*
With a view to carrying out the shopfitting for my new shop, located at ........... I require a loan of 5,000 euros.

*Pourriez-vous me consentir un prêt sur une durée de 5 ans, et dans quelles conditions?*
Would you be able to offer me a loan over a period of 5 years, and under what conditions?

*Je reste à votre disposition pour tout renseignement complémentaire,*

Please do not hesitate to contact me for further information,

*Veuillez agrèer, Monsieur, l'expression de ma considération distinguée,*
Yours sincerely

### Letter Offering Someone a Job

*Monsieur/Madame/Mademoiselle*

*Suite à notre entretien du ..... nous avons le plaisir de vous confirmer que votre candidature à été retenue.*
Following our meeting of ..... we have pleasure in informing you that your application has been successful.

*Cet engagement est fait pour une durée déterminée de 1 an, à titre d'un contrat de jeunes.*
Your employment will be for a fixed period of 1 year, on the basis of a *Contrat de Jeunes* [or other type of short-term contract].

*Votre contrat débutera le ..... et arrivera à échéance le .....*
Your contract will commence on .... and end on .....

*Les horaires de travail sont de 9h30 à 18h30 du lundi au vendredi.*
Working hours are from 9:30 in the morning to 6:30 in the evening from Monday to Friday.

*Vous recevrez une rémunération mensuelle de .....*
You will receive a monthly salary of .....

*Nous vous prions d'agréer, Monsieur/Madame/Mademoiselle, l'expression de notre considération distinguée,*
Yours sincerely

## Letter Complaining About Late Payment

*Messieurs*

*Nous sommes au regret de devoir vous informer que nous n'avons toujours pas reçu le règlement du solde de .... euros restant dû sur notre facture de .....*
We regret to have to inform you that we have until now not received payment for the amount of .... euros which remains outstanding on our invoice of ......

*Au cas où vous n'auriez pas reçu ce dernier facture, nous vous adressons ci-joint une photocopie.*
In the event that you did not receive this latest invoice, we are sending you herewith a copy of the invoice.

*Souhaitant que vous régliez rapidement, nous vous prions d'agréer, Messieurs ....*
Hoping that you will settle this account speedily, we remain....

(Adapted from *250 Modèles de Lettres pour l'Entrepeneur Solo* by Gérard Roudaut, publ. Jeunes Editions).

## Letter Giving Someone a Power of Attorney to Carry Out Certain Acts

*Je soussigné M. ............. demeurant à ............................. constitue par les présentes pour mandataire: M. ............................ demeurant à ................................... dont vous trouverez la signature ci-dessous.*
I, the undersigned ............ residing at ...................... grant by this document a power of attorney to the following: ................... residing at ........................ whose signature is given below.

*M. ...................... est mandaté pour effectuer les opérations suivantes: .................................................*

Mr .................. is authorised to carry out the following acts
.....................


*Ce pouvoir est à durée illimitée. Il prendra fin par révocation expresse.*
This power of attorney is for unlimited duration and will expire when
an express cancellation is issued.

*Fait à .............. en ............. originaux.*
Done and signed at ................ with ........ originals.

*Lu et approuvé – Bon pour pouvoir.*
Read and agreed – Valid for power of attorney.

*Signature*

> *J'accepte le pouvoir ci-dessus – Lu et approuvé*
> I accept the power of attorney stated above – Read and agreed

> *Signature*

(Adapted from *300 Modèles de Lettres 2001;* publ. Prat).

# Tax, Social Security and Other Matters

## CHAPTER SUMMARY

○ **Accountants.** Almost all foreign-run businesses use an accountant.

○ **UK Tax.** First inform the UK authorities that you are leaving their tax jurisdiction.

○ **Tax Regimes.** As a small business you have a choice of tax regimes.

○ **Micro-Entreprise.** A favourable and easy tax regime for very small businesses.

○ **Three-year Cycle.** Taxes are paid retrospectively. Planning ahead is vital, otherwise you may not last three years.

○ **Local Taxes.** Local services are funded from taxes that are raised by the central government and then redistributed.

○ **Capital Gains Tax.** The system was reformed in 2003 for residential property.

○ **Tax Evasion.** This is very common with the self-employed, but best avoided by foreigners.

○ **Social Security.** The system appears to be incomprehensible to a layperson, but there is no real need to understand the details.

○ **TVA.** Raises more money than income tax for the French state.

○ **Insurance.** Compulsory for all businesses.

# BOOKKEEPING/ACCOUNTANTS

One piece of advice that almost everyone gives to new entrepreneurs in France is to get an accountant or *expert comptable*. Most foreign businesspeople simply hand everything over to the accountant and let them get on with the job of dealing with income tax returns, etc. For a newcomer without any accountancy training, trying to deal with the Byzantine tax laws in France, and in French, is simply more than they can handle, so it seems this advice is best heeded. Accountants are not allowed to advertise in France, but they are easily found in the yellow pages under *expert comptable,* or by word of mouth.

## THE NEED FOR AN ACCOUNTANT

Jane Smith ran both an import-export business and a hotel in France for more than 30 years.

*When you start a business here you should think that you are both going to make a fortune, and lose all your money. Personally, the best piece of advice is to get a good accountant. No one can do their accounts properly without help. The best accountant is someone who does the work themselves, not a big firm who use trainees. There is no such thing as a cheap or expensive accountant: they are indispensable. The accountant is in contact with the tax office and should know what's going on. The best accountants are those who have worked for the tax office before. The accountant's reputation is on the line, not yours, if something goes wrong. From time to time your books are going to be checked and inevitably they are going to find something wrong, so the accountant can take the blame. But remember that the taxpayer still has to pay the bill if the accountant makes a mistake. At the end of the day the most the accountant will do is refund their fees if they have made a serious error.*

You can, if you wish, have your accounts dealt with by a *Centre de Gestion Agréé*. CGAs are non-profit organisations to be found in every Chambre de Commerce. Businesses liable to pay *impôt sur le revenu* (income tax), whether commercial, artisanal or industrial can join a CGA as long as they do not pay tax under the *micro-entreprise* regime. If you are a sole trader then you gain an abatement of 20% on the first €113,900 of your profits as long as you follow the CGA's rules; this makes up for the 20% abatement that you would have received as a salaried worker. The main requirement is that you agree to accept payments by cheque made out in your name, and that cheques go directly into your bank account. This does not exclude payment in cash. Your accounts will have to be inspected by an accountant approved by the CGA. The fact that you belong to a CGA will appear on your business stationery. To qualify for the advantages of the CGA in a calendar year you need to join before March 31st. The charge for belonging to a CGA is about €120-200, which is tax-deductible.

# TAXATION

French taxation is an extremely complex subject, and not something that one can easily summarise in a few pages. A French accountant or lawyer can save you a lot of money, as they will know all the ins and outs of the system, which is far from transparent. There are annual changes to the system. These are announced at the end of July and come into force from 30 December.

While French income tax might appear exorbitantly high, this is not really the case, because of all the exemptions and allowances that are applied. Most taxes in France are raised through social security contributions and TVA, which are more difficult to avoid than income tax. About half of French families pay no income tax at all. In order to stimulate economic growth, income tax has been cut: by 5% in 2002, 1% in 2003, and 3% in 2004.

# MOVING TO FRANCE

**Procedure for UK Residents.** The situation is reasonably straightforward if you are moving abroad permanently. You should inform the UK Inspector of Taxes at the office you usually deal with of your departure and they will send you a P85 form to complete. The UK tax office will usually require certain proof that you are leaving the UK, and hence their jurisdiction, for good. Evidence of having sold a house in the UK and having rented or bought one in France is usually sufficient. You can continue to own property in the UK without being considered resident, but you will have to pay UK taxes on any income from the property.

If you are leaving a UK company to take up employment with a French one then the P45 form given by your UK employer and evidence of employment in France should be sufficient. You may be eligible for a tax refund in respect of the period up to your departure, in which case it will be necessary to complete an income tax return for income and gains from the previous 5 April to your departure date. It may be advisable to seek professional advice when completing the P85; this form is used to determine your residence status and hence your

UK tax liability. Once the Inland Revenue are satisfied that you are no longer resident or domiciled in the UK, they will close your file and not expect any more UK income tax to be paid.

France has a double taxation agreement with the UK, which makes it possible to offset tax paid in one country against tax paid in another. While the rules are complex, essentially, as long as you work and are paid in France then you should not have to pay UK taxes, as long as you do not spend more than an average of 91 days a year in the UK spread over 4 years. For further information see the Inland Revenue publication IR20 *Residents and non-residents. Liability to tax in the United Kingdom* which can be found on the website http://www.inla ndrevenue.gov.uk. Booklets IR138, IR139 and IR140 are also worth reading; these can be obtained from your local tax office or from:

*Centre for Non-Residents (CNR):*   St John's House, Merton Rd, Bootle, Merseyside L69 9BB; ☎ 0151-472 6196; fax 0151-472 6392; www.inlandrevenue.gov.uk/cnr.

### Aspects of Tax Residence

It is important to understand that the French authorities make no distinction between 'residence', 'ordinary residence' and 'domicile' in the way the British tax authorities do. In the British sense, the country where you have your longest-lasting ties is your domicile; this is a concept not defined in the UK Tax Acts, but rather based on precedent. In French, *domicile* simply means residence, and is based on facts, such as the number of days you spend in a place, or where you have the main centre of your economic interests.

The French tax authorities define tax residence (*domicile fiscal*) differently from the British. If your household – *foyer fiscal* – is in France, e.g. your family lives there, then you are tax resident there. The other test of tax residence is where you have your principal residence – *séjour principal*. If you spend more than 183 days a year in France then you are tax resident there. You may even be tax resident in France if you spend less than 183 days a year there, if you have spent more time in France than in any other country. Whether you have a *carte de séjour* or not does not enter into the assessment. If the main centre of your economic interests is in France, or your main employment is there, then you are certainly tax resident there.

Situations may arise where one married partner is tax resident in the UK and the other in France. Partners are considered separately as far as tax residence goes, even though the location of your household is the main criterion for establishing tax residence. In this case you have a choice between being taxed together in the usual way, or being treated separately, so that the resident spouse will declare their income to the local *centre des impôts* and the other to the *Centre des Impôts des Non-Résidents* in Paris. This is a possibility, since under French law, those married in the UK and US are assumed to come under the regime of separate estates – *régime de séparation des biens*. It is advisable to make a declaration that you are married under the separate estates regime before a notaire.

As a basic principle, tax is levied on a household as a whole – the *foyer fiscal* – rather than on separate persons. It is not usual for a husband and wife to pay tax separately, unless they are in the throes of divorce and have separate households, or are married under the separate estates regime. If you have entered into a PACS – a civil partnership contract – you will have to wait for three years before you can be assessed as one household. If you are simply living together *en concubinage* you are treated as two separate households. Each of the *concubins* can have their own dependants, who will be taken into account when their tax is calculated.

## CHOOSING YOUR INCOME TAX REGIME

When you register your business you will be asked to state whether you want to pay *impôt sur le revenu* (income tax) or *impôt sur les sociétés* (corporation tax). Small businesses generally opt for IR. If you are a sole trader you can only pay IR. The pros and cons of IR and IS are dealt with under IS below. If you expect to make substantial profits from your business then it is essential to discuss the advantages and disadvantages with your accountant or lawyer. Should your financial year not be the calendar year, then you will pay the tax at the rate in force for the larger part of your financial year. The main thing to bear in mind is that it is easy to switch from paying IR to IS, but you cannot switch back again.

| Company | Tax regime |
|---|---|
| *Entreprise Individuelle* | only IR |
| EURL | IR or IS |
| SARL | IS |
| | IR for SARL *de famille* |
| | IR for minority director's salary (*géant minoritaire*) |
| | IR on other directors' remuneration |

Partners or directors are considered salaried employees if they have a contract with a SARL. Their remuneration is tax-deductible from the SARL's profits. Partners' shares in profits, dividends etc. are subject to corporation tax. A SARL *de famille* is considered fiscally transparent: members are taxed on their real income, but no one outside the family is allowed to buy shares, otherwise the fiscal regime automatically changes to IS.

## Tax Returns

There are several different types of tax returns – *déclarations fiscales* – for different types of income. The forms can be viewed on the government website www.service-public.fr, and can also be obtained at any time from your *Centre des Impôts* or *mairie*. The basic form is No.2042, the *déclaration des revenus*. If you are self-employed, have capital gains to declare, or rent out property, you also have to fill in No.2042C, the *déclaration complément*. Beyond that there are forms where you give more detail about your business profits.

---

### Accounting Requirements and Tax Regimes (IR)

**Micro-entreprise**

Keep a daybook (*livre-journal*), and a register of all expenses, supported by receipts etc. No requirement for full accounts or balance sheet. Invoices to clients will state that you are exempt from TVA: 'TVA non applicable, article 293 B du CGI'.

**Régime réel simplifié**

Complete double-entry bookkeeping required with daybook, inventory, full accounts (*grand livre*) and annual balance sheet. Accounts to be published at the end of the year. Sole traders can apply to keep super-simplified accounts. Companies can dispense with annual balance sheet if their turnover is less than €153,000 (sales) or €54,000 (services). TVA must be stated on invoices.

**Régime réel normal.**

Full accounts and annual balance sheet. Accounts to be published. TVA must be charged.

If you choose to pay income tax (IR) rather than corporation tax (IS) you will need to choose between three types of regimes: *micro-entreprise, régime simplifié,* and *régime réel.* There are two versions of the *micro-entreprise* regime. *Micro-Bénéfices Industriels Commerciaux* only applies to commercial professions. Liberal professions can use the *Micro-Bénéfices Non-Commerciaux* regime. If you are taxed as a *micro-entreprise* you also fill in form No.2042P. If you run more than one business then you will fill in a form for each.

***Micro-BIC.*** The basic idea is that you accept a fixed deduction from your turnover, in exchange for a super-simplified bookkeeping regime. The thresholds depend on what type of business you run. If you sell goods or provide furnished lodgings (which includes running *chambres d'hôtes/gîtes*), and your pre-tax turnover is under €76,300 annually, then you can choose to be taxed on turnover after an abatement of 72% is taken off. You effectively pay IR on 28% of your turnover. Capital gains are not included in the calculation. Commercial services can choose to be taxed on their turnover (*chiffre d'affaires*) after an abatement of 52%, but their turnover is limited to €27,000. This regime is not obligatory – you can choose to be taxed on your real income (*régime simplifié* or *réel*). It is important to realise that because you are only taxed on a fixed percentage of your turnover, you will pay very much smaller social security contributions and tax than someone who chooses to deduct their real expenses from their turnover and who is then taxed on the remainder. However large your expenses may be you will still win out as a *micro-entreprise*. Another great advantage is that you only need to keep a very basic record of all your expenses and income, in a standard daybook, but you do not have to present full accounts at the end of each year. You simply enter your total turnover on form No.2042C, and the type of services supplied at different locations. If you exceed the limit during one year, then you are taxed on the excess at the usual IR rates. In the year after you will no longer qualify for *Micro-BIC*, unless the two years taken together average out at less than the *Micro-BIC* threshold.

As regards *gîtes* and *chambres d'hôtes*, if the net income from rentals exceeds €23,000, or constitutes more than 50% of your household income, then you are considered a professional landlord; you will be required to register as a business and you will pay higher social security taxes on the income.

The *micro* regime is not only related to your turnover. If you opt to make TVA declarations then you are excluded from the *micro* regime. Companies that pay IS are always excluded, as are companies where the partners pay IR on their income, such as SARLs *de famille*. You cannot declare a loss under the *micro* regime, neither can losses be carried forward. If you start your business in the middle of the year then you are assessed pro rata, on a proportion of €76,300 or €27,000, as the case may be.

**Micro-BNC.** This is open to liberal professions and is also called a *déclaration spéciale*; you are taxed on turnover minus 37%. Your turnover cannot exceed €27,000 per annum if you want to stay in this category. Liberal professions do not have the option of choosing the *régime simplifié* or *régime réel*. The next step up is a *déclaration controlée*.

**Micro-BA.** Farmers have their own *micro* regime, otherwise called a *BA forfait*. To qualify your turnover has to be below €76,300. The *forfait* or fixed sum on which you are taxed is calculated according to standardised figures of production per hectare. If you have no revenues other than those coming under *bénéfices agricoles* you can fill in the basic tax declaration No.2042. Most farmers are involved in some form of commerce and have to fill in No.2342 as well. In the case of natural disasters, farmers using the *Micro-BA* can still apply to deduct their real losses from their lump sum income. There is also a scheme in place for young farmers who do not subscribe to *Micro-BA* whereby they can be taxed on only 50% of their annual income for the first 5 years.

**Régime réel simplifié.** Where your turnover before taxes exceeds

€76,300 (commercial), or €27,000 (services and liberal professions), you have no choice but to move to the *régime simplifié*. You have the option of moving up to the *régime réel* (i.e. *réel normal*) if you want. You will be required to make a TVA declaration at the end of each year, and to make 3-monthly estimated TVA payments. You can pay IR on your real income, and deduct your real expenses. You are required to keep accounts.

The tax annex form you require is No.2031 for BIC or No.3035 for BNC. You can still belong to a CGA and claim your 20% abatement.

**Régime réel normal.** Once your turnover exceeds €763,000 (commercial) or €230,000 (services) you are in the realms of the *réel*. Here you need to hire an accountant (unless you are an accountant yourself), maintain full accounts, and publish annual balance sheets. You are also required to make monthly TVA payments and declarations. In other respects there is not that much difference between the *réel* and *simplifié*, just more paperwork. Your tax annex form is No.2031.

**Micro-Foncier.** This is more correctly called the *régime simplifié de déclaration des revenus fonciers*. It enables you to put your income from letting unfurnished property directly into the basic tax declaration form No.2042, instead of using form No.2044. It only applies to landlords who earn less than €15,000 net in one calendar year from their lettings. You are given an automatic 14% deduction from the gross letting income for the year. If your real expenses add up to more than 30% of letting income during the year you will be better off with the normal *foncier* regime (i.e. you simply file tax annex form No.2044). There is a useful calculator for *micro-foncier* on the site www.patrimoine.com. Once you opt for the normal *foncier* regime you are obliged to remain in it for 5 years.

**Main Tax Deadlines**

|  | Declaration | Form | Payment |
|---|---|---|---|
| IR *Micro* | 31 March | No.2042 | 3 instalments/final payment 15 September |
| Réel simplifié BIC | 30 April | No.2031 | as above |
| Réel normal BIC | 30 April | No.2031 | as above |
| BNC (*déclaration controlée*) | 30 April | No.2035 | as above |
| Taxe professionnelle | 30 April | No.1003 | 31 May/final payment 1 December |
| Taxe foncière | when received | variable | variable |
| Taxe d'habitation | when received | variable | variable |

*Other tax annex forms.* There are a number of other tax forms that one **may** be required to fill in:

No.2044 for *revenus fonciers* – property income

No.2047 for foreign income

No.2049 for capital gains (IPV)

No.2065 for corporation tax (IS)

No.1810 for fixed minimum corporation tax (IFA)

No.2074 for capital gains on investments

## CALCULATION OF IMPOT SUR LE REVENU

Non-salaried workers and businesses pay tax on their annual profits, arrived at by subtracting actual expenses from revenues. Salaried workers enjoy a basic 20% abatement, plus another 10% for their expenses. Non-salaried workers declare business outgoings. They can still enjoy a 20% abatement if they have joined up with a CGA. Those who opt for the *micro* regime have a fixed percentage deducted from their turnover.

IR is levied on a range of sources of income, whether you are salaried or non-salaried. Bank interest and income from some savings accounts and life insurance are taxed at source.

| **Types of income subject to IR include:** | |
|---|---|
| Wages, salaries, remunerations, pensions, life annuities | *Traitements, salaires, rémunérations assimilées, pensions, rentes viagères* |
| Investment income | *Revenus de capitaux mobiliers* |
| Capital gains (short-term) | *Plus values à court terme* |
| Industrial and commercial profits | *Bénéfices industriels et commerciaux(BIC)* |
| Non-commercial profits | *Bénéfices non-commerciaux (BNC)* |
| Property income | *Revenus fonciers* |
| Agricultural profits | *Bénéfices agricoles (BA)* |
| Certain directors' remunerations | *Rémunerations des dirigeants de sociétés* |

○ Benefits in kind are taxed at the same rate as wages, salaries, pensions and life annuities, according to their market value. There are fixed limits to the amounts allowable for meals and corporate hospitality, to prevent avoidance of social security contributions.

○ Commercial profits – BIC – covers income from running a business, small-scale manufacturing and trading, as well as letting out shops or furnished properties. Profits from running *chambres d'hôtes* and *gîtes* come under BIC.

○ Non-commercial profits – BNC – concerns income from liberal professions, i.e. doctors, architects, lawyers, and other services.

○ Property income concerns the letting of houses, offices, factories, etc., agricultural land, lakes, forests, as well as hunting rights.

## Exemptions

Certain kinds of income are exempt from income tax, notably:

○ Rental income, if you rent out rooms in your own home on a long-term basis, as long as the rent is considered 'reasonable'.

○ Up to €760 rental income generated from short-term letting of rooms in your house.

○ Income from certain savings plans, and investments in industry, under certain conditions: e.g., PEP, PEA, CODEVI and *Livret A*.

○ Social security benefits, some maternity benefits, disability benefits,

incapacity benefits.
o  Redundancy payments.

Although you may not pay income tax on the above, income from investment plans is still subject to social security taxes totalling 10%.

## Deductions

Before any tax is calculated you are entitled to certain deductions, notably:

o  Maintenance payments to parents and children, including adult children, if they can be shown to be in need.
o  Child support and alimony payments to divorced partners.
o  Voluntary payments to children up to a reasonable limit.
o  Voluntary payments to persons over 75 living in your home.
o  Losses on certain business investment schemes, qualifying for tax breaks.
o  Accountant expenses up to €915 including the cost of belonging to a CGA.

If your income falls under wages, salaries, pensions, etc. there are further items to deduct from your gross income before tax is calculated:

o  Professional expenses – including travel to and from work, meals, hotels. These will be part of your business expenses if you are a non-salaried worker. Otherwise you can claim a fixed 10% of your gross income, up to €12,500, or more subject to proof.
o  Salaried workers receive a 20% abatement up to a limit of €23,800 in 2002.
o  The interest on loans contracted in order to invest in a new company can be deducted from the salary paid by the company.
o  Private pension contributions up to €46,000 (indexed).

## Methods of Calculation

The basis of the calculation is the total income of the household added together. In order to compensate taxpayers with dependants or low earners in their household, the French use a 'family quotient' system – *quotient familial* – calculating tax according to *parts* assigned to members of the family. The total income is divided by the number of *parts*, which has the effect of calculating the tax as if each member of the family earned the same amount. Once the tax has been worked out on a sliding scale, it is multiplied by the number of parts to arrive at the final figure.

As a single person, you have 1 *part*. If you are married then you have 2; if one partner is disabled the couple receives 2.5 *parts*; if both are disabled 3 *parts*. There are numerous different categories of *parts*. Dependants (*personnes à charge*) are (to put it simply) children under 21, students under 25, children doing their military service, and disabled children whatever their age. They are only accepted as dependants if they are based at home and still require some support from you. In the first three cases they may be 're-attached' to the household, even though they are living and working away from home, and you will receive an additional 0.5 *parts* for each of them. Since 2003, divorced or separated parents can receive 0.25% of the *parts* if they share custody.

The most commonly used *parts* are given in the table below:

|  | Married couple | Single, widowed, or divorced |
|---|---|---|
| None disabled | 2 | 1 |
| 1 disabled | 2.5 | 1.5 |
| 1 dependent child | 2.5 | 1.5 |
| 1 disabled dependant | 3 | 2 |
| 2 dependent children | 3 | 2 |
| 2 dependants including 1 disabled | 3.5 | 2.5 |
| 2 disabled dependants | 4 | 3 |
| 3 dependent children | 4 | 3 |
| 4 dependent children | 5 | 4 |

As a rule, each additional child or dependant gives a further 0.5 *parts*. Three children or dependants give 1 *part* apiece, plus 0.5 *parts* if one is disabled. There is a limit to the amount that you can save with this system. If your saving is more than €2,086 (indexed) per half *part* above your base *parts*, then you do not qualify for the *quotient familial*, and your tax has to be calculated differently. Single parents and those with disabled dependants are treated more generously.

## The Tax Calculation by tranches

The French tax system resembles other systems in that tax is calculated progressively on the amount per *part*. The amount per slice or *tranche* has to be multiplied by the *parts* to arrive at a final figure before tax credits and rebates are applied. The following figures apply to income earned in 2003. They are revised annually depending on inflation.

|   | Slice or *tranche* | Net income |
|---|---|---|
| 1 | 0-4,262 | 0% |
| 2 | 4,263-8,382 | 6.83% |
| 3 | 8,383-14,753 | 19.14% |
| 4 | 14,754-23,888 | 28.26% |
| 5 | 23,889-38,868 | 37.38% |
| 6 | 38,869-47,932 | 42.62% |
| 7 | 47,932 and over | 48.09% |

## Tax Credits

There are various tax credits and reductions, too numerous to go into in great detail. Note that these are all subject to conditions and limits. All are subject to having the correct paperwork. The more usual ones include:

o 50% of the cost of domestic help, child-minding, gardeners, cleaners, etc. up to a maximum credit for all domestic employees of 50% of €10,000.
o Child-minding expenses outside the home.
o Charitable donations; but no more than 10% of your taxable income.
o Renovations, extensions, repairs to the principal residence, and

to tourist accommodation in certain designated rural areas, up to 15% of the purchase price of the property.

○ A 25% tax credit for the costs of installing heavy equipment for the home.

○ Environmentally friendly vehicles.

○ Investments in small and medium-sized businesses.

## LIMITED COMPANY TAX CALCULATION

Mr English runs a small shop and Mrs English owns property that generates €18,000 income. Mr English is the single partner in an EURL limited company; his income is the same as the business's net profits. The basis for calculating tax for a business in the *régime réel* is the *revenu brut d'exploitation* – the turnover minus raw materials and goods.

| | |
|---|---|
| Shop income (BIC) | 38,000 |
| Unfurnished rental income | 18,000 |
| 20% abatement for belonging to a CGA | 7,600 |
| Centre de Gestion Agréé | |
| Income tax | 8,398 |
| Social security taxes | 1,440 |
| Local taxes | 3,000 |

## *The Décote*

If your tax liability is below €786 (indexed) you are eligible for a rebate – *décote* – of the difference between €393 and half the tax liability. Thus if your tax liability is €600, you will have a rebate of €93 and your liability is reduced to €507. If your liability is under €393 you pay no tax at all.

## *Complete Exemption from Income Tax*

Certain persons are completely exempt from paying income tax. If your income after deduction of professional costs is below €7,250 you pay no tax.

## EXAMPLE OF A TAX CALCULATION

Mr Gallomane is a sole trader running a bed and breakfast with his wife. Together they have a taxable income income of €50,000; they have opted to pay income tax under the *Micro-BIC régime*. Their grown-up children live in the UK, so they have 2 *parts*. They have no investments and have not realised any capital gains in the tax year in question. For the sake of simplicity it is assumed that the couple divide the social security contributions between them. Mrs Gallomane is a *conjoint collaborateur* (i.e. has no separate salary).

| | | |
|---|---|---|
| Income | | €50,000 |
| actual expenses **not taken into account** | (20,000) | |
| 72% fixed deduction | | 36,000 |
| Taxable amount | | 14,000 |
| halved for two parts | | 7,000 |
| Tax on 0-€4,262 @ 0% | 0 | |
| on €4,263-8,382 @ 6.83% | 187 | |
| Tax per *part* | | 187 |
| multiply by 2 | | 374 |
| Tax refund because of *décote* | | (206) |
| *Prime pour l'emploi* (premium for working) | | (101) |
| Income tax | | 67 |
| *Contribution sur les revenus locatifs* (lettings tax) at 2.5% | | 350 |
| Social security contributions + social security taxes | | 6,100 |
| Income after tax | | 43,483 |
| Real expenses | | 20,000 |
| Local taxes (average amount) | | 3,000 |
| Actual disposable income | | 20,483 |

If the Gallomanes chose to pay according to the *régime réel* they could deduct social security contributions, and benefit from the 20% abatement for belonging to a Centre de Gestion Agréé, but would be €3,000 worse off than in the *Micro régime*. About €3,000 in private pension payments is also tax deductible on this turnover for each person.

### Where Do You Pay Your Taxes?

Tax declarations and demands are issued by the Centre des Impôts. There are two different organisations that collect your taxes, the Trésor Public and the Centre des Impôts, and each has its own inspectors and controllers. Since 2004, the term Recette des Impôts is no longer officially used, having been replaced by the term Centre des Impôts; people will continue to refer to the Recette des Impôts. You can now fill in your tax return on-line, but this is not permitted for the first year of your business activity.

| Type of Tax | |
| --- | --- |
| *Droits de mutation* (transfer tax) | Centre des Impôts |
| *Droits d'enregistrement* (registration tax for businesses | Centre des Impôts |
| IR | Trésor Public |
| IS | Centre des Impôts |
| ISF (wealth tax) | Trésor Public |
| *Taxe d'habitation* | Trésor Public |
| *Taxe professionnelle* | Trésor Public |
| *Taxes sur les salaires* (payroll tax) | Centre des Impôts |
| TVA | Centre des Impôts |

## SOCIAL SECURITY TAXES

The basic tax is the CSG (*Contribution Sociale Généralisée*) which is applied at a rate of 7.5% after a deduction of 5% for professional costs (i.e. 7.5% of 95% of gross income). All earned and unearned income is subject to this tax, which is in many cases a withholding tax. A contribution to repaying the social security system's debt, the CRDS or *Contribution pour le Remboursement de la Dette Sociale,* is levied at 0.5% on similar terms to the CSG. Most types of income are also subject to an additional 'social contribution', the *Prélèvement Sociale* at 2%.

Social security contributions are entirely separate from social security taxes and are dealt with below.

## *Paying in Instalments*

The French tax system works on the basis that you pay income tax (IR) in instalments on your income for the previous year, calculated on the basis of your income in the year before that. There is, therefore, a delay before a foreign resident starting work in France for the first time pays any tax. If you have been resident in France, there will be no break in your tax payments, unless you have been unemployed. You will be paying tax on your previous year's salary during the year that you start your business. If you come from abroad you will pay for the first time by September 15 **in the year after you start up.** You are then hit with the entire tax bill in one go for the previous year.

No tax is paid in advance (except for taxes withheld at source on savings etc.). If you work for an employer, tax can be deducted at source throughout the year. Businesses pay IR in three instalments in February, May and September – the *tiers provisionnels,* as do many salaried workers. Strictly speaking the first two payments are due on 31 January and 30 April, but it has become the custom to extend the deadline to 15 February and 15 May. Normally you will receive your final assessment during September. You cannot be required to pay your final instalment before 15 September. Since 2003 you are required to pay within 45 days of an assessment. If you fail to pay in time then there is a 10% penalty.

All French residents must be registered with the local *inspecteur des impôts.* You are liable for tax on your worldwide income from the day you arrive in France. It is up to you to request a tax return (*déclaration fiscale*) if you do not receive one automatically. Small businesses are given more time to submit their tax returns. For the *micro* regime the final date is 31 March. For BIC and *déclaration controlée* (BNC) it is 30 April. If you file your tax return even one day late, you automatically receive a 10% penalty.

# WEALTH TAX (ISF)

ISF or *Impôt de Solidarité sur la Fortune* only affects those with net assets over €720,000 if they are resident or have assets in France on 1st January of any tax year. The tax is levied on the fiscal household, defined as:

o Single persons, divorced, widowed, unmarried or separated from their partners.
o Married persons, including dependent children under 18.
o Persons who are known to be living together (*concubinage notoire*), and their children.
o Those who have entered a PACS (partnership contract) and their children.

The household's net assets as of 1st January are calculated by the householder him or herself; they include the assets of everyone in the household. The declaration, accompanied by payment in full, is due by 16 July for EU citizens, and 15 June for French citizens. Other foreigners (e.g. US citizens) have until 1st September to pay. Variations in the value of your assets during the year cannot be taken account when calculating your liability.

All your assets, including cars, yachts, furniture, etc. must be included. You will need to produce receipts and insurance policies in order to justify your valuations. You are expected to calculate the 'fair market value' (*valeur vénale réelle*) of your property on the basis of prices in your area. The tax authorities have their own ways of assessing your net worth.

There are a number of items exempt from wealth tax, of which a few are given here in a simplified form:

o Antiques over 100 years old.
o Copyrights on works of art, literature, music.
o Personal injury compensation.
o Movable and sometimes immovable property that you require to carry on your profession.
o Shares in companies of which you are a director, with more than 25% voting rights.

It may be possible to have assets that you need to run *gîtes* or *chambres d'hôtes* exempted from wealth tax. You are allowed a 20% reduction on the household's principal residence (not more than one house). Wealth tax is generally payable on shares in French companies and foreign companies owning property in France.

Since the basis on which ISF is calculated is your net worth, any debts can be deducted from the total. This includes any property loans. Any money you owe to builders or other tradesmen can be deducted, as can the taxes you owe for the previous year (including the ISF itself). Money that is owed to you is added to the total. There is a limitation on wealth tax, inasmuch as your total tax liability (including income tax) cannot exceed 85% of your net taxable income for the previous year.

## WEALTH TAX TARIFFS (AS OF 2004)

| Net Taxable Assets | Tariff |
| --- | --- |
| below €720,000 | 0% |
| €720,000–1,160,000 | 0.55% |
| €1,160,000–2,300,000 | 0.75% |
| €2,300,000–3,600,000 | 1.00% |
| €3,600,000–6,900,000 | 1.30% |
| €6,900,000–15,000,000 | 1.65% |
| €15,000,000 and above | 1.80% |

Since 2004 there have been some measures to encourage investment in small businesses by lessening ISF. In particular if you hold under 25% of the shares in a small or medium enterprise you may be exempt from ISF on these shares if they represent more than 50% of your total gross taxable wealth. There is also a 50% exemption for minority shareholders provided that the total of their shareholding represents at least 20% of the shares in a listed company or 34% in an unlisted company, with certain conditions attached.

**Payment and Penalties.** Your wealth tax return and payment have to be made to the local Centre des Impôts by 16th July. If you are not resident in France payment is made to the: Centre des Impôts des Non-Résidents, 9 rue d'Uzès, 75094 Paris Cedex 02. If you reside in Monaco it is made to the Centre des Impôts in Menton.

In the unlikely event that you cannot pay the tax, you can give works of art instead. The penalties for submitting a false return, or late payment, are very high. Any assets that are not declared will be taxed under the inheritance laws as though they were gifts, and interest and other penalties will be levied.

## TOO TAXING?

The French tax system is certainly intimidating even to the French, but as long as you have an accountant there is not too much to worry about. If you are interested in understanding more of the details, the following book is highly recommended: *Taxation in France 2003* by Charles Parkinson, from PKF Guernsey (see www.pkfguernsey.com). If you rent out property, the companion volume *Letting French Property Successfully* by Stephen Smith and Charles Parkinson is also recommended. There are also tax simulation programmes on the internet; the best for businesses is www.impots.gouv.fr. Simulation programmes are not entirely reliable since every profession pays different amounts of social security contributions, which can reduce tax liability.

# IMPOT SUR LES SOCIETES

This is the French equivalent of corporation tax, and is known as IS. In very general terms, most French companies pay IS. The list of those that do not is given above under *Impôt sur le Revenu*. IS is levied at two rates:

33.33% + a non-deductible 1% contribution = 34.33%

15.45% on the first €38,120 profit as long as the company's capital was paid up in full at the time of incorporation, and at least 75% of the shares are held by natural persons (i.e. not other businesses).

As a measure against tax avoidance, companies subject to IS are required to pay a graduated basic minimum of €750 on turnover above €76,000 which can later be claimed back if they actually pay IS. This is the *impôt forfaitaire annuel*. New businesses can in some circumstances claim exemption.

Companies are expected to calculate and pay their IS themselves without any demand from the tax office. There are numerous deductions of costs and expenses to be applied. Salaries paid to directors or partners can be deducted from the company's IS bill. The directors and partners then pay IR on the salaries and dividends they receive. You also have the option of carrying over losses, using depreciation and provisions for debts and a great deal more to reduce your tax bill. The services of an accountant are compulsory.

### IR or IS?

Making a decision about whether to opt to pay IR or IS needs careful consideration and the advice of a professional. As a general rule if you run a company and your income tax bill exceeds 34.33% of your profits then you should consider paying IS. For this to happen you will most likely be a single or married person without dependants, and with a high income. As your income increases you will pay less and less social security contributions, and have the freedom to reinvest your profits in your company or put them into your company's legal reserve.

## LOCAL/REAL ESTATE TAXES

Most local taxes are real estate taxes. There are some minor taxes that are not dealt with here in detail, namely, regional development tax, the tax to finance local chambers of commerce, and the refuse collection tax. The main real estate taxes come under three headings:

*taxe d'habitation*
*taxes foncières*
*taxe professionnelle*

These are local taxes raised for the benefit of local *communes, départements* and *régions*. The rates of tax are set by the local administrative collectivities, up to specific limits set by the national government. The rate for your area can be found in the annual publication *Impôts Locaux,* published at the start of November. See www.guideducontribuable.com.

## Taxe d'Habitation

The *taxe d'habitation* is payable by anyone who has premises at their disposal subject to this tax. This includes both principal residences as well as any secondary homes that are available for your use. Whether you rent or own the property, if you occupy the property on 1 January you are liable for the entire year's tax. It follows that if you move house during the year, the person whose dwelling you are taking over pays the tax for the year.

Any types of premises that are furnished so as to be habitable, as well as garages, parking spaces, gardens, staff accommodation and other outbuildings within one kilometre of the main building are assessed for the *taxe d'habitation.*

Some buildings are exempt from *taxe d'habitation*:

○ buildings subject to the *taxe professionnelle*
○ farm buildings
○ student accommodation
○ government offices

The tax is calculated by the local authorities on the basis of the cadastral value on 1 January, cadastral value being the nominal rental value of the property or *valeur locative*. If you own an empty habitable rental property, then you pay the *taxe d'habitation*, otherwise the tenant pays.

How much you pay depends on the assessed nominal rental value of your property. Average values range from €1,500 up to €8,000 in the very expensive Paris suburb of Neuilly. The commune sets a percentage of the nominal rental value, which varies widely from some 5% to 35%. Generally percentages are higher where properties have the lowest average nominal rental value; one could be looking at sums of €300 to €1500 per annum.

**Exemptions.** Those on very low incomes are exempt. Also exempt is anyone who is over 60, widowed, or disabled and unable to work. Anyone subject to Wealth Tax (ISF) cannot claim exemption.

**Reductions.** The tax is reduced using the system of family *parts* outlined above; single persons do not qualify for this particular reduction. If the taxable income for the first family *part* does not exceed €16,290, there is a reduction of €3,533. There are further reductions for subsequent half *parts*. The family reductions only apply to principal residences, not to holiday homes.

The local commune may grant reductions to anyone whose principal residence is in the commune, and reductions for low earners.

### Taxes Foncières

There are two land taxes, or *taxes foncières:*

o   tax on unbuilt land
o   tax on built-up land

### Un-built Land

Agricultural land is subject to the element of the tax that goes to the *commune,* but not those parts that go to the *département* and *région.* There are exemptions for certain kinds of forests and tree plantations for fixed periods of time.

### Built-up Land

Types of buildings and constructions subject to the *taxe foncière* include:

o   Anything that has the character of a permanent construction.
o   Warehouses.

O Private roads.

O Hard standings.

O Boats with permanent moorings.

O Grounds used for industry or commerce.

O Land with advertising hoardings.

Buildings used for farming or non-profit public services, are exempt. New buildings, or converted buildings, or extensions to buildings, are exempt from the tax for two years from the date of completion, as regards the regional and *département* element of the tax. As far as the *commune's* part of the tax goes, there may be a two-year exemption for new residential property, or the *commune* may collect the tax.

The owner of the property pays the *taxe foncière*. If the property remains empty through circumstances outside your control for more than three months, you may obtain a rebate of the tax proportional to the time it has stood empty. If you buy a property, you can agree to divide the *taxe foncière* for the year *prorata temporis* with the vendor, unlike the *taxe d'habitation*.

Built-up land is assessed on the basis of 50% of the nominal rental value, the *valeur locative cadastrale*. Un-built land is assessed at 80% of the cadastral value. There are exemptions for the over-75s and the disabled, subject to certain conditions. Percentages vary widely, but the *taxe foncière* is generally much more than the *taxe d'habitation*, and is comparable to British council tax, going up to €2,000 a year or more.

### *Taxe Professionnelle*

The *taxe professionnelle* is by far the most lucrative for the local authorities, and accounts for about half their income. The tax is levied on individuals (*personnes physiques*) and companies (*personnes morales*) that regularly carry on a non-salaried business. Members of partnerships and so-called fiscally transparent companies (whose members are assessed individually for income tax), are assessed in their own names.

There is a long list of persons exempt from the tax, some of which could be relevant to foreign residents:

- Writers, artists, and teachers.
- Recognised private schools.
- Artisans working as sole traders or in an EURL subject to income tax, or with an apprentice under contract, or family members, or only using basic manual techniques.
- Correspondents on local newspapers.

There are temporary exemptions for new businesses in some areas of the country. The most significant exemption (if granted) is for people who rent out *chambres d'hôtes* and *gîtes,* who fall under the category of *loueur en meublés*. Rooms rented out in your principal dwelling to another person who uses them as their own principal dwelling are always exempt from the *taxe professionnelle*. The tax is calculated on the basis of the cadastral rental value of the premises, with 16% of the value of fixed assets added on. There are reductions for artisans who employ no more than three salaried workers. The percentages that are used vary from *commune* to *commune*. The average amount is similar to the *taxe d'habitation*. The poorest cities charge the highest rate of *taxe professionnelle*.

It is a moot point whether you will be liable for the *taxe professionnelle* if you rent out *gîtes* and *chambres d'hôtes*. There are three cases where exemption may be granted by the local administration, namely:

- The renting out of *gîtes* for six months or less per year in a principal or secondary dwelling.
- Premises classed as 'furnished premises for tourists' which form part of your principal dwelling.
- The renting out of any part of a dwelling, not covered by the former.

There is no certainty that you will receive this exemption; it depends on local practice. **The taxe professionnelle is likely to be abolished in 2004.**

## *Taxe Locale d'Equipement*

This is a tax payable on the completion of new buildings, and also on extensions and reconstructions. It is levied by *communes* with more than 10,000 inhabitants. Other *communes* may or may not levy it. The *Certificat d'Urbanisme* which comes with your planning permission will tell you whether you have to pay this tax, and what the amount is.

The tax is assessed at between 1% and 5% of the nominal value of the building calculated on a fixed scale per square metre. One half of the tax is payable within 18 months of delivery of the building permit, and the second half within 36 months.

The main exemptions from this tax relate to building work done with certain state-approved loans, and buildings in certain zones earmarked for industrial development. The only exemption likely to apply to foreign residents or non-residents, is for rebuilding a house destroyed by a natural disaster. The local Division Départementale de l'Equipement can let you know if you are eligible for any reduction.

## Taxation of Real Estate Owned by Foreign Companies

The French authorities have instituted an annual tax of 3% of the market value of real estate in France owned by non-French companies, more than 50% of whose assets consist of property, as a measure against tax evasion, and to discover the identities of the owners of the real estate.

## Contribution sur les Revenus Locatifs

If you are considered a professional landlord (your income from letting is more than €23,000 a year, or more than 50% of your income) you become liable for a tax that was once known as the *droit de bail* (letting tax), but which is now called the *contribution sur les revenus locatifs* (CRL). The basis of calculation is the net income exceeding €1,830 attributable to each location. If you run *chambres d'hôtes* or a hotel, then this means each room; if you rent out a block of apartments, then it is each apartment. The tax only amounts to 2.5% of the net income and is only levied on properties over 15 years old. You are not liable for CRL if you charge TVA on rentals. There are a number of other exceptions. CRL is declared on your basic income tax return (form No.2042).

# CAPITAL GAINS TAX

Where a private person makes a profit on the occasional sale of certain valuable items, they become liable for French Capital Gains Tax, or *Impôt sur les Plus Values* or IPV. Three categories of transactions are subject to IPV, namely, those concerning *immeubles* (buildings and land), *meubles* (movable items) and *parts de société* (company shares). Under *meubles* are understood:

- furniture and other movable goods
- antiques and works of art
- precious stones and precious metals

A distinction is made between short-term gains – *plus values à court terme* and long-term gains – *plus values à long terme*. Short-term gains on property are those made within 5 years of acquisition. The following deals with the taxation of land and buildings. Companies 50% or more of whose assets consist of property are treated as properties. IPV on immovable property was radically reformed starting from 2004, so any information from prior to this time is invalid. IPV is also payable on *fonds de commerce* (intangible parts of a business). This is dealt with in chapter 11, *Selling On*.

## Method of Calculation

The *plus value* on your property sale is worked out by deducting the original purchase price – *prix d'achat* – from the selling price – *prix de cession*. The costs associated with buying the property are added on to the original purchase price, thus reducing your liability. You can opt for a lump sum of 7.5% to cover such a costs. Also added on is the cost of building work, extensions, renovations, etc. if you have owned the building for more than 5 years. It is advisable to have all the original receipts and invoices from when the work was done. If this is not possible, a state-appointed expert may produce a valuation of the work, or you may opt for a flat rate 15%. If you or your family did the work yourselves this can also be taken into account, either using a valuation by an expert, or by multiplying the price of the materials you used by three. Secondary items, such as painting, wallpapering, carpeting, etc. will not be taken into account. The purchase price and associated costs are no longer indexed to the rate of inflation, as of 2004.

Your capital gain is taxed as income at 16%, with a further 10% in social security taxes also payable. If you sell the property within 5 years of acquiring it, or it is repossessed, the gain from the sale of the property is added directly to your income tax liability, and the tax has to be paid immediately. Since 2004, where there is a long-term gain, the capital gain is payable at the time of signing the final deed of transfer (*acte de vente*). The notaire will take the amount of IPV out of the sale proceeds. Sellers are no longer required to enter a special declaration for IPV. The tax cannot be deferred as was the case before 2004.

There are two main methods of reducing IPV. In the first place, the gain is reduced by 10% for every full year after 5 years since the purchase of the property. Thus after 15 years there is no more IPV to pay. Secondly, there is a flat rate deduction of €1,000 from your gross capital gain (but only on one transaction per year). There are also deductions for holiday homes that have been owned for more than five years, which you have always had at your disposal. The deduction is €6,100 per married couple, and another €1,525 per child. A single person enjoys a deduction of €4,600.

Non-residents are taxed at 16% on their capital gains from the sale of property; the EU does not permit France to charge the 10% social security taxes to non-residents, on the grounds that non-residents do not benefit from France's social security benefits. If a non-resident is considered to have been trading in property then IPV is payable at 50% on the capital gain. The provisions of France's Double Taxation Agreement with your country may apply.

There is a complete exemption from IPV in some situations, e.g.:

○ You are a pensioner or officially incapacitated and not liable for income tax.
○ The property has been your habitual principal residence since you bought it, or at least five years (even if owned through a SCI).
○ You have owned the property for more than 15 years.
○ The sale price of the property is under €15,000.
○ Your property has been acquired by the state or local government.

If you can show that the sale of the property was forced on you by family circumstances or because you had to move to another part of the country, you can claim exemption. No IPV is payable if you receive the property as an inheritance, as a gift, or through a divorce settlement. If you originally received the property free of charge, the fair market value at the time you acquired it is taken as the purchase price. There are no deductions for any taxes paid at the time on the transfer of the property.

You can also claim exemption on the sale of a secondary residence the first time that you sell a property in France under certain conditions:

○ you or your spouse do not own your principal residence directly or indirectly
○ the property is sold at least 5 years after it was completed or acquired
○ you have not sold your principal residence in the previous 2 years
○ you have been tax-resident in France for at least 1 year in the past.

For IPV on sales or transfers of businesses, see chapter 11, Selling On.

> **Tax Evasion**
>
> There is no doubt that tax evasion is very common in France. The difficulties of running a business and keeping the profit inevitably encourage some people to disguise some of their business activity. For example, a baker may buy a proportion of his flour unbilled from a miller and keep a double cash book, so the procedure does not appear in the accounts of either party. Foreigners starting up a business should be very cautious, because the tax inspectors will be keeping a close watch on you; they are aware that foreigners have difficulty understanding the French tax and social security system.

# VALUE ADDED TAX (TVA)

The French invented TVA; the *taxe sur la valeur ajoutée* generates 45% of the state's tax revenues. Most businesses are required to collect TVA and make payments to the Centre des Impôts. At the same time you deduct the TVA you pay on your purchases from the total you collect. You have the right to opt out of TVA if you are a *micro-entreprise*. The rates in continental France are:

- 0% TVA is payable on residential lettings.
- 2.1% on medicines refunded by the social security system, news-papers, TV licences, etc.
- 5.5% on agricultural and fishing products, water, hotel accommodation, books, medicines not refunded by social security, renovation expenses on residential properties, etc.
- 19.6% charged on all other items.

Corsica has 6 rates of TVA ranging from 0.90% to 13%.

Within the first 15 days of starting business operations you are obliged to go to the Centre des Impôts to obtain a TVA number which will appear on your invoices (unless you are a *micro-entreprise* in which case you can claim exemption). Note the following TVA deadlines:

| Declaration Form | Payment |
|---|---|
| *Régime réel simplifié* | monthly CA3 at the time of three-monthly declaration |
| *Régime réel normal* | annually CA4/CA12 at the time of declaration |

If your annual TVA liability falls below €4,000 then you can opt for three-monthly declarations/payments in the *régime réel normal.*

## SOCIAL SECURITY

The world of French social security is, by any stretch of the imagination, a forbidding one. Without someone to hold your hand, you could soon get lost in the labyrinth of acronyms the French love so much. The reality is that you do not need to know a lot about the system. Once you have registered with the local Centre de Formalités des Entreprises, you will hear from the organisations you have to pay contributions to.

When you register as self-employed, you also make a declaration that you are a non-salaried worker (*travailleur non-salarié*). You are obliged to make contributions to cover for:

- *allocations familiale*      family benefits
- *maladie-maternité*        illness and maternity
- *retraite*              pension

No one who is resident in France is exempt from making these payments. The organisations that collect payments and distribute benefits are either state bodies, or private organisations that work with the state (*organismes conventionnés*). They are organised at national, regional and departmental level and according to profession. You will be informed where to pay your contributions.

## *Healthcare Cover*

There is a common misconception that if you have private health insurance then you are not required to pay into the French state system. It is illegal to replace French state cover with private health insurance. If you intend to stay for more than three months in France but are not yet making contributions to the social security system, then you have to contribute to a local organisation known as CPAM (*Caisse Primaire Assurance Maladie*) which collects compulsory healthcare contributions.

Contributions to the state social system will allow you to reclaim about 75% of healthcare costs. Precise tables can be found on the website www.canam.fr. For the remaining 25% you need to take out additional insurance with a *complémentaire* or *mutuelle*. If you have very limited resources then you can go to your local CPAM and ask for your costs to be reimbursed under the system known as *Couverture Maladie Universelle* (CMU) which is intended to ensure that everyone in France has complementary healthcare cover. The salary threshold is €6,798 for a single person in 2004, more if you are married or have dependants.

When you first go to France you can use form E111 (obtainable in a UK post office) to obtain refunds for medical treatment. This extends for 3 months and covers unexpected illnesses. After that you are supposed to pay contributions to the French system. People who are not working in France can in practice continue to rely on the NHS in the UK and use the E111 for anything up to 2 years. Once you start paying into the French system and are no longer tax-resident in the UK then you are not officially entitled to go back to the UK to be treated free of charge on the NHS.

**Child Benefit.** As regards *allocations familiales,* you make your contributions to your nearest URSSAF office. Benefits coming under *allocations familiales* – in particular child benefit – will be paid to you by the Caisse Nationale des Allocations Familiales (www.caf.fr). The following table gives some idea of what kinds of payments you have to make. Pensions are dealt with separately below.

| | *Allocations familiales* | *Maladie-maternité* |
|---|---|---|
| Benefits | family benefits | illness and maternity |
| Contributions | *allocations familiales* CSG/CRDS/CFP | *maladie-maternité* *indemnités journalières* |
| Information from | URSSAF www.urssaf.fr | CANAM www.canam.fr |

## Unemployment

You are not obliged to take out insurance against unemployment if you are a non-salaried worker. You can make voluntary contributions to either the *Association pour la Protection des Patrons Indépendants* (APPI – www.appi.fr) or *La Garantie Sociale des Chefs d'Entreprises* (GSC – www.gsc.asso.fr). If you are a salaried director or partner, then your employer is generally not permitted to make payments to the national unemployment fund, ASSEDIC. You can try to approach ASSEDIC to see if they will accept you, but the chances are slim. You are usually bound to pay to APPI or GSC.

## Occasional Work

If you do self-employed work for less than 90 days a year you are still required to pay social security contributions as a non-salaried worker. This minimum contribution is calculated on the basis of 40% of the social security annual threshold, which was €29,712 in 2004. A new pro-rata system is being introduced in 2004, greatly reducing the payments.

# PENSIONS

While working in France you pay contributions towards your old-age pension (*assurance vieillesse*) to the state social security organisation URSSAF, which entitles you to a basic pension (*retraite de base*) and the supplementary pension (*retraite complémentaire*). Contributions to the basic pension are more or less the same for salaried workers, *commerçants* and artisans (16.35% of the social security threshold), but less for liberal professions. The intention is that you will be able to receive 50% of your average salary for your highest earning years at the age of 60 or 65. Entitlement is based on the number of *trimestres* or three-monthly periods you have contributed for. At the current time the number of qualifying *trimestres* is being progressively increased from 150 to 160 in 2008 (i.e. a full 40 years). From 2008 your pension will be calculated on the basis of your 25 highest-earning years, whereas in the past it was based on your 10 highest-earning years.

There is a multitude of organisations dealing with your *retraite complémentaire*. On top of that you have to pay contributions to cover incapacity (*invalidité*), and towards *capital-décès*, a lump sum paid to surviving dependants when you die. The following table will give you some idea where to look for information:

|  | Artisans | Commerçants/ industriels | Liberal professions |
|---|---|---|---|
| Pension rights | retraite de base | retraite de base | retraite de base |
|  | complémentaire | complémentaire | complémentaire |
|  | obligatory | optional | obligatory |
| Contributions | assurance vieillesse | assurance vieillesse | assurance vieillesse |
|  | invalidité-décès | invalidité-décès | invalidité-décès (not all) |
| Information from | CANCAVA | ORGANIC | CNAVPL |
|  | www.cancava.fr | www.organic.fr | www.cnavpl.fr |

If you are a non-salaried *commerçant* or *artisan*, pension contributions are made by using percentages adding up to some 20% of the *plafond de sécurité sociale* (indexed social security threshold; €29,712 in 2004). If you are a salaried director of a company then you will pay contributions into the same pension funds as salaried workers, namely ARRCO and AGIRC. Payment systems are more complex for liberal professions (see www.cnavpl.fr) and farmers (see www.msa.fr).

The French state pension is paid tax-free. You will still have to pay tax on other sources of income, i.e. UK pension.

## WHEN AND WHAT DO I PAY?

Social security contributions are often cited as a cause of small businesses collapsing by their third year, because they increase steeply over time. To give some idea of the situation the following table compares contributions paid by non-salaried and salaried directors/partners on the basis of a taxable income of €34,000 after deduction of business expenses, taking 2004 as Year 1.

*Entrepreneur Individuel*/Single partner EURL/Majority director of SARL

|  | Year 1 | Year 2 | Year 3 | Year 4 |
|---|---|---|---|---|
| Income tax | zero | €1,629 | €539 | €212 |
| Personal SS contributions | €3,115 | €11,245 | €17,630 | €8,435 |
| Net income | €30,885 | €21,126 | €15,831 | €25,353 |

Salaried minority director of SARL/Salaried chairman of SAS

|  | Year 1 | Year 2 | Year 3 | Year 4 |
|---|---|---|---|---|
| Income tax | zero | €145 | €145 | €145 |
| Personal SS contributions | €4,873 | €4,873 | €4,873 | €4,873 |
| Employer's SS contributions | €9,579 | €9,579 | €9,579 | €9,579 |
| Net income | €19,548 | €19,403 | €19,403 | €19,403 |

The basic system is that during the first two years of your self-employment, you will pay lump sum rates until your actual income is known. In the first year your contributions are calculated on the basis of an annual income of €6,364 (indexed), which gives a basic contribution of €1,227 (rate for 2004) to which are added the pension contributions that apply to your profession; total €2,580 for *commerçants*; €2,950 for *artisans* (2004). The contributions in the first half of year 2 are based on a notional income of €9,546, so you pay €920 (2004) for the first 6 months (plus pension contributions). From the second half of the second year the amount will be adjusted to reflect your real income. During the third year you will be taxed on your real earnings, but you will pay on the basis of what you earned one or two years before. This means that you need to have money in reserve to meet a sudden increase in the social security contributions, as is evident from the table above.

Payments are made monthly, three-monthly or half-yearly. If you earn very little then your contributions are reduced. For example if you earn less than €11,674 then your health insurance contribution is only €817. If you benefit from the ACCRE scheme, which helps unemployed people to start or take over a business, you may be freed from making some social security payments if your income does not exceed 120% of the minimum wage or SMIC.

There has been a change in the system in that the authorities have recognised the problems created by making high social security demands when someone has just started out as an *indépendant*. From 1 January 2004 non-salaried workers – i.e. entrepreneurs – will be able to defer social security payments for the first 12 months of their start-up, and spread out the payments over 5 years. This applies to businesses created or taken over from 1 January 2004. As a further measure, those who choose to pay tax under the *micro-entreprise* regime can in future ask to pay contributions on the basis of their real income, rather than making advance payments on the basis of what they earned in the year before last.

## SOCIAL SECURITY DEADLINES

| Contributions | Deadlines |
|---|---|
| Maladie-maternité | 1 April/1 October |
| Allocations familiales | |
| + CSG/CRDS taxes | 15 May/15 August/15 November/15 February |
| Assurance vieillesse de base | 15 February/31 July |
| Assurance vieillesse complémentaire | varies according to profession |
| Invalidité-décès | 15 February/31 July |
| (only commerçants/artisans) | |

# INSURANCE

Insurance is compulsory for properties used to run a business. While the risk of burglary is quite low in many areas, there are serious risks from flooding, subsidence and fire in some areas. It pays to take this into account before you buy your property.

While you can add your French property to your UK insurance, it is more convenient to insure with a local company in France who are able to handle claims in English, so that you get a quick response in case of problems. There are English-speaking agents in many parts of France who can arrange insurance for you. Some agents only sell policies for one company (*agents généraux*), and others deal with several (*courtier d'assurances*). For general information see www.cdia.fr.

### House and Contents Insurance

The basic house and contents insurance is the *assurance multirisques habitation,* also often called *assurance multirisques vie privée* or *la multirisque.* This will include cover against natural disasters as a matter of course. Insurance is calculated on the basis of the surface area of your property or the number of rooms. Civil liability insurance – *responsabilité civile propriétaire* – is essential, in case an event on your property affects your neighbours. Your possessions also need to be insured. This kind of policy does not insure you against personal accidents, unless you ask for it. There are numerous formulas for the *assurance multiris-*

*ques*, depending on your requirements.

It is assumed that you will take over the existing insurance from the previous owner of the property you are buying. If you do not wish to continue the same insurance policy – generally the wisest course of action for foreign buyers – you are required to present another policy to the notary before you can sign the final *acte de vente*. It is normal to insure the contents of your property as well. The current market value or *valeur vénale* of the items is used to work out the amount of cover; depreciation is taken into account.

## Insurance and Tenants/copropriétés

If you rent a property for a long period the owner will ask you to take out an *assurance multirisques habitation* to cover the building and any risks that could affect neighbours, e.g. floods, fire, explosions. You should ask the owner whether you need insurance well before you sign a tenancy agreement. You are free to choose any insurance company you want. In the case of a *copropriété* the building insurance will be taken care of by the manager of the property, and your share of the premiums will appear on the monthly charges. You are responsible for insuring your own possessions and for third-party insurance.

## Commercial Properties

Whether you are the owner or the tenant it will not be possible to take over a building to start a business without having an insurance policy. Businesses need the same types of insurance as homes: property and contents insurance is basic. If you have customers visiting your premises then third-party liability insurance is a necessity. In addition, you will need to insure your stock, and if you think it wise, also take out insurance against interruption to your business if your premises cannot be used for a certain period. Insurance brokers will give you a quote for an all-in policy.

If part of your business is offering potentially hazardous sports activities such as ski-ing or canoeing, then you are required to inform your insurer. Those who work in liberal professions, e.g. estate agents, architects etc., must have professional indemnity insurance.

## Terms and Conditions

**Thefts.** It is a condition of insurance policies that you report thefts within 24 hours to the police, or as soon as possible, if you want your claim to be taken seriously. The police will give you a form – *déclaration de vol* – with the details of what you have lost. You need to inform the insurers within two working days of the theft and send the receipt of the *déclaration* by registered post (*recommandée avec avis de réception* – RAR). It is advisable to telephone the insurer immediately and they will send you a confirmation. You then draw up a list of the stolen goods and send it by registered post.

**Natural Disasters.** There is a whole raft of regulations about which natural events count as disasters or *catastrophes naturelles*. The amount of time you have to report a disaster ranges from four days for hail to 10 days after a storm, if this has been declared a *catastrophe naturelle* in the official journal. Your house or business insurance should cover not only *catastrophes naturelles* but all kinds of other natural risks. Check that the policy covers damage to electrical items as well.

**Checking the Small Print.** Look carefully at the small print in the policy to see what conditions are set for reporting damage, thefts, etc., and any exclusions. Check for the *franchise* or excess, i.e. the first part of the claim that is not paid. Taking videos and photos of property is an eminently sensible precaution to make sure you are paid in full. You can use a bailiff – *huissier* – or an insurance expert to prepare a report on damage to your property. The insurance company will normally send their own expert to draw up a report on your loss.

Policies are renewed automatically (*tacite reconduction*); you are given a period of time before the renewal date when you can cancel the policy. Once the date has passed it is too late to cancel. Premiums should be paid by standing order, within 10 days of the set date. You will receive a warning (*mise en demeure*) from the insurer. If you haven't paid within 30 days your policy will be cancelled, but you will still be liable for the outstanding amount and the insurer's costs.

# UTILITIES

Electricity and gas supplies are supplied by the state monopoly organisation EDF/GDF. In most of France there is no mains gas (*gaz de ville*), so you have the option of installing a large *citerne* (2 cubic metre tank) and having liquefied gas delivered, or using bottled gas. For more information see www.gazdefrance.com.

## *Electricity*

Many foreign property-buyers take little notice of the state of the wiring in the property that they are thinking of buying, something that can prove to be an expensive mistake. Almost all pre-1970s houses have potentially hazardous wiring, unless they have been rewired. The main problems are lack of, or insufficient earthing, corroded wiring and unsuitable circuit-breakers. In older properties you can still find WWI-style cotton-covered wiring. Apart from any risk of electrocution, if you are taking over an older property it is essential to find out whether the wiring can handle heavy-amperage equipment such as washing machines and electric cookers. If you need to run electric heating at the same time as other heavy equipment such as an electric cooker, water heater, washing machine etc., then you will require a supply of at least 12 KvA (kilovolt amperes or kilowatts), for which heavier wiring is needed to the electricity meter. Where you are planning a business that involves using heavy equipment, then you need to consider whether your supply is going to be adequate.

If the power supply to your property has been cut off before you buy it then you will require a *certificat de conformité* or CC from the electricity safety organisation Consuel to certify that the system is safe before EDF will reconnect your supply. Consuel does not inspect an electrician's work unless there is a good reason, neither does it certify that your system conforms to a certain level. They will only test the earths and the consumer unit (*tableau principal*). If you buy a house without an electricity supply, the French state monopoly, Électricité de France (EDF), will connect you to the grid. There is a basic charge of €600 for a new connection, plus €1,500 for every new electricity pole that has to be erected. If you cannot see an electricity pylon nearby then your connection could cost more than the property itself.

If you are intending to buy a property in France, it is in your interest to ask the seller to allow a *Diagnostic Confiance Sécurité* to be carried out. This is a 40-minute inspection covering a list of 53 points resulting in an objective assessment of the state of the wiring of your house. Once the inspection has been carried out, you can call in an electrician to give an estimate (*devis*) of the cost of any work needed. The DCS only costs €80 including taxes. Needless to say, if your prospective seller refuses to allow a DCS then you should be suspicious. Do not under any circumstances take the seller's word for it that everything is fine with the wiring. A DCS can be arranged by calling an EDF advisor on 0801 126 126, or through Promotelec who carry out the DCS, on 0825 046 770 or through their website www.promotelec.com. Information about different tariffs can be found on EDF's websites: http://monagence.edf.fr and www.mamaison.edf.fr.

## Water

The mains water supply is safe to drink, if not always that tasty. The French consume a lot of bottled mineral water, on average 100 litres per person per year.

Mains water is supplied by Générale des Eaux and other local companies around France. Lyonnaise des Eaux is well-known and owns some UK water suppliers. There have been water shortages in central and southern France in recent years during hot weather. The water supply is metered and can cost twice as much as in the UK. There will be a meter outside the property. It is essential to check the reliability of the supply if you are buying property. Water leaks should be reported quickly.

If there is no water supply to a property, one can either arrange for a connection to be made, or try to sink a well – *puits* – on the land, or tap into an underground spring. The quality of the water has to be analysed first before you can use it. Water with a high nitrate content – where there is intensive agriculture – presents a real health risk.

On average, mains water costs €2.8 per cubic metre. The average person in the north of France uses 43 cubic metres a year, while on the Côte d'Azur the figure is 74 cubic metres. In Paris it is 66 cubic metres.

Evidently, it is worth investing in water saving measures if possible. To find out the local price of water, and the nearest supplier, look at the website www.generale-des-eaux.com.

For large-scale use of the water supply for activities such as brewing your system will have to be inspected by the Police d'Eau (water police). If you generate large amounts of waste water you will need to build natural filtration tanks – *lagunage* – and have your facilities approved.

### Septic Tanks/Fosses Septiques

The state of one's septic tank is a favourite subject of conversation with foreign residents in France. Septic tanks exist in the UK, but they are more common in France, where many properties are far from the main sewage system. There is a trend in France to connect more properties to the main sewage system, known as *tout à l'égout*. Cesspits – *puisards* – where all the waste simply goes into a hole in the ground, are being phased out, and it is no longer legal to build one. All *fosses septiques* are supposed to meet a new government standard by the year 2005.

The idea of the septic tank is to process the waste from toilets, and other used water, through the natural action of bacteria, so that eventually only fairly harmless water is left. All the waste runs into the first settling tank, or septic tank, where the solid matter sinks to the bottom, while scum forms on the surface. The naturally present bacteria break the waste matter down, releasing methane. The remainder goes into a second settling tank, which should be half the length of the first tank, and then into a 'drain field' or system of soakaways, with a series of drain pipes or drain tiles laid on gravel. The drain pipes or tiles are perforated so that the effluent filters away into the ground. Before the effluent reaches the soakaways, there has to be an inspection chamber, or *regard de visite*. The solid matter in the septic tank has to be emptied once in a while, the so-called *vidange*. The interval depends very much on how well the tank is maintained. The local municipality will recommend at what intervals the tank should be emptied, but there are no hard and fast rules. Anywhere between two and 10 years is possible.

The soil has to be tested for percolation properties before the *fosse septique* is built. Too much clay or too much sand will have a detrimental effect on the percolation. The system must not be built within 100 feet of a well, or within 50 feet of a watercourse. It also needs to slope downwards away from the property to help the throughput. One is not obliged to use commercial preparations to maintain the bacteria level, since waste water is already full of bacteria. Bleach and other chemicals will tend to reduce the amount of helpful bacteria, but only temporarily. Cooking oil and grease are particularly noxious to a *fosse septique.*

If you are looking at country properties, make sure to find out whether there is a *fosse septique.* If there is none you will be required to install one. Since the whole contraption extends at least 70 feet from the house, it is essential to have enough land to build one. The larger your *fosse septique* the less trouble it will give you. You cannot construct anything over the *fosse septique,* and there should be a minimum of trees around it. You should also look at the slope of the land, and make sure that the water table is not too close to the surface. Generally, *fosses septiques* work better in hotter climates, which favour the breakdown of the wastes. The price of new *fosses septiques* is going up rapidly because of ever more stringent regulations. A new one, including the cost of installation, can cost €5,000. For suppliers look at French property magazines, or the website www.profosse.com.

# TELEPHONES AND INTERNET

## *Telephoning*

For the moment the telephony scene in France is straightforward: France Télécom is the only company that can install your phone and you will make your calls through them. There are plans to privatise France Télécom, and this may not be entirely positive, especially if you live in a country area. Up until now there has been no difference in the price of having a new phone line installed in a city, or in the remotest parts of the hinterland. Sooner or later, France Télécom may decide it cannot spend 1,000s of euros on connecting rural customers to the nearest exchange. You can use other telephone services providers, e.g. Onetel and 9 Télécom. The comparison of the prices can be found on the website www.comparatel.com.

British handsets need an adaptor to work in France; the British variety has three wires, while the French ones have only two. The keys on French telephones are much the same as on British ones. The only point to note is that the hash symbol is called *dièse* – the same as a 'sharp' in music – needed for cheap-rate telephone cards. Both business and private phone numbers are on the internet. The Yellow Pages are on www.pagesjaunes.fr and private subscribers on www.annuaire.com or www.annu.fr. There is also Minitel, which is expensive but can be used free in post offices. There is always Directory Enquiries: dial 12.

## Mobile Phones

Mobile phone contracts are a subject of some controversy in France. Unless you are prepared to stay with one company for a certain time, you will not be able to keep the same phone number or list of numbers if you buy another phone. If you spend any amount of time in France you will want to rent or buy a mobile phone there, but before you sign a contract it is worth considering the small print. You can try to have the SIM card in your phone replaced with a French one, so you can carry on using the same phone. If your phone is 'SIM-locked', i.e. the card cannot be changed, then you need a French mobile. Unless you are officially resident in France, French mobile phone companies will only let you use a phone with a pre-paid card, on production of your passport. The well-known deals are Orange La Mobicarte, SFR La Carte, and Bouygues Carte Nomad.

To buy a phone you need a proof of identity and a proof of address. You also have to produce an RIB – a bank account number – which is in any case unavoidable if you pay by direct debit. You will also be asked to produce a cheque written out to you that has gone through your account, or a French credit card.

As France is relatively thinly populated in comparison to the UK, mobile phone coverage is not guaranteed, and there are areas in the countryside where you will not have any reception. Out of the three main phone companies, Orange and SFR are supposed to have better coverage than Bouygues Télécom in country areas. All three claim to cover 98% of the population and 87% of the land area.

The mobile phone market is competitive and rapidly changing. For a clear overview of the different deals on offer, look at the website www.comparatel.com. From this it is evident that there is not that much to choose between the three main operators, although Bouygues comes out slightly better if you are a light user. For the three main companies see: www.orange.fr, www.sfr.fr and www.bouyguestelecom.fr.

## *Internet*

It would be fair to say that France is some years behind the UK in terms of internet use and availability. This is to some extent because of the pioneering system known as Minitel started in 1985, which provides a service similar to the internet. Minitel is a keyboard and screen that sit alongside your telephone; although it is expensive to use it is still popular. You can access Minitel from the UK, by logging on to www.minitel.fr. If you are travelling around in France it can be difficult to find cybercafés outside the big towns. The French government has had the bright idea of installing internet terminals in 1,000 post offices. Unfortunately, many of these terminals do not work properly, and you can only use the post office's own webmail, www.laposte.net in any case.

The French are still trying to decide on a word for 'e-mail'. The Académie Française favours *courriel*, an abbreviation of *courrier électronique*, but almost no one has taken this up. Most people prefer the ugly-sounding *mel*; a lot of companies use the word *e-mail*, but it is not likely to become the standard written form of the word here.

Once you have settled in to your new home in France, you can look at the different internet service providers' offerings, which are more limited than what you would find in the UK. If you are a light user, you may do well with Wanadoo.fr or Club-internet.fr. Wanadoo (owned by France Télécom), Club-internet, Tiscali, Free and Freesurf also offer 'free' packages where you only pay for the telephone call. If you are connected to cable, you can get good deals with Noos. For the moment you will only be able to have ADSL (high-speed connections) in certain areas. Even if your modem speed is 56kbps it may effectively be only 10kbps or less. The French government is committed to providing ADSL all over the country, which may mean having small aeroplanes flying overhead in remote districts 24 hours a day. For more information about different ISP charges, look at the website www.comparatel.com or some back issues of the French consumer magazine *Le Particulier.*

# Employing Staff

## CHAPTER SUMMARY

o **Local Workers.** Many Anglo-Saxons bring in foreign labourers rather than using local workers.
o **Availability.** With high unemployment there is no difficulty finding staff.
o **Social Security.** Employers pay 60% on top of employees' wages.
o **Incentives.** There are various incentive schemes in place for employing young people and the long-term unemployment.
o **Contracts.** Employment contracts should be written down in some form or other.
o **Terms of Employment.** Employees are protected against sudden dismissal and will receive compensation if wrongfully dismissed.
o **Spouses.** Spouses of company founders or partners can receive social security benefits on the basis that they work with their partners in a business.

Taking on staff is likely to become a necessity at some point during your business career. The formalities involved are considerable, and the burden of social security costs means that you can double the basic salary if you want an idea of how much an employee will cost you. For that reason, many businesses avoid taking on long-term staff. It is certainly the case that many small businesses start to struggle when they have to take on the responsibility of permanent staff.

Being an employer entails taking on a lot more paperwork than if you work alone. It is, on the other hand, not true to say that employers are required to make a lot of rules in the workplace. There are actually far fewer regulations governing workers' conduct on the shopfloor than in the UK or USA. The French view is that workers and employers should be able to thrash out their differences without having to rely on written rules. A French worker is more likely to tell their employer what they think they should do than one in the UK (at least according to sociologists). Personal relationships are paramount, while at the same time there is a much stricter separation between private and working life than in the UK. It is most important to understand the French concept of personal honour, and hope it applies to your employees.

Northern Europeans often say that the French simply do their own thing, or that they are a nation of anarchists. They are certainly impulsive to a fault. You will often meet foreigners in the southern part of France who swear that they will never employ another French tradesman, and bring in Portuguese or Irish or British workers. Making a plan and then sticking to it is not really the French way. First make your plan, then throw it out of the window and improvise as you go along is more the way things are done. Making plans is fun, but they shouldn't get in the way of work.

## FINDING STAFF

In a country with high unemployment like France, there is no shortage of staff. Your first port of call is the state employment centre or ANPE (www.anpe.fr) whose function is to find work for the unemployed. Your advertisement for a worker can be put on their website (see *Recrutement*). There are also the local newspapers.

## HIRING AND FIRING

When hiring a new worker you are required to submit a single document – the *document unique d'embauche (DUE)* – which contains 9 different formalities connected with hiring. The DUE is to be submitted to URSSAF – the body responsible for collecting social security contributions – or MSA in the case agricultural workers, by letter, fax or internet on www.due.fr. The first part of the DUE has to be received by URSSAF eight days at the earliest before the worker actually starts: this is the *déclaration préalable à l'embauche (DPAE)*. Your employer cannot legally start work until URSSAF have received the DPAE. You will receive a confirmation of receipt (*avis de réception*) from URSSAF informing you that you have taken the necessary steps to employ a salaried worker.

## BASIC FORMALITIES WHEN HIRING WORKERS

All these formalities will be carried out for you when you submit your *déclaration unique d'embauche.*

- DPAE – declaration that you intend to employ a salaried worker
- declaration that this is your first salaried worker
- request to register the worker with the social security regime through URSSAF
- request for membership of the unemployment insurance organisation ASSEDIC
- registration with a health and safety organisation
- request for a compulsory visit from a medical service
- list of workers with a view to establishing DADS (annual declaration of company details).

Beyond this, you may also need to submit declarations in order to receive reductions on your social charges for a first employee, or a part-time employee.

Your DUE will be passed on to relevant bodies, such as the CPAM (*Caisse Primaire d'Assurance Maladie*) for health insurance, the DDTEFP (*Direction Départementale du Travail, de l'Emploi et de la Formation Professionnelle*) the labour inspectorate, the tax office, and to ARRCO, which will inform you to which organisation you have to make pension contributions for your worker. You are required to register with ARRCO within three months of setting up any company. The pension fund you contribute to depends on what type of business you run. You may in some cases be able to choose for yourself, or have one assigned to you. If your employee is classified as a manager then you will also need to be affiliated to AGIRC, the equivalent organisation to ARRCO for managers and the higher paid.

The percentages of your employee's salary that you as the employer are liable to pay – the *part patronale* – varies depending on the type of business you are in. If you employ a director then you are not required to make any contributions to an unemployment fund. Overall the employer can expect to pay anything up to 60% on top of the salary that the employee receives. The social security payments come to some 50%, and there are additional taxes payable by employers (see below), as well as insurance against accidents. The employee also pays their part of the contributions.

In order to find out what kind of payments you will have to make it is useful to register with the on-line payments site www.net-entreprises.fr. It is possible to make your social security declarations on-line using the *déclaration unifiée de cotisations sociales* (DUCS). If you use this system you can have payments made by direct debit on the date due. It also saves you having to send cheques to 3 or 4 different organisations.

## EMPLOYER'S SOCIAL SECURITY PAYMENTS

As a general principle social security contributions are paid monthly 5 days after the salary has been paid, although this can be stretched to 10 days. Sole traders and SARLs employing fewer than 10 workers can make payments every three months, on the 15th of the month following the three-monthly period (i.e. 15 April, 15 July, 15 October, 15 January). The following are the basic payments:

| | |
|---|---|
| *Maladie-maternité* | URSSAF |
| + CSG/CRDS taxes | URSSAF |
| *Invalidité-décès* | included in *maladie-maternité* |
| *Allocations familiales* | URSSAF |
| *Assurance vieillesse de base* | URSSAF |
| *Assurance vieillesse complémentaire* | fund assigned by ARRCO/AGIRC |
| *Assurance chômage* (unemployment contributions) | ASSEDIC |

Precise dates are given on the website www.apce.com.

### *Holiday Pay and the 35 hour week*

French law requires employers to give 5 weeks paid holiday per year to their workers (not including public holidays and weekends). Payment is either the same as worked days, or 10% of annual salary for the 5 weeks, which comes to the same thing. Employees will, under normal circumstances, take their holidays during the *période légale* – 1 May to 30 October. If they are made to take their holiday outside this period then they are entitled to 1 additional day off for 3-5 days' holiday taken outside the legal period, or 2 additional days for 6 or more days of holiday taken outside the legal period.

Since the passing of the first Loi Aubry in 1998, a 35-hour week has been imposed on many employees. This is a bone of contention for employers, and the current right-wing government is giving them more and more leeway to make their employees work longer hours. In managerial positions the 35-hour week is generally replaced by a system where the employee works 39 hours a week and takes additional holidays in lieu. There is, however, a law that no employee can take more than 4 weeks' holiday in one go.

**Minimum Wage.** France has had a minimum wage since 1980, known as the SMIC, the *Salaire Minimum Interprofessionnel Croissance*. It stands at €1090.48 for a 151.67-hour month, which at the current exchange rate adds up to £8,750 per year.

## INCENTIVES FOR EMPLOYING SALARIED WORKERS

There are some financial incentives for employing long-term unemployed and the socially disadvantaged. There are many conditions attached. Grants and exemptions are more generous in depressed areas, such as Zones de Redynamisation Urbaines, or Zones de Redynamisation Rurale. The local employment centre (ANPE) will give you further information, as will the work inspectorate – DDTEFP. The following is only a sample of the possibilities:

***Contrat Jeunes.*** If you take on a young person between 16 and 23 on a permanent contract of indeterminate duration (CDD) you will receive €225-292.50 per month for the first two years of employment, and 50% for the third year, depending on the wage. You are required to pay at least the minimum wage (SMIC) or the minimum wage as laid down in the collective labour agreement for your industry, known as the *salaire minimum conventionné* (SMC). The contract can also be less than part-time, but at least 50% of a full-time contract. Only young people who have not gained their *baccalauréat* qualify. They can have vocational qualifications such as the CAP or BEP or none at all.

***Contrat Initiative Emploi (CIE).*** This aims to return the long-term unemployed who are over 25 or have dependent children to the workplace. Contracts of unlimited duration or of limited duration between one and two years are allowed. To qualify the employee should have been unemployed at least 18 months of the previous 36 months, or 12 out of 18 in urban areas. Depending on the type of employee, the employer will receive a subsidy of €330 or €500 per month for up to two years. The employee can themselves continue to receive some unemployment benefits while also receiving a salary, to make up for the difference between their unemployment benefit and their salary.

***Contrat d'apprentissage.*** If you take on a young person between 16 and 25 who is studying towards a vocational qualification, then you can benefit from some exemptions from employer's social security payments. The contract is for 1-3 years. You are required to pay 23-78% of the minimum wage, and to ensure that the apprentice receives suitable training. Part of the apprentice's time will be spent doing training at the *Centre de Formation d'Apprentis* (CFA). The employer will receive a lump sum at the start of €915, plus €1,525 annually to subsidise training (and further advantages). The employer is not required to pay any social security contributions on behalf of their trainee. There is a trial period of 2 months after which the contract cannot be broken except in case of a serious fault by either party. A similar type of contract is the *contrat de qualification.*

***Association Loi 1901.*** If you run a non-profit *association* then there are considerable advantages if you want to employ young salaried workers.

The *association* can enter into a contract with a young person between 18 and 22 for three years, after which the employee leaves without any redundancy payment. Young persons can be employed after the age of 22 but they have to leave before they reach the age of 25. The current *emploi-jeunes* scheme started operation in 2003. When you employ an unemployed young person you enter a *Contrat d'insertion des jeunes dans la vie sociale* which entitles you to receive a subsidy from the state of up to 33% of the current SMIC (minimum wage). The amount can be as much as 66% if you employ someone to work in certain socially beneficial areas, such as with the handicapped or the aged. The state particularly likes to encourage young people with a business plan of their own to work for *associations* to gain experience.

### Not Your Average Bar

Englishman Tony Pidgeon owns a bar, Le Manhattan, in Ribérac, Dordogne.

*I was going to retire, but then I got to know a young French couple who were unemployed. As I knew the owner of the bar and had some experience of this kind of work, I decided to take it over and employ the couple; but then they split up and I carried on. The bar was owned by a SARL (limited company). I started a new SARL so I wouldn't be held liable for any of the former owner's misdemeanours. All the profit goes into the SARL. I don't draw any salary. Officially I'm a tourist, and I can stay here for 9 months of the year without any problem. The SARL has to have an accountant which entails more costs; I use a firm in Bordeaux which is half British-owned. The SARL registers annual accounts.*

*I left the bar and its name exactly as it was. I haven't tried to cater specially for foreigners. When I started, the local Commission de Sécurité came around and told me what I had to put right, i.e. fire doors and extinguishers etc. I have a licence to sell any kind of alcohol. The only restriction is that I have to be closed 4 hours out of every 24. The main difficulty about running a business here is the cost of hiring staff. In England you can hire students and if they earn less than £80 a week there is no tax or NI. Here you have to pay another 50% in social charges on top of salary, regardless of what they earn. You have to register anyone you want to employ first; you can't just ask someone to come in if you need them. Every month I have to pay 6 cheques to different organisations, such as URSSAF, Assedic, the pension fund, and so on. In England you would only pay one.*

*We are no longer registered for TVA because we're below the threshold. We were registered once; it was a pain because I had to pay back all the TVA that I didn't have to pay when I did up the bar. I've made a lot of friends here, all the old characters who come in here, and what's more our pool team are the champions of France.*

### Sickness and Maternity Leave

By virtue of making payments to the social security system, the employee becomes eligible for sickness pay (*indemnités journalières*) once they have made enough payments during the course of the year. The first 3 days they receive nothing. It is also usual for the employer to make additional payments for sickness leave. The employee has to provide the employer with a medical certificate within 2 days. If the employer is also making sickness payments then they have the right to submit the employee to an independent medical examination. After 6 months' absence, the employee can be made redundant following the usual process of dismissal.

Pregnant women receive 16 weeks' leave on full pay (6 weeks before and 10 weeks after the delivery) in normal circumstances. An additional 6 weeks can be taken if there are medical complications. The father can take 11 days off, and receive basic state sick pay as of right.

## CONTRACTS

An employment contract is only obligatory if you are taking someone on for a limited period of time (*contrat à durée déterminée*), or if you are applying for subsidies or exemptions from social security payments. In the case of the contract of unlimited duration (*contrat à durée indéterminée*), the letter offering the job counts as a contract. You are legally required to provide the employee with a letter confirming their employment which should give details of their working hours, salary, holidays, etc. An example is given in the following chapter under 'Business Letters'. A copy of the *déclaration unique d'embauche* – social security declaration – can be given to the employee.

In certain sectors you do not have total freedom to make any contract you want: you will have to follow a ready-made model imposed by the collective labour convention. This is the case with café/hotel/restaurant workers; see www.chr-link.com for details.

## EMPLOYMENT CONTRACT

The contract should mention at least the following:

*Entre les soussignés ..... et .....*
The undersigned .... and ....

*il est convenu que:*
it is agreed that:

*Fonctions*
Job function

*Rémunération*
Remuneration

*Horaires*
Working hours

*Congés payés*
Paid holidays

*Jours fériés*
............... *percevra la totalité de son salaire pour tous les jours fériés*
Public holidays
................. will receive their salary in full for public holidays

*Clause de non-concurrence*
Non-competition clause

*Fin de contrat*
Conditions for termination

## *Contrat à durée déterminée*

Short-term contracts can only be used in certain specific circumstances. They are illegal where the employee is taking on a regular position in a company without any special circumstances. Justifications for a CDD include:

o the employee is replacing a permanent worker whose post will disappear within a predictable time
o the employee is standing in for a worker who is yet to be appointed
o the employee is replacing a worker who is absent for a determined period of time
o the employee is required to fulfil an urgent order or to deal with a temporary increase in business
o the nature of the work is seasonal

The CDD is for a maximum time of:
o 18 months in general
o 9 months if waiting for a future appointment, or in case of urgent work
o 24 months if the post is going to disappear

The minimum period is generally 6 months, but can be shorter if, for example, the job is only for the summer season or a festival. The CDD can be renewed once for the same period. Another type of contract, the *contrat de travail temporaire* has no definite length, because of the nature of the situation. It is used in areas of work where it is impossible to draw up a fixed contract, or where the work is intermittent.

Failure to respect the rules concerning CDDs results in the contract being requalified as a permanent one. The employee can break the contract if they have been offered a permanent job; they still have to give 1 month's notice. The employee can also be dismissed for gross misconduct or because of circumstances beyond the employer's control. The employee and employer can agree to end the contract at any time.

## DISMISSALS

There is an elaborately worked-out system of *'fautes'* for which one can dismiss an employee. The employee can also cite the employer for breach of contract or some other *faute* in front of an employment tribunal. The *chef de l'entreprise* – which is anyone who owns a registered business – has disciplinary powers. In the first place you can give a warning (*avertissement*), followed by a second warning (*blâme*) followed by suspension (*mise à pied*), either temporarily for 14 days, or with a view to dismissing the miscreant. If you intend to sack the worker, then you are required to invite them to a meeting either by handing them a letter or by post (registered letter with confirmation of receipt). Following the meeting you can send a registered letter giving the precise reasons for dismissal. If you find yourself in such a situation, then you would be well advised to take legal advice. Failure to give adequate reasons, or to inform the employee of their right to be assisted at the hearing will give rise to heavy penalties. If the employee fails to appear at the meeting then you will be able to dismiss them immediately without indemnity. If you prefer not to have your errant worker on the premises, you may pay them salary in lieu of notice and ask them not to darken your door again.

Dismissal can be motivated by three kinds of *faute: faute simple, faute lourde* and *faute grave.* You are not required to give any notice in the case of *faute lourde* and *grave.* It is accepted that the employee can no longer work for you because of theft, violent conduct, refusal to work, repeated lateness, etc. in the case of *faute grave.* The *faute lourde* implies that the employee deliberately harmed the interests of their employer without having committed an act that could render them liable to prosecution. In the case of *faute simple* (incompetence) you have to pay redundancy money equivalent of 10% of monthly salary (or sometimes 20 hours' salary) per year of employment. There is also a period of notice of 1 month if the person has been in your employ for over 6 months, and 2 months if they have been employed more than 2 years.

The burden of proof always lies with the employer. For that reason one would need to be very cautious about dismissing employees. If you fail to prove the grounds for dismissal then the employee can demand compensation.

Where there are genuine economic reasons for making an employee redundant then there are also procedures to be followed. Apart from having to show that your business is in difficulties, you have to set up a plan to try to retain the employee – *plan de sauvegarde de l'emploi* – and try to find the employee alternative work. Naturally, if you go into official administration – *redressement judiciaire* – there is no burden of proof. You are also committed to re-employ that person if your business recovers within one year. The redundancy payment is higher than in the case of dismissal on grounds of incompetence; generally, it is 20% of monthly salary per year of seniority, and more if the worker has been with you for over 10 years.

## Employment Tribunals

It is an unfortunate fact of life that half of all dismissals end up in front of the *conseil des prud'hommes* or the employment tribunal. The term *prud'hommes* means something like 'wise men'. Half the members of a tribunal are elected by employees and half by employers. In the first instance the *prud'hommes* hold a private hearing to try to resolve matters by conciliation. Where that fails, there is a public hearing, where the matter is decided by a majority vote; failure to reach a decision means putting the case before a panel of five judges. Dealing with *les prud'hommes* is something that one would want to avoid since it requires having legal representation.

## Trade Unions

There is a well-known myth that the French trade unions have immense power, which is not really true any longer. For one thing, only 9% of French workers are unionised, against 30% in the UK, but most union members are in the public sector where they can cause a great deal of disruption if they are feeling militant. The laws allow trade unions to go on strike without warning and give them all sorts of freedoms that disappeared with Margaret Thatcher as far as the British went. The closed shop is still very much present.

As a small business you are unlikely to have any dealings with a trade union. Naturally, your workers have the right to belong to one, but you would have to become quite a large business before you needed to be concerned about union activities. The worst that can happen is that the trains go on strike and your employees cannot get to work. You can also join an employers' trade union, such as MEDEF.

## Business and Love

Very often a one-person business is really a couple working together. To cover this eventuality the French have thought up three different regimes for your spouse: the *conjoint collaborateur,* the *conjoint associé* and the *conjoint salarié.* The term *conjoint* only covers married partners. If you enter into a notarised civil pact – a PACS – with someone then your 'partner' does not enjoy the same rights as someone you have married, at least as regards pensions. From a business point of view, being in a PACS with someone is of no great significance, except that you and the other person can choose to be taxed jointly since you share the same *foyer fiscal.* There are some advantages as regards transferring property and inheritance. If you are in a common-law partnership or *union libre,* also known as *concubinage notoire,* then you can make a declaration at the *mairie* informing the authorities of your shared existence. There are implications as regards social security, but as far as business or taxation goes you are treated as strangers.

**Conjoint collaborateur:** this status is open to you if you run an *entreprise individuelle* (but not agricultural), or you are the single partner in a EURL, on condition that your spouse (*conjoint*) works for you without being paid, and does not have another salaried activity that would take up more than half the working week. To prevent abuses of the system the spouse will need to be able to prove that they do in fact work with you in your business. For EIs it is preferable to inform the Registre de Commerce that your partner is working with you. The *conjoint collaborateur* has the right to act on their partner's behalf as though they were a director of the company. In all cases you need to present a sworn statement – *attestation sur l'honneur* – to the social security bodies you deal with to confirm that you are working with your partner. The advantage for the spouse is that they will receive healthcare and maternity benefits free of charge as the partner of someone paying self-employed contributions.

Concerning pensions, the spouses of artisans and *commerçants* who have been registered with the Registre de Commerce, can opt to pay contributions at one of three rates:

○ on 33.33% of the annual social security threshold (indexed) which was €29,712 in 2004.
○ on 33.33% or 50% of the business income
○ divide their contributions with the owner of the business

Spouses of the single partner of a EURL only have the first two options. There is a further advantage in that the spouse can also make voluntary pension contributions as well as the business founder, both of which are tax-deductible up to around €45,000 per year (indexed), along with the compulsory social security payments.

After 10 years as unpaid *conjoint collaborateur* the spouse are also entitled to a capital sum up to the equivalent of three times the annual minimum wage when the business founder dies (some €42,000 in 2004) but not more than 25% of the business assets. This constitutes a 'deferred salary' for all the years of unpaid work. Once the business founder has died the business is liquidated and the amount taken out of the inheritance. The deceased partner's pension rights also revert to the surviving partner (*réversion de droits*). These matters are however further complicated by the inheritance laws. If you are the partner of someone exercising a *profession libérale* your rights are not quite as advantageous.

**Conjoint associé.** As the name suggests, this status is only open to a spouse who is a partner in your company, which can be a SNC, SARL, SELARL or SAS. The spouse is required to contribute to the capital of the company by investing their labour, cash or other assets in the company, but they are protected from creditors beyond the amount of their real contribution. The spouse-partner can be made a director of the company, and has the right to continue your business if you die before they do. If they are a director of the company they pay social security contributions in the same way as any other director, i.e.

minimal compulsory social security contributions for a majority director, and the full contributions if they are a salaried minority director (except for unemployment).

*Conjoint salarié.* The spouse has a salaried post in the business and has to be paid at least the minimum wage, or a reasonable amount according to the work they do and their qualifications. They are treated as salaried workers for the purposes of social security. The spouse's entire salary can be deducted from the business's taxable income if the company is subject to corporation tax (IS). Where the company is subject to income tax (IR), the full salary is deductible if the couple are married under the separation of assets regime. If you are married under the common assets or *participation aux acquêts* regime, then a sum of up to 36 times the monthly minimum wage is deductible if you belong to a Centre de Gestion Agréé (state-sponsored accountancy organisation), or only €2,600 if you do not.

## DOMESTIC STAFF

Apart from your business, you may also want to hire a babysitter, gardener, handyman etc. The rules require domestic employees to enjoy the same rights as other workers. You are expected to draw up a written contract, specifying the number of hours and nature of the worker's duties. The minimum level of remuneration is determined by a *Convention Collective Nationale* for all workers employed in the home, covering cooks, cleaners, nurses, handymen/women, nannies, babysitters, governesses, butlers and chauffeurs, amongst others, but not gardeners and caretakers.

Often the person working for you will be working for other people as well, but this makes no difference to the amount of social security charges you have to pay. To take a simple example: if you pay a babysitter €100, you may pay €70 in social security charges. For anyone on an average income, half the charges, the employer's part, are refunded by the Caisse d'Allocations Familiales. Half the rest is refunded as tax credits: effectively you pay €17.50 of the total. The employer is not liable for payroll tax if they pay no more than €10,000 to domestic employees in total (this amount may change in the future).

Half of what you pay, up to a maximum of €5,000 is tax-deductible.

Domestic workers enjoy the same protection as every other worker: they cannot be dismissed without a good reason. The law regarding workers who are paid in kind or partly in kind is less specific. In principle the remuneration should reflect the value of the work, but it cannot fall below the minimum wage. If you take someone into your house and they do work in exchange for board and lodging then the total value of their payment in kind has to reflect the minimum wage. If you help out your neighbour or a relative then this is not regarded as paid employment and there is no obligation to declare the work to the taxman. You should not underestimate the zealousness of the tax inspectors in tracking down cash-in-hand workers; there is a general culture of informing on your neighbours in France, and the person you employ may inform the authorities if you do not pay their social security contributions.

In order to ensure that domestic employees are correctly paid, town halls will provide a ready-made cheque-book, the Chèque Emploi-Service, specifically for domestic employees. The cheques have two parts: one section is to pay the employee; the other is a declaration to send to the URSSAF, the authority that collects social security contributions. By using the cheques you can meet your obligations as regards social security payments and avoid breaking any laws.

## ADDITIONAL BUSINESS TAXES

Employing salaried workers also entails paying some additional taxes, as well as the social security contributions.

*Taxe sur les salaires.* This is payroll tax. It is in principle payable by businesses that are exempt or partially exempt from collecting TVA. *Micro-entreprises* – businesses with a turnover of less than €76,000 in commerce, or €23,000 in services, are also exempt. The tax is based on the total salary used to calculate social security contributions, but after taking off certain benefits-in-kind and social security entitlements. The basic rate of payroll tax is 4.25%, increased to 8.5% between €6,675 and 13,337, and to 9.35% above €13,337 (indexed). The tax does not have to be paid if it comes to less than €690. The tax is to be paid spontaneously by the business itself by 15 January every year, using form No.2052.

**Taxe d'apprentissage.** This tax is meant to fund training and apprenticeships. For that reason small business employing apprentices are exempt. The tax is payable by businesses subject to income tax (IR) that are classed as *commercial, artisanal* or *industriel,* meaning most businesses that are not liberal professions. All businesses subject to corporation tax (IS) suffer this tax. The basis is the gross salary on which social security contributions are paid; the tax is levied at 0.50% of this sum. Payment is to be made by 30 April, using form No.2482.

**Participation à la formation professionnelle continue.** The tax is to fund professional training and is levied on virtually all companies based in France. The basis is the same as for the *taxe d'apprentissage*; the amount is 0.15%, or 0.10% if you pay the *taxe d'apprentissage.* Payment is to be made by 30 April, with form No.2486. You can claim partial exemption if you spend money on training your employees.

**Participation à l'effort de construction.** Employers are also expected to contribute to making it possible for workers to buy houses. If you make investments in housing for your workers, or make voluntary payments, or provide loans, then you can claim almost total exemption. You will still have to pay one-ninth of the tax to fund housing for immigrant workers. The basis is the same as the previous two taxes; the rate is 0.45%. Payment is made by 30 April with form No.2080.

**Taxe sur les voitures de société.** All companies, except non-profit Associations Loi 1901, are subject to this tax, which concerns passenger vehicles less than 10 years old. There are a number of exemptions, but if you use an ordinary passenger car belonging to your company, then you will be liable. The annual sum is levied depending on the number of 'fiscal horses' (*chevaux fiscaux*) the car is rated at. Therefore:

O  under 7 fiscal horses: €1,130 annually
O  over 7 fiscal horses: €2,440 annually.

It can also be paid by three-monthly periods. Payment is to be made by 30 November, accompanying form No.2855. The tax is levied on vehicles in the company's possession between 1 October and 30 September.

There is a further tax levied on legal persons (i.e. companies) owning more than three vehicles. It is also levied on natural persons with vehicles weighing more than 3.5 tonnes. Another tax is levied on heavy vehicles above 12 tonnes.

There are tax deductions for use of company cars, or use of cars for business, also based on fiscal horses. A table of amounts allowed as tax deductions is published every year: the *barème kilométrique*.

# Marketing your Business

# MAKING A NAME FOR YOURSELF

Becoming known is obviously essential. However good your *gîtes* or *chambres d'hôtes* may be, if no one knows about it then you are not going to make a living. The classic way for small businesses to become known is to leave small flyers under windshield wipers, or in libraries or cafés, and other places where a lot of foreigners go (if you are looking to other expatriates). The French term for canvassing potential customers is *faire la prospection*. There are also English-language newspapers and magazines which are likely to generate business for you. If you make wine, cider, beer, or cheese or produce some other delicacy, then a very popular and very French way of becoming known is to enter a *concours* or competition as a way of promoting your business. Winning the gold medal at the local *concours* is quite a big deal for the locals and it looks good on your website, if you have one. You do not have to set up your own website, but one way or another, being listed on an internet site can be the most efficient way of reaching potential customers. It is more or less essential if you are trying to bring people from the UK to your door.

# BED AND BREAKFASTS

The usual way to advertise your *gîtes* or *chambres d'hôtes* is to sign up with Gîtes de France, who will put you in their catalogue, which is used by all tourist offices. French tourist offices may only know about *gîtes* and *chambres d'hôtes* that are in GdF catalogues. You are required to pay an annual subscription to the departmental *relais* or branch of GdF, as well as 12-15% of your takings, in return for being listed. There are a lot of other strings attached to gaining grants and backing from GdF, which have been explained in both chapter 2, *Types of Business* under *gîtes* and *chambres d'hôtes,* and in chapter 6, *Finance* under 'Grants'. Once you have done what you are required to in order to receive a rating from GdF, you will appear in GdF's regional catalogue. As long as you adhere to the conditions for membership of GdF then you remain in their catalogue, but you can be instantly thrown out if you do something too heinous, and you must be prepared to be inspected from time to time. Your *gîtes* or *chambre d'hôtes* will also come up on GdF's on-line catalogue so you will attract customers from the UK and elsewhere. There is a widespread view that GdF attracts some of less desirable customers because of its very extensive coverage. Whether this is true or not, you will in any case never know who is going to turn up on your doorstep, but there may be means of targeting specific kinds of customers by being listed in more exclusive catalogues.

Some foreign owners find the demands of Gîtes de France intolerable and look for other ways of publicising their *gîtes* or *chambres d'hôtes*. There are other organisations that will handle your publicity, notably Chez Nous in the UK, but whoever you deal with you will have to pay fees. The alternative is to sign up with a website or advertise in UK magazines and newspapers (also expensive)), or even in local shops. Some websites will also offer to handle your booking for you; others just give your contact details. If your *chambres d'hôtes* are outstanding then you might be taken up by a specialised catalogue or guide, such as Alastair Sawday's *Special Places to Stay in France,* but few qualify for this kind of honour. Other organisations and websites include:

www.abritel.fr.
www.chateauxandcountry.com.
www.cheznous.com.
www.clevacances.com.
www.dordogne-vacances.com.
www.e-gites.net.
www.francophiles.co.uk.
www.frenchconnections.co.uk.
www.holiday-rentals.co.uk.
www.stopoverconnections.com.
www.villarama.com.

You can always create your own website and back it up with adverts in the French property magazines, but you will almost inevitably have to use the services of a website designer, who can be based in any country (see below). Whichever way you go about it, you have to expect to spend several hundred euros a year on publicity. It takes a long time before you can rely on word of mouth to bring in the customers.

# NEWSPAPERS AND MAGAZINES

English-language publications in France, as well as the UK-based property magazines, are widely read by foreign residents and carry a lot of advertising. You can also have your advert featured on the magazine's websites. The cost depends on whether you use colour or are just putting in a line advert. *French News'* prices for single colour small adverts start at €170.

Most *gîtes* and *chambres d'hôtes* will advertise in UK-based magazines rather than the English-language press in France. Property magazines generally carry adverts for professional services rather than holiday homes or bed and breakfasts. The following are some magazines worth considering:

## UK-based

*Everything France.* Monthly magazine; www.efmag.co.uk.
*Focus on France.* Monthly magazine; www.focusonfrance.co.uk.

*France.* Monthly magazine; www.francemag.com.
*French Property News.* Monthly magazine; www.french-property-news.com.
*Living France.* Monthly magazine; www.livingfrance.com.

### French-based

*The Connexion.* Monthly Riviera news, entertainment free mag; www.theconnexion.fr.
*The English Yellow Pages.* Annual directory for Paris and Riviera; free small ads for businesses; www.englishyellowpages.fr.
*French Times:* Quarterly published from Dordogne; www.french-times.com.
*FUSAC.* Leading free weekly in Paris; stands for France-USA Contacts; www.fusac.fr.
*The Irish Eyes.* Free monthly in Paris; www.irisheyes.fr.
*New Riviera-Côte d'Azur.* Glossy up-market magazine published every three months; e-mail newriviera@smc-france.fr.
*French News:* Monthly. www.french-news.fr; essential reading for expat residents.
*Paris Voice:* Free monthly. www.parisvoice.com.
*Riviera Reporter:* Monthly. www.riviera-reporter.com.
*Riviera Times:* Monthly. www.mediterra.com.

## A WEBSITE OF ONE'S OWN

Being visible on the internet is more and more of a must these days. There are situations where having a website may be quite pointless, e.g. you sell fruit and vegetables in a small town, but most foreign-run businesses can benefit from some internet exposure. To some extent one can have free exposure, in that the French telephone directory is available to everyone on the internet free of charge, and lists businesses by category. Many towns and villages have a site which lists all the local businesses. Moreover, one can have a free mini-website via www.microentreprises.net. This minimal presence is not, however, all that useful as you will never be picked up by internauts browsing with search engines. Everyone with an Internet Service Provider is given some free webspace to make their own internet page(s), but not many people have the knowledge or patience to try to construct their own page, even if it costs them nothing. Web addresses which start with a Service Provider's name tend to be missed by search engines in any case. The crucial point is that someone out there needs to know your website address, after which they can always find you again.

The solution is evidently to use the services of a professional who will construct your site using the photographs you give him/her and advise you on a suitable logo and wording. A basic 5-page website will cost from around £400, and then there are regular maintenance charges. There is also the annual cost of registering a domain name which should be minimal: £10 for a .fr or .co.uk name, and £20 for a .com name. The website designer should charge you for your domain name at cost. Before you think about a domain name (e.g. www.frenchhols.com, which is already taken by the way), you can look at the site www.whois.net to see whether the name you have thought of has not already been taken. The name you choose should preferably be one word without dots and hyphens, and memorable as well.

## WHAT MAKES A GOOD WEBSITE?

Web designer Mike Stickland (www.sticklandweb.co.uk) has the following words of wisdom:

*The website acts as a source of information about your business that is accessible from anywhere in the world. It tells people who and where you are and what you offer. It should reflect the style of your business in terms of colours, pictures and textures, and should show examples of what you do.*

*The website needs to load quickly and should be interesting and professional. Navigation of your website should be easy and clear, so that people can find the information that they want with a minimum number of mouse clicks; they can contact you by e-mail or on-line form if required. Your site needs to be easy to find on the internet, and should be constructed with a view to achieving high listings with search engines. Many businesses now achieve higher sales via their website than from any other source.*

In order to get a large number of hits, your website designer can register your site with free search engines like Google or Jeeves. It is most important to keep the website simple; the longer it takes to download the more likely that surfers are going to give up and look elsewhere. Complicated coloured backgrounds to text should be avoided as it can put readers off. Printing white on black is an absolute no-no as it can trigger off epileptic fits in some people. There is also the matter of keeping your website printer-friendly; too many frames can make it impossible to print the whole page off.

It is worth having your website text checked to make sure it does not contain glaring spelling or grammatical mistakes. If you have to reproduce French words then at least try to get them right. It appears to make no difference for search engines whether words have accents or not, so do put them in.

Finally there are so-called 'hosting costs', namely your website has to reside somewhere on a computer that is running 24 hours a day, and for this service there is a charge of £5 a month or so. You can also pay popular websites (e.g. French property and leisure magazines) to have your site included via a link.

## Website Designers

There are not many English-speaking website designers living in France, but it makes no difference really where your designer lives, unless you want to go to talk to them in person. The following is a small list of designers who specialise in websites for French-based businesses run by foreigners:

*One the Web:* www.onetheweb.com; e-mail info@onetheweb.com; ☎ 05 53 36 97 92 (FR).
*Spice of Life Web Design:* www.spiceoflifewebdesign.com; e-mail info@ spiceoflifewebdesign; ☎ 02 96 86 00 44 (FR).
*Stickland Web Studio:* www.sticklandweb.co.uk; e-mail mike@sticklandweb.co.uk; ☎ 01424 775021 (UK).
*What Another Web Design:* www.whatanotherwebdesign.com; e-mail jay@whatanotherwebdesign; ☎ 06 11 19 78 71 (FR).

# Selling On

## CHAPTER SUMMARY

o **Properties and Businesses.** These are treated more or less as the same in French law when selling.

o **Estate Agents.** It is usual to give an estate agent an authority to act on your behalf.

o **Valuations.** It is advisable to have your property or business independently valued.

o **Notaires.** At some point a notaire has to be involved in selling your property.

o **Payments.** All payments should go through an estate agent or notaire's blocked account.

o **VAT.** French VAT is payable on first sales of property.

o **Capital Gains Tax.** CGT is payable both on property sales and on sales of business goodwill.

o **Exemption.** Transfers of businesses can be exempt from CGT if a member of your family carries on your business without a break.

The idea of selling up and moving on is far from one's mind as one approaches a French venture, but a number of Britons and other foreigner do sell up every year or are forced to leave by financial circumstances. Some cannot settle down in France, or split up from their partners and do not want to remain. Others have gambled on setting up a successful business and not succeeded. If you have really cut your ties with the UK then it can be very difficult to return. While property prices have been going up in the UK, your French property may not have gone up, so trying to buy a property back in the UK may be impossible. For those who are committed to remaining in France there is usually some way or other to remain here. Once you have been contributing to the French social security system for a while, it may be best to stick it out in France, as you will be in the comfort zone for the rest of your days.

# SELLING A PROPERTY OR BUSINESS

Because properties – *immeubles* – and businesses – *fonds de commerce* – are treated virtually the same in French law as regards buying and selling it is possible to deal with both subjects under one heading.

The first question to consider is whether you want to try to sell the property yourself, or whether you are going to use the services of an *immobilier* (estate agent) or notaire to handle the sale. Once you advertise a property for sale then you will be approached by estate agents who would like you to give them an authority (*mandat de vente*) to negotiate the sale on your behalf. They may claim to have a client who is interested in your property, even though it has only just appeared in the newspaper. Sometimes private persons will be interested in buying your property and selling it on to someone else, in the hope of making a quick profit. There are also the *marchands de biens*, professionals who buy and sell property on their own account for profit.

There is another factor, however, which is the valuation. of the property. An owner who has invested a lot in improving their property will tend to overlook its faults and put it on the market at an inflated price. They may believe that they need to add on something to the price so that they have a basis for negotiation.

It is wise to have your property or *fonds de commerce* valued by an expert, for which you will have to pay a fee. If you intend to give an *immobilier* an authority to sell your property, then he will do the valuation free of charge. You can also ask an *immobilier* to come and give an estimate of the price without committing yourself to take him on to sell your property, which could have an undesirable effect, as he will be more likely to overvalue the property as a way of making sure that you will not be able to sell it quickly. French *immobiliers* receive a higher percentage than those in the UK of the selling price, but this does not necessarily mean that they will overvalue your property. The *immobilier*'s fees start from a minimum of around €2,000 and are on a sliding scale going down to a minimum of 3% of the purchase price.

It can also happen that he doesn't want to disappoint you by giving a price that is lower than you had hoped for. There is more to be said for an independent and objective valuation. A proper valuation consists of a report of several pages. Qualified valuers can be found by looking under *expert immobilier* in the yellow pages. Notaires often have valuers working with them.

As with any other selling operation, one needs to consider the amount of time and trouble that it is going to cost you to have a lot of prospective buyers coming to look at your property who will be put off by an inflated asking price. There is also the seasonal factor. Once the autumn has arrived it may be difficult to sell a property before the following spring. There is more to be gained by putting a realistic price on the property, rather than advertising it as 'negotiable' or *à débattre*.

### Authority to Sell

You are not limited to using an *immobilier* to sell your property. Notaires often deal with property sales, especially in the countryside. Some will have special degrees in handling property sales, which they will display prominently: the '*Conseil en Gestion de Patrimoine*'. Those who will not have anything to do with property sales may have a sign stating '*non marchand*'.

Whether you deal with an *immobilier* or a notaire, you need to give him/her the authority to negotiate on your behalf, the *mandat de vente*. Unlike in Britain, a French-based estate agent must have professional qualifications and have a licence from a Chambre de Commerce. You should check that the *immobilier* is above board and has the necessary guarantee fund and professional indemnity insurance. The seller who gives the authority is known as the *mandant* (the 'principal' in English legal parlance), while the intermediary who accepts the authority is the *mandataire* (the 'agent').

There are two kinds of *mandat de vente*: the *mandat simple* (or *non-exclusif*) and the *mandat exclusif*. In the first case you can give several agents a *mandat simple* to sell property on their behalf, which can be at different prices. The agent who succeeds in finding you a buyer is the one who receives the commission. Legally speaking, if they showed the prospective buyer around the property or made the greatest amount of effort in finding the buyer then they have the right to the commission. The *mandat* that you give to the *immobilier* will state whether you have the right to sell your property yourself to anyone you wish, but if you try to make a private deal with a buyer who has been shown around by an *immobilier* then you can be sued.

The agent who has a *mandat exclusif* is the only intermediary permitted to negotiate the sale. The contract will state whether or not the seller can find a buyer for themselves. Where the agent has the exclusive right to sell the property you will see *en exclusivité* on the contract and advertisement.

The *mandat de vente* always has a time limit, which is normally three months. The *mandat* can be cancelled with a notice period of 15 days, otherwise it continues for fixed periods of time until the seller gives 15 days' notice that he wishes to cancel. Naturally, if the property is sold, the *mandat* ceases of its own accord, but the seller must still inform the other *mandataires* of the sale by registered letter.

It is best to take a draft of the *mandat de vente* home with you to check its terms. There is a difference between a *mandat* that is signed at the *mandataire's* office and one that is signed elsewhere. In the latter case you have the right to cancel the *mandat* within 7 days if you change your mind, and the *mandat* must include a statement to this effect. If it is signed in the *mandataire's* office you have no right of retraction.

## Private Sales

You have the right to sell your property without using an intermediary, but there are risks involved if one does not know the French law. In an ideal situation, you will show someone around your house, agree on a price, and write out an agreement on a piece of paper which states the address, the price, who will pay the fees and where and in front of whom the pre-contract is to be signed. There is a get-out for both parties in that the pre-contract has to be signed within a set number of days, which is normally eight days. An agreement of this sort is binding on both parties for the time agreed. Verbal agreements are also binding.

It is not possible to go through the selling process without the intervention of a notaire, however. Only a notaire can register the sale of a property with the *bureau des hypothèques*. On top of that it is highly advisable that a pre-contract, a *compromis de vente* or *promesse de vente* is signed in front of a notaire, who should preferably draw up the contract. Signing the pre-contract is equivalent to buying the property, with the proviso that get-out clauses can allow the buyer to escape from its implications. This has been dealt with in chapter 5, *Acquiring a Business or Property*. A *compromis de vente* or *promesse de vente* can also be signed 'under hand', or *sous seing privé*, in which case it is only binding on the buyer, the seller and their inheritors. It is not binding on third parties, and cannot be recommended.

The most serious mistake any seller can make is to accept any deposit or part-payment themselves before the final transfer has been signed. Any payment made in advance of the transfer deed is considered to be an *acompte* or non-returnable deposit, which binds both seller and buyer. There is no means of preventing the sale from going through in such a case. In the normal course of events the deposit and final payment are made through a notaire's or *immobilier's* blocked account, and no funds are released until all fees have been paid and any possible objections to the sale have been examined.

### Contracts

In the first instance, the *compromis de vente* or *promesse de vente* (promise to sell) should be signed with a notaire or *immobilier* as the witness. You may be offered a standard pre-printed contract to sign; it is better not to use such a form, but may be unavoidable.

With the 'promise to sell' the seller commits himself to selling within at least one month, or more usually within two to three months. In return the potential buyer will pay an *indemnité d'immobilisation*, a sum that compensates the seller for temporarily taking his property off the market. The usual amount is 10% of the sale price. If the *promesse* is signed privately, then it is to be signed in triplicate, and one copy is deposited with the *Centre des Impôts*. The *indemnité d'immobilisation* should be paid into a blocked account held by a *notaire* or *immobilier*, and not directly to the seller. If the buyer exercises their option to purchase – *lever l'option* – the *indemnité* will be deducted from the sale price. If the deal falls through the *indemnité* will be returned to the buyer if one of the get-out clauses can be invoked within the allotted time.

The *compromis de vente* is a two-way contract which binds both parties equally; the correct term is a *promesse synallagmatique*. The buyer pays 5-10% of the sale price as a deposit or *indemnité*, normally into a blocked account – *compte séquestre* – held by a notaire or by the estate agent. The nature of the deposit is important. If it is an *arrhes*, then the buyer can withdraw from the agreement but will forfeit the deposit. If the seller decides not to sell, then they are required to pay the buyer twice the amount of the *arrhes* as compensation. A variation on this type of deposit is a *dédit*, a specified sum that is forfeited if the buyer pulls out of the deal. The other type of deposit, the *acompte* – which can be translated as 'down-payment' or 'instalment' – means that the sale is legally enforceable on both buyer and seller.

The *conditions suspensives* in a pre-contract are also of concern to the seller. The most significant one is that the sale is dependent on the buyer obtaining a loan in time. If the seller can prove that the buyer did not make reasonable efforts to obtain a loan, then they can claim compensation. Certain buyers may sign a pre-contract and look around for another buyer who has the money to buy the property at a higher price, and then pocket the difference. If a buyer (or their partner) has ever been an *interdit bancaire*, i.e. had an unauthorised overdraft which they have failed to deal with in time, then they will quite probably be refused a mortgage. The seller can be entirely unaware of this. Making enquiries about whether the buyer is likely to receive a loan may not help much.

The notaire has the task of ensuring that the mortgage on a property has been cancelled. A property cannot be sold with a mortgage charge attached to it. It is also the notary's job to check on any third-party claims to the seller's assets, and on 'easements' or *servitudes*, meaning rights that others might have in relation to a property, such as a right of way, the use of a well, or the like.

The seller or his representative will be present at the signing of the *acte final* or final deed of transfer. It takes some time for all formalities to be completed and the sale amount to come through. While the buyer is responsible for the so-called 'notary fees' (most of which do not actually go to the notaire), it is a matter of local custom whether the buyer or seller pays the *immobilier*'s fees. The practice in the past was for the buyer to pay, but it is becoming more usual for the seller to pay. The difference is not negligible.

## Selling a Fonds de Commerce

There are certain differences between selling an immovable property and a business, in the sense of the *fonds de commerce,* which is mainly the intangible assets. The sale is called a *cession de fonds de commerce* rather than a *vente.* Once the actual *acte de cession de fonds de commerce* has been signed, it is registered with the nearest *centre des impôts* or tax office. The tax office has to be informed immediately if you plan to sell a business in any case, as does the Tribunal de Commerce (Commercial Court) where your business is registered. You are required to enter a tax declaration within 60 days with the figures for the final year of business activity.

Once the business is sold, the act must be published in a local newspaper that is authorised to publish such advertisements (known as a *journal d'annonces légales*) within 15 days. Both buyer and seller have to inform the local Registre des Commerces et Sociétés of the change to the status of the business, using the form *Mutation de Fonds de Commerce ou de Clientèle.* The clerk of the commercial court will have the details published in the national BODACC journal at the buyer's expense within one month. Starting from the date of publication in BODACC, the seller's creditors have 10 days to enter an *opposition* to the sale with a court to obtain what they are owed. If a creditor believes that the sale of the *fonds* will not raise enough money to satisfy his claim, then he can make a bid for it equalling the selling price plus one-sixth (*surenchère du sixième*). This leads to the enforced auction of the *fonds.* The bidder is obliged to buy the *fonds* if no one else makes a bid for it.

The buyer is jointly liable with the seller for a period of up to 6 months for any unpaid taxes or any other money that is owed to third parties. The seller can take back the business if the buyer cannot pay the full purchase price. Once again it is essential to use the services of a lawyer or an estate agent.

## TAXES ON SALES OF PROPERTY OR BUSINESSES

Sellers of properties have to beware of two possible taxes that they can be hit with when they sell up. The first is TVA (Value Added Tax), which is payable on the first sale of a 'new' property after the owner has moved into it. A 'new' property is defined as one which is less than 5 years old. There are two criteria for deciding the starting date for the 5-year period during which TVA is payable, one being the date on which the buyer signed the *certificat d'achèvement* (completion certificate) and the other the date that the buyer actually moved in, roughly speaking whichever is earlier.

If a buyer has ordered a house from plans to be built, he then pays 19.6% TVA on the purchase. If he then sells within 5 years, he pays 19.6% TVA again on the sale price, but with the proviso that the original amount of TVA is deducted from the second payment of TVA. If the property rises in value, the seller only pays TVA on the difference between the buying price and the selling price. Thus:

| | |
|---|---|
| Purchase price 2000: €100,000 | TVA €19,600 |
| Sale price 2004: €120,000 | TVA €23,520 |
| Net TVA payable | €3,920 |

TVA is not payable in the unlikely event of a subsequent sale within the 5-year period.

### Impôts sur les Plus Values (IPV)

The French equivalent of Capital Gains Tax was radically reformed starting from 2004 as regards residential property, and this is explained in detail in chapter 8, *Tax and Social Security*. The system for taxing professional capital gains is also changing. All businesses make capital gains or losses when they sell fixed assets. Such gains are treated as profits and taxed accordingly, but there are various ways of reducing or deferring tax for each tax year. Over time, the business builds up 'latent capital gains' (*plus values latentes*), which are only realised when the business is sold. If a business is handed on free of charge and continues as a going concern, then there is no IPV to pay since there is no capital gain, as long as the valuation of the business is not changed.

When you sell a *fonds de commerce* (i.e. the intangible part of the business), then you are liable to pay IPV on the difference between the purchase price and the selling price. In the case of business assets that appear on your balance sheet the basis for the calculation is the depreciated purchase price subtracted from the selling price. IPV is payable at 16% + 10% social security taxes, making 26% in all. Exemption from IPV is granted if the business turnover did not exceed €250,000 for a commerce and €90,000 for other businesses, as long as the business was going for at least 5 years.

As a general principle, the notaire handling the sale of your business will take the IPV that you owe out of the selling price and pass it on to the taxman.

**Valuation.** The state takes an interest in the price that is paid for *fonds de commerce,* in order to prevent under-the-table payments. If the price appears to be too low then both the seller and the buyer can be fined. The starting price for shares in a company is fixed according to the average value of the shares over the lifetime of the company, which can be a disadvantage if they have gone up a lot in value. The starting price for a business you have created can be determined by taking its value during the first years of its creation worked out from the turnover according to standard formulas that are used by professionals valuing businesses.

## Taxation of Sale of Company Shares

Profits or income from the sale of shares in a company are treated as business income and taxed accordingly. The basis of the calculation is the actual acquisition price, subtracted from the selling price. Income tax or corporation tax is payable on short-term gains on shares (shares that have been held for less than 2 years). For long-term gains, IPV is paid at 16% + 10%. The French government intends to limit IPV on transfers of companies from 2004.

Private persons are exempted from paying IPV on share sales if they reinvest the proceeds in similar shares and do not sell the newly acquired shares within 5 years.

# ACRONYMS AND ABBREVIATIONS

| | |
|---|---|
| AGIRC | *Association Générale des Institutions de Retraites de Cadres* |
| ANPE | *Agence Nationale Pour l'Emploi* |
| APCE | *Agence Pour la Création d'Entreprises* |
| ARRCO | *Associations des Régimes de Retraite Complémentaire* |
| ASSEDIC | *Association pour l'Emploi dans l'Industrie et le Commerce* |
| | |
| BA | *bénéfices agricoles* |
| BFR | *besoin en fonds de roulement* |
| BIC | *Acquiring* |
| BNC | *bénéfices non-commerciaux* |
| BODACC | *Bulletin Officiel des Annonces Civiles et Commerciales* |
| | |
| CA | *chiffre d'affaires* |
| CANCAVA | *Caisse Autonome Nationale de Compensation de l'Assurance Vieillesse des Artisans* |
| CC | *code civil* |
| CCI | *chambre de commerce et des industries* |
| CDI | *centre des impôts* |
| CFE | *centre de formalités des entreprises* |
| CGI | *Code Général des Impôts* |
| CMU | *Couverture Maladie Universelle* |
| CPAM | *Caisse Primaire Assurance Maladie* |
| CRAM | *Caisse Régionale d'Assurance Maladie* |
| CRDS | *contribution au remboursement de la dette sociale* |
| CSG | *contribution sociale généralisée* |
| | |
| DATAR | *Direction de l'Aménagement du Territoire* |
| DDASS | *Direction Départementale des Affaires Sanitaires et Sociales* |
| DDCCRF | *Direction Départementale de la Concurrence de la Consommation et de la Répression des Fraudes* |
| DDE | *Direction Départementale de l'Equipement* |
| DDTEFP | *Direction Départementale du Travail, de l'Emploi et de la Formation Professionnelle* |
| DOM-TOM | *Départements d'Outre-Mer et Territoires d'Outre-Mer* |

| DRIRE | *Direction Régionale de l'ndustrie de la Recherche et de l'Environnement* |
| DUE | *document unique d'embauche* |
| EI | *entreprise individuelle* |
| FC | *fonds de commerce* |
| HT | *hors taxes* |
| INPI | *Institut National de la Propriété Industrielle* |
| INSEE | *Institut National de la Statistique et des Etudes Economiques* |
| IR | *impôt sur le revenu* |
| IS | *impôt sur les sociétés* |
| ISF | *impôt de solidarité sur la fortune* |
| JO | *Journal Officiel* |
| LJ | *liquidation judiciaire* |
| MSA | *Mutualité Sociale Agricole* |
| ORGANIC | *Caisse Nationale du Régime d'Assurance Vieillesse Invalidité Décès des Non-salariés de l'Industrie et du Commerce* |
| PACS | *pacte civile de solidarité* |
| PDG | *Président Directeur Général* |
| PME | *Petites et Moyennes Entreprises; SMEs* |
| PV | *plus values* |
| RAR | *(Lettre) Recommandée avec Avis de Reception* |
| RCS | *registre du commerce et des sociétés* |
| RJ | *redressement judiciaire* |
| RMI | *revenu minimum d'insertion* |
| SAFER | *Sociétés d'Amènagement Foncier et d'Etablissement Rural* |
| SA | *Société Anonyme* |

| SARL | *Société Anonyme à Responsabilité Limitée* |
|------|---------------------------------------------|
| SAS | *Société par Actions Simplifiée* |
| SMIC | *salaire minimum interprofessionnel de croissance* |

| TGE | *taux global effectif* |
|-----|------------------------|
| TNS | *travailleur non-salarié* |
| TTC | *toutes taxes comprises* |
| TVA | *taxe sur la valeur ajoutée* |

| UNEDIC | *Union Nationale pour l'Emploi dans l'Industrie et le Commerce* |
|--------|----------------------------------------------------------------|
| URSSAF | *Union de Recouvrement des Cotisations de Sécurité Sociale et d'Allocations Familiales* |

| ZA | *Zone Artisanale* |
|----|-------------------|
| ZI | *Zone Industrielle* |
| ZFU | *Zone Franche Urbaine* |
| ZRP | *Zone Rurale Prioritaire* |
| ZRR | *Zone de Revitalisation Rurale* |
| ZRU | *Zone de Redynamisation Urbaine* |

# FRENCH BUSINESS GLOSSARY

| *acompte* | refundable deposit |
|-----------|--------------------|
| *à concurrence de…* | up to a limit of… |
| *actif* | assets |
| *actif net comptable* | net assets |
| *action* | share |
| *actionnaire* | shareholder |
| *actionnaire propriétaire* | owner shareholder |
| *agencement* | fitting-out of premises |
| *agencer* | to fit out premises |
| *aisances et dépendances* | easements and outbuildings |
| *amorti(s)* | depreciated; written-off |
| *amortissement* | depreciation |
| *amortissement dérogatoire* | accelerated depreciation |
| *arrêté (municipal)* | by-law |
| *arrhes* | non-refundable deposit |

| | |
|---|---|
| *assemblée générale annuelle* | Annual General Meeting |
| *assurance dommage ouvrage* | 10-year insurance on new buildings |
| | |
| *bail (pl. baux)* | lease; leasehold |
| *bailleur* | lessor |
| *bail précaire* | tenancy at will; short-term let |
| *besoin en fonds de roulement (BFR)* | working capital requirement (WCR) |
| *biens* | property |
| *biens meubles* | movable property; chattels |
| *bilan comptable* | balance sheet |
| *bilan synthétique* | concise balance sheet |
| *billet à ordre* | promissory note |
| *bon pour accord* | agreed |
| | |
| *cadastre* | land registry |
| *cadre* | manager |
| *capital libéré* | paid-up capital |
| *cession de biens* | assignment of property |
| *Centre des Impôts* | local tax office |
| *Code civil* | book of basic laws |
| *Code général des impôts* | book of tax laws |
| *Commissionaire aux comptes* | company auditor |
| *comptabilité* | accounts |
| *comptable* | accountant |
| *comptes sociaux* | unconsolidated accounts |
| *conseil de gestion* | management board |
| *conseil de prud'hommes* | employment tribunal |
| *coût de revient* | cost price; production price |
| *créances* | amounts due (from creditor's viewpoint) |
| *créancier* | creditor |
| *crédit bail* | lease to own; lease financing |
| *croupier* | sleeping partner |
| *curatelle* | guardianship; supervision |
| | |
| *débit* | debit |
| *débiteur* | debtor |
| *découvert* | overdraft |
| *dégrèvement fiscal* | tax relief |
| *délai de carence* | deferral period |

| | |
|---|---|
| *détournement de fonds* | embezzlement |
| *dette* | debt (from debtor's viewpoint) |
| *dirigeant* | senior executive |
| *dol* | fraud |
| *dolosif* | fraudulent |
| *DOM-TOM* | overseas départements and territories |
| *droit au bail* | leasehold right |
| *droit de bail* | tax on leases |
| *droit de nantissement* | lien on goods |
| | |
| *en bon père de famille* | with due diligence |
| *encadrement* | management |
| *encours* | outstanding debt |
| *enseigne* | shop-sign |
| *escroc* | swindler |
| *escroquerie* | swindling |
| *ester en justice* | to sue |
| *état des lieux* | inspection report on rental property |
| *expert comptable* | accountant |
| | |
| *faillite* | bankruptcy |
| *filouterie* | deception |
| *fonds de commerce* | intangible and (sometimes) movable assets of a business |
| | |
| *gage* | pledge |
| *gérant* | director (of a limited company) |
| *greffe du tribunal de commerce* | clerk of the commercial court |
| *grève* | strike |
| *grevé* | encumbered |
| *grèvement* | charge; encumbrance |
| *hors taxes* | net of tax |
| *huissier* | bailiff |
| | |
| *incident de paiement* | payment irregularity |
| *inexécution* | breach of contract |
| | |
| *jouissance* | peaceful use; rights |

| | |
|---|---|
| *lettre recommandée avec avis de reception* | registered letter with confirmation of receipt |
| *libératoire* | discharging; final |
| *liquidation judiciaire* | winding-up; liquidation |
| *local/locaux* | premises |
| *louer à bail* | to let out |
| *loyer* | rent |
| | |
| *mandant* | principal |
| *mandat de vente* | authority to sell |
| *mandataire* | agent |
| *mandataires sociaux* | board members |
| *marge brute d'autofinancement* | net cash flow |
| *mise en demeure* | warning to pay; final notice |
| *montage financier* | financial package |
| *montant forfaitaire* | lump sum |
| | |
| *nanti* | pledged; secured |
| *nantissement* | pledge; collateral |
| *nue propriété* | reversion of freehold; ownership without use of property |
| | |
| *obligation* | bond; debenture |
| *OPCVM* | unit trust |
| *opposable* | binding on; invocable against |
| *ordonnance* | court order; decree |
| *ordonnance de ne pas faire* | injunction to desist |
| *ordre du jour* | agenda |
| *ORGANIC* | pension fund for *commerçants* |
| | |
| *paiement libératoire* | final payment |
| *pas-de-porte* | premium |
| *passible de* | punishable by |
| *Président Directeur Général* | chairman and managing director (CEO) |
| *pleine propriété* | freehold |
| *pli R.A.R.* | registered mail with confirmation of receipt |
| *plus values* | capital gains |
| *point chaud* | busy spot |
| *pouvoir* | power; authority |

| | |
|---|---|
| *prélèvement libératoire* | once and for all levy |
| *président* | company chairman |
| *prêt bonifié* | soft loan |
| *privilège* | lien; privilege |
| *procédure en référé* | summary proceedings |
| *procès verbal (PV)* | minutes (of a meeting); written report |
| | |
| *quote-part* | share; proportion |
| | |
| *raison sociale* | business name |
| *redressement judiciaire* | official administration |
| *recette principale des impôts* | pre-2003 term for main tax office; now called *centre des impôts* |
| *rupture de contrat* | breach of contract |
| | |
| *seuil de rentabilité* | profit threshold |
| *servitude* | easement; servitude (e.g. right of way over your land) |
| *SICAV* | unit trust |
| *siège social* | registered office |
| *soustraitant* | subcontractor |
| | |
| *taux de rentabilité* | rate of return |
| *taux global effectif* (TGE) | APR; annualised percentage rate |
| *taxe sur la valeur ajoutée* (TVA) | value added tax (VAT) |
| *toutes taxes comprises* (TTC) | including all taxes |
| *travailleur non-salarié* (TNS) | non-salaried worker; self-employed person |
| | |
| *valeurs mobilières* | transferable securities |
| *valoriser* | promote |

# Complete guides to life abroad from Vacation Work

## Live & Work Abroad

## Buying a House Abroad

## Starting a Business Abroad